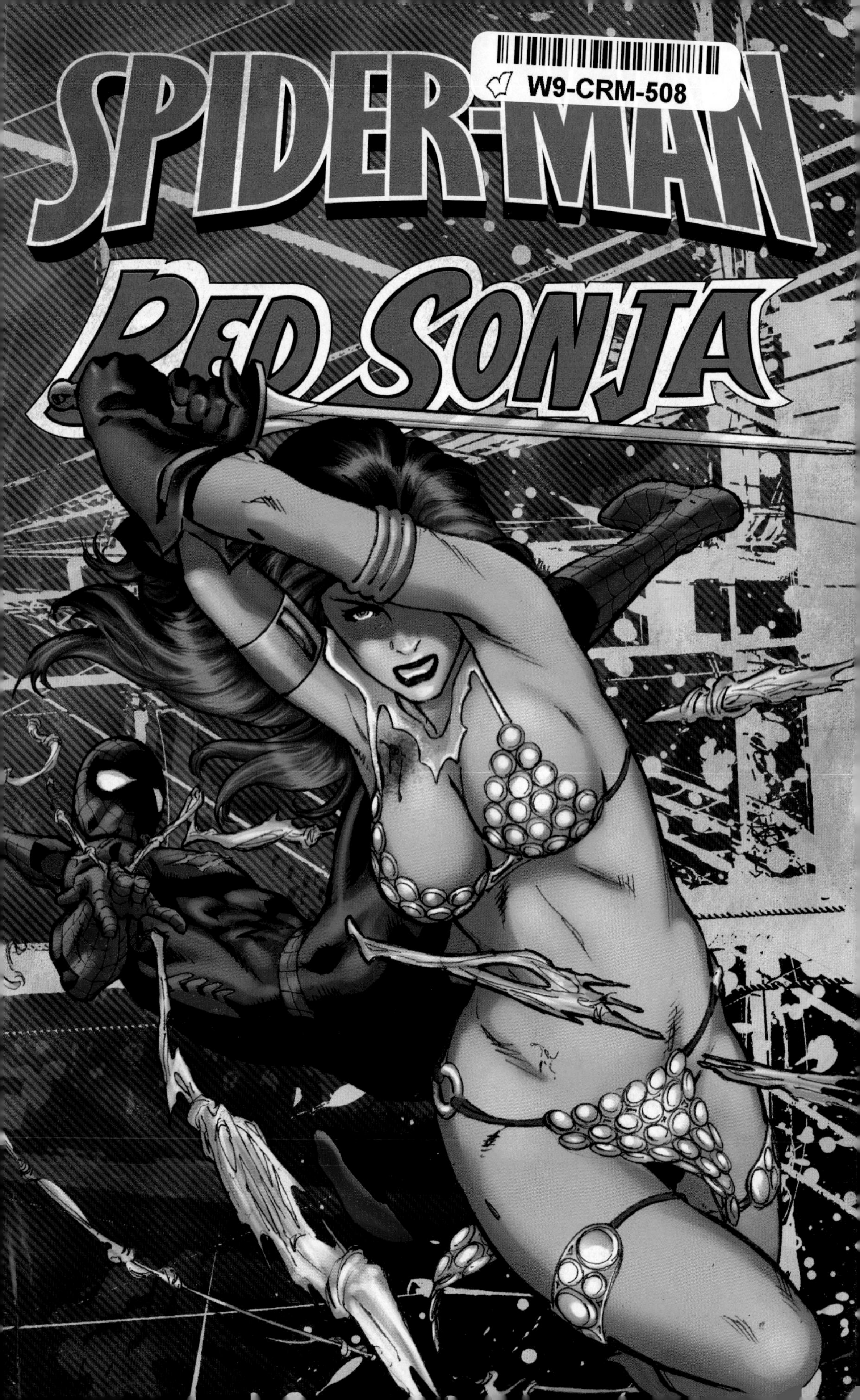
SPIDER-MAN
RED SONJA

# SPIDER-MAN

# RED SONJA

*Writer:* MICHAEL AVON OEMING
*Artist:* MEL RUBI
*Colorists:* BRIAN BUCCELLATO
*Letterer:* SIMON BOWLAND
*Covers:* MICHAEL TURNER
*Assistant Editors:* ALEJANDRO ARBONA
& LAUREN SANKOVITCH
*Editor:* BILL ROSEMANN

*Consulting Editor:* JOE RYBANDT
*Special Thanks to:* TOM BREVOORT, JOSH JOHNSON,
JUAN COLLADO, NICK BARRUCCI, JASON
ULLMEYER, ARTHUR LIEBERMAN *and*
LUKE LIEBERMAN

---

*Marvel Team-Up #79 (March 1979)*
*Writer:* CHRIS CLAREMONT
*Co-Plotter & Penciler:* JOHN BYRNE
*Inker:* TERRY AUSTIN
*Colorist:* GLYNIS WEIN
*Letterer:* TOM ORZECHOWSKI
*Editor:* AL MILGROM
*Consulting Editor:* ROY THOMAS

Red Sonja is based upon
the heroine created by
ROBERT E. HOWARD

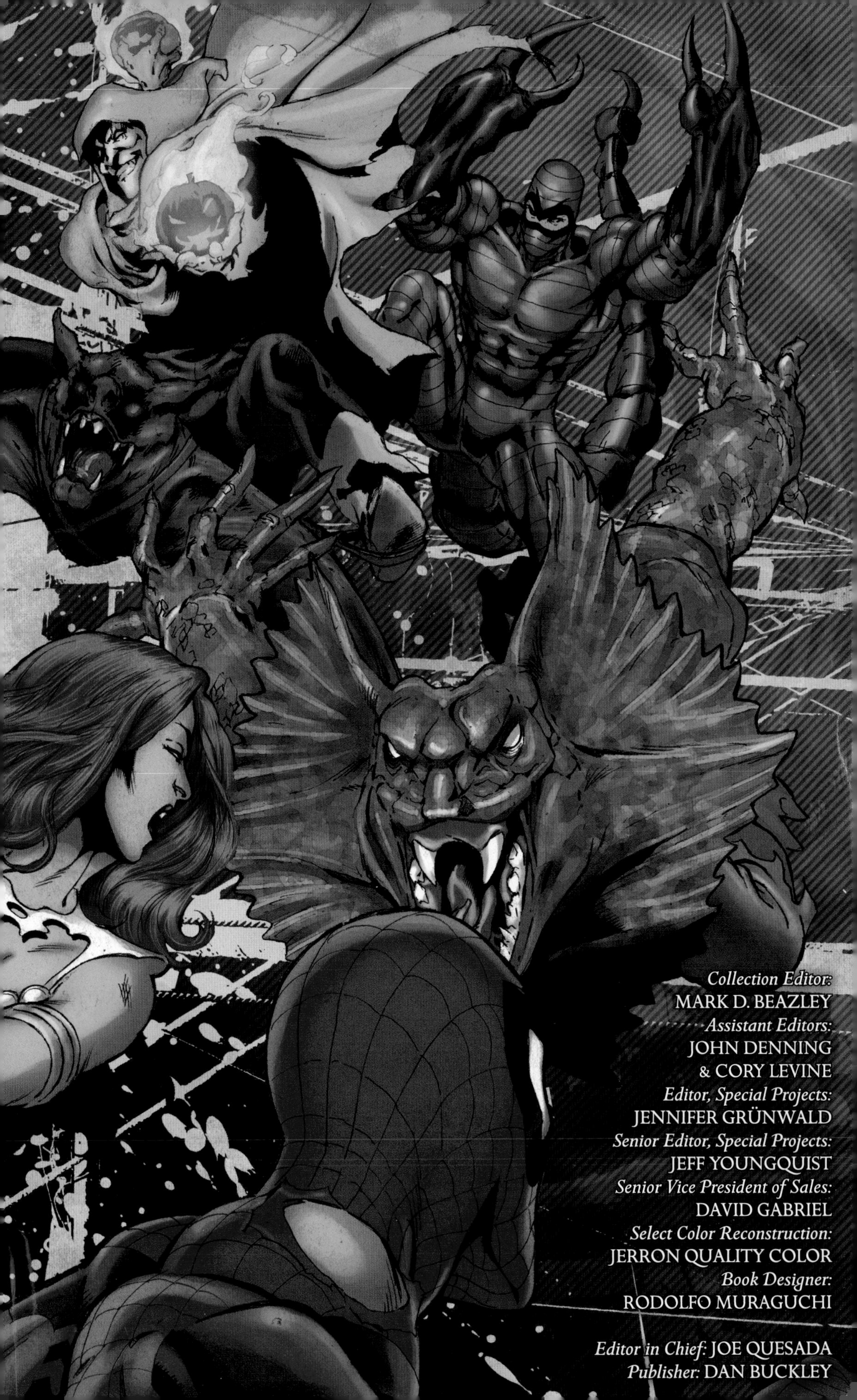


*Collection Editor:*
MARK D. BEAZLEY
*Assistant Editors:*
JOHN DENNING
& CORY LEVINE
*Editor, Special Projects:*
JENNIFER GRÜNWALD
*Senior Editor, Special Projects:*
JEFF YOUNGQUIST
*Senior Vice President of Sales:*
DAVID GABRIEL
*Select Color Reconstruction:*
JERRON QUALITY COLOR
*Book Designer:*
RODOLFO MURAGUCHI

*Editor in Chief:* JOE QUESADA
*Publisher:* DAN BUCKLEY

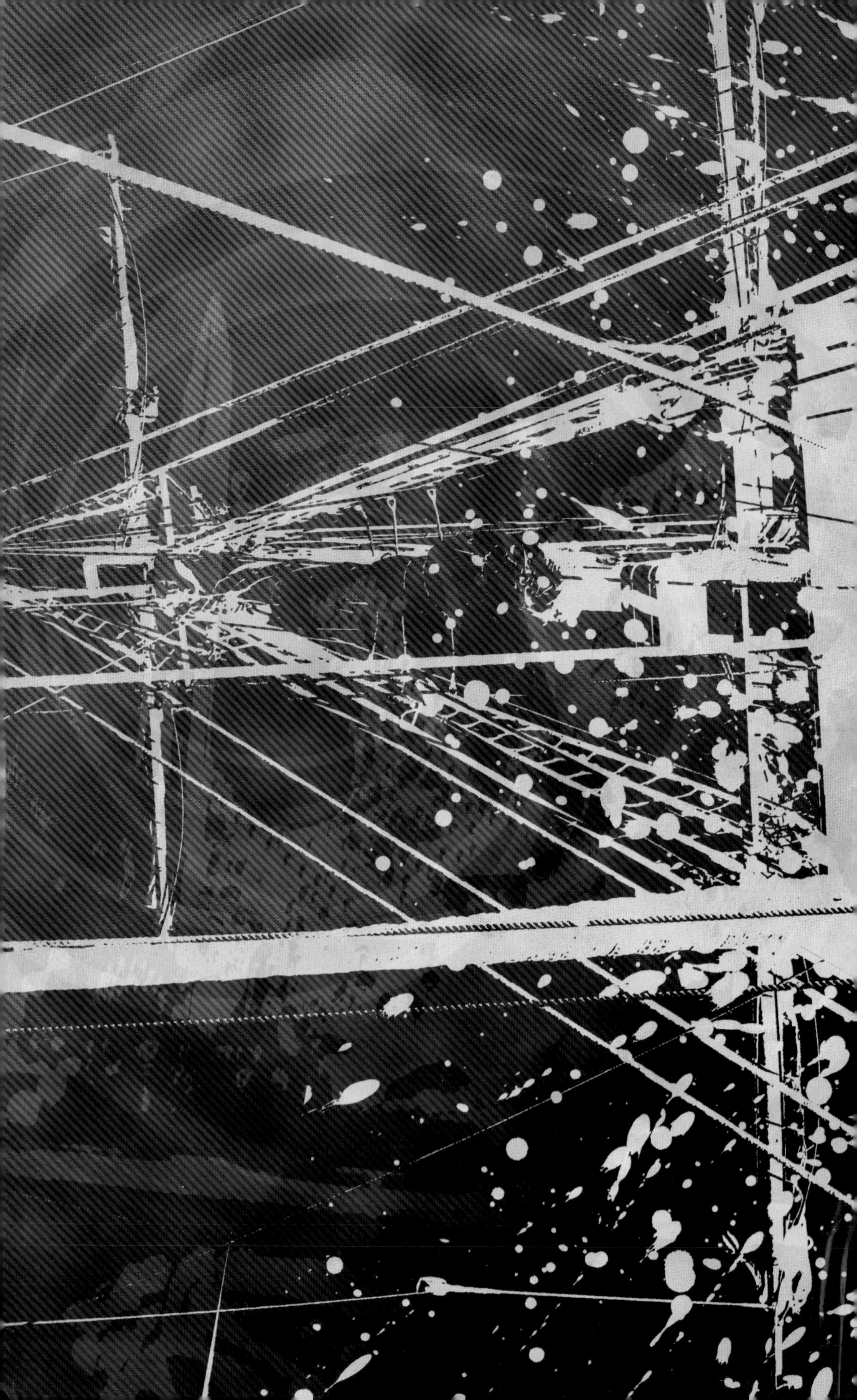

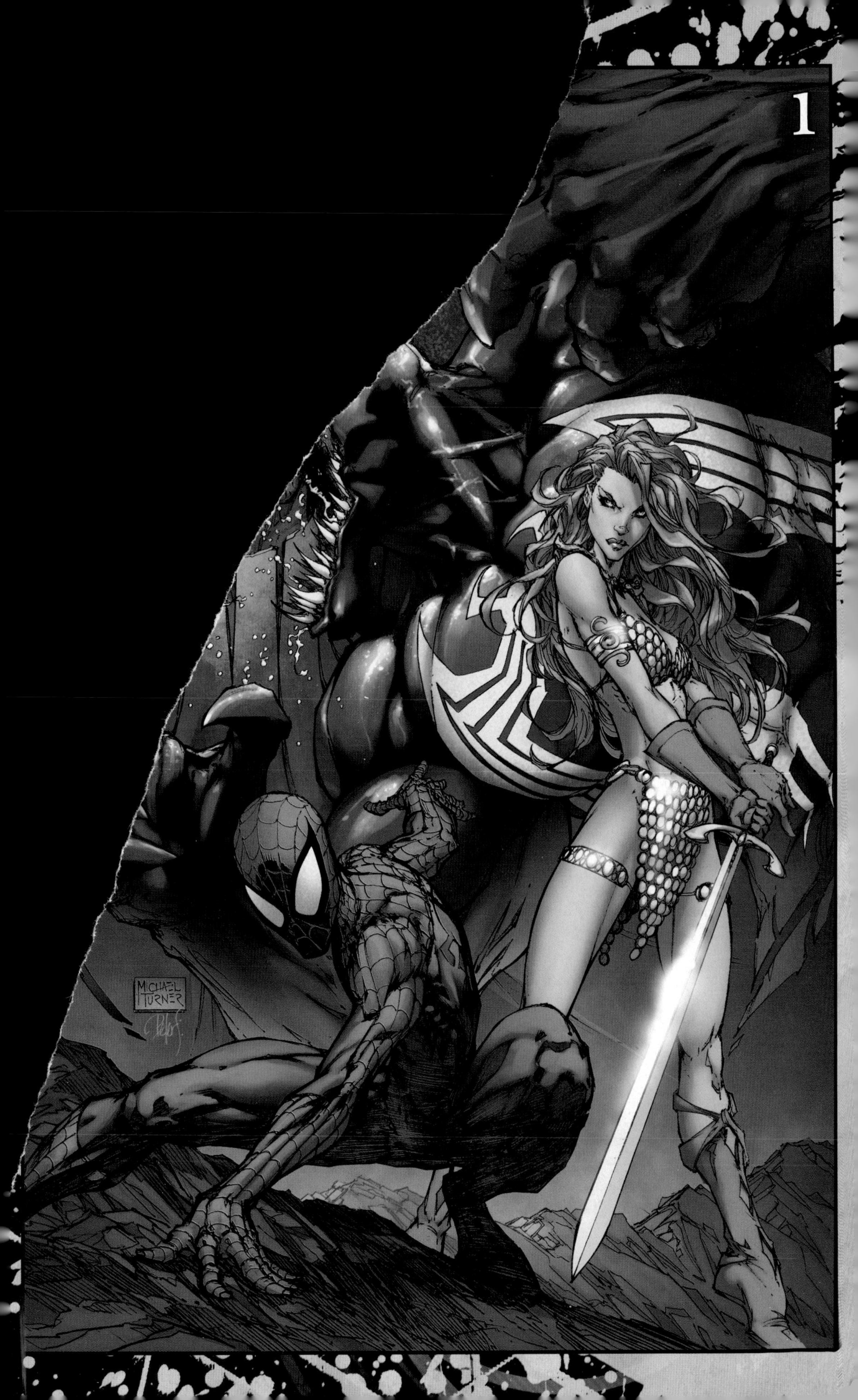
1
MICHAEL TURNER

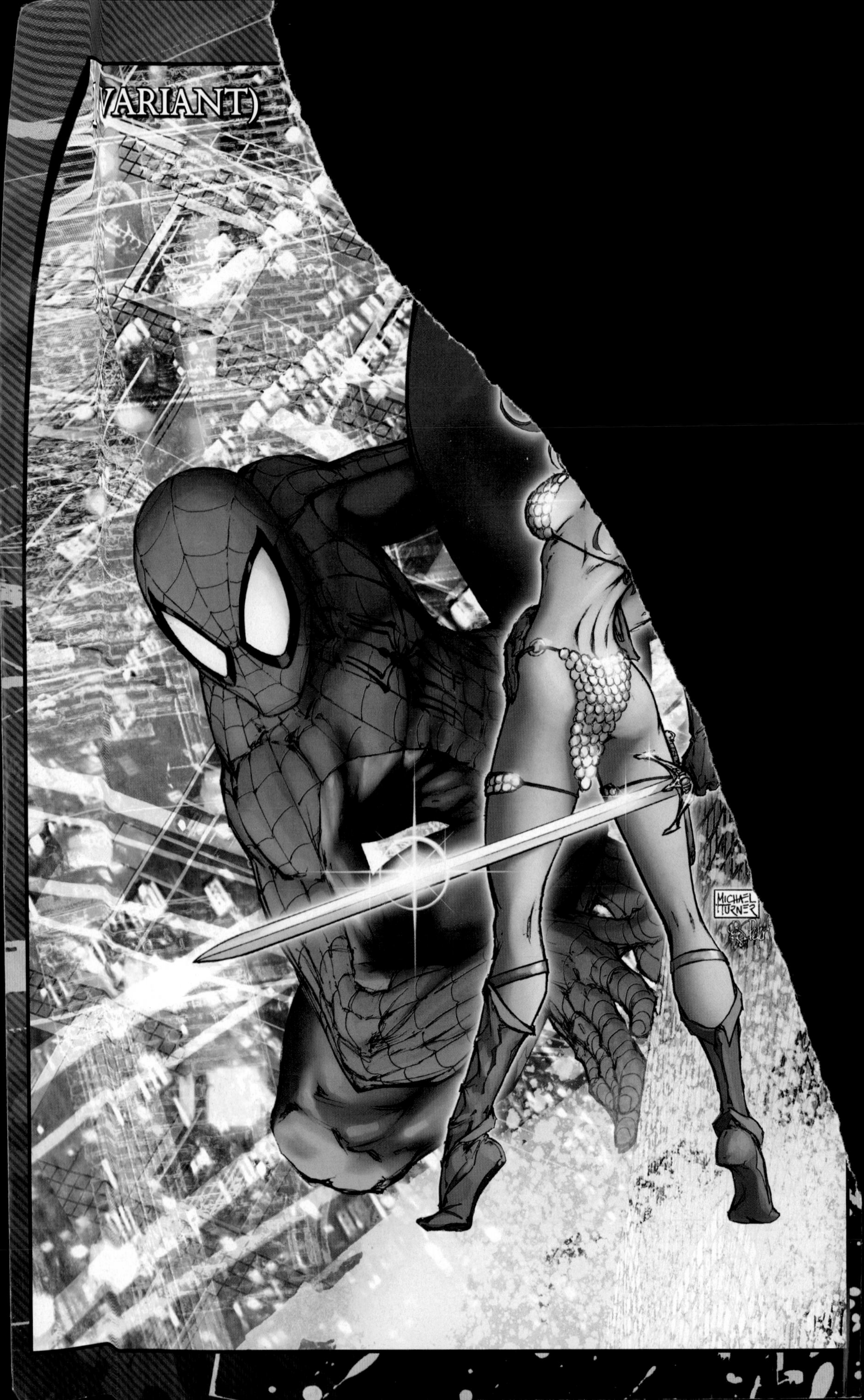
(VARIANT)
MICHAEL TURNER

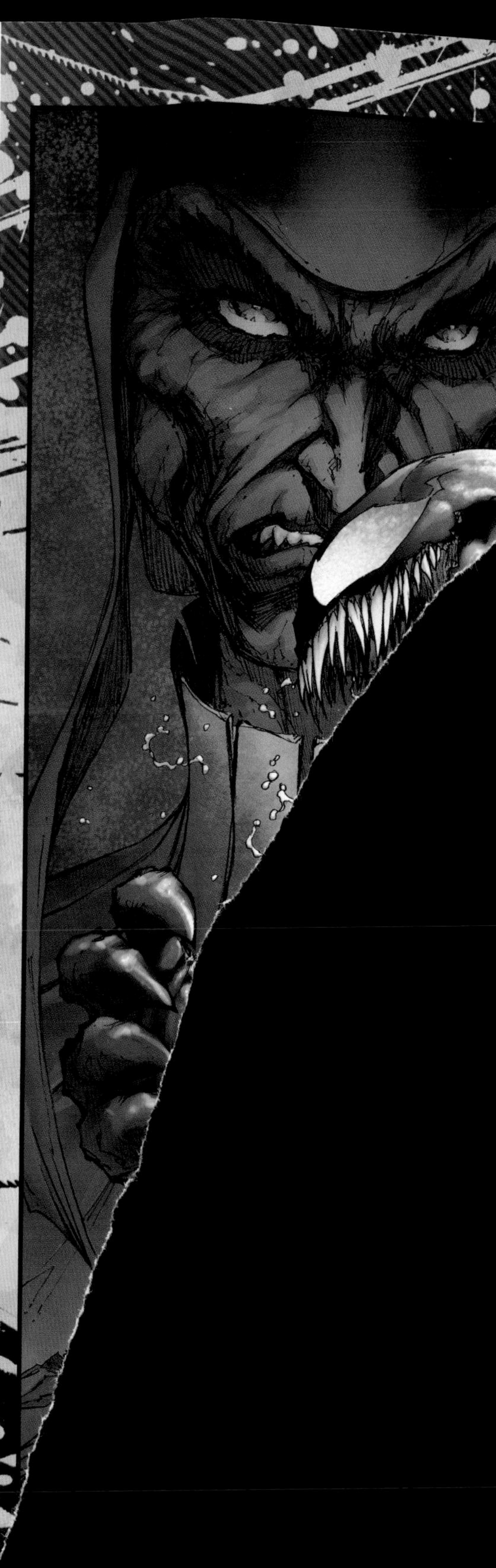

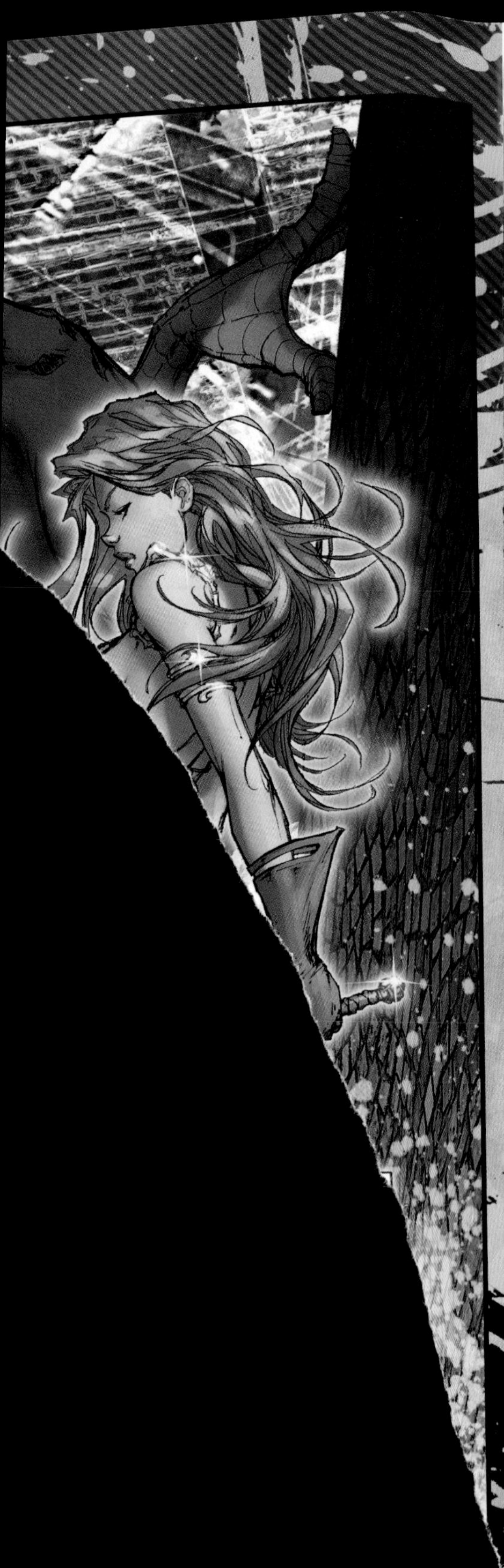

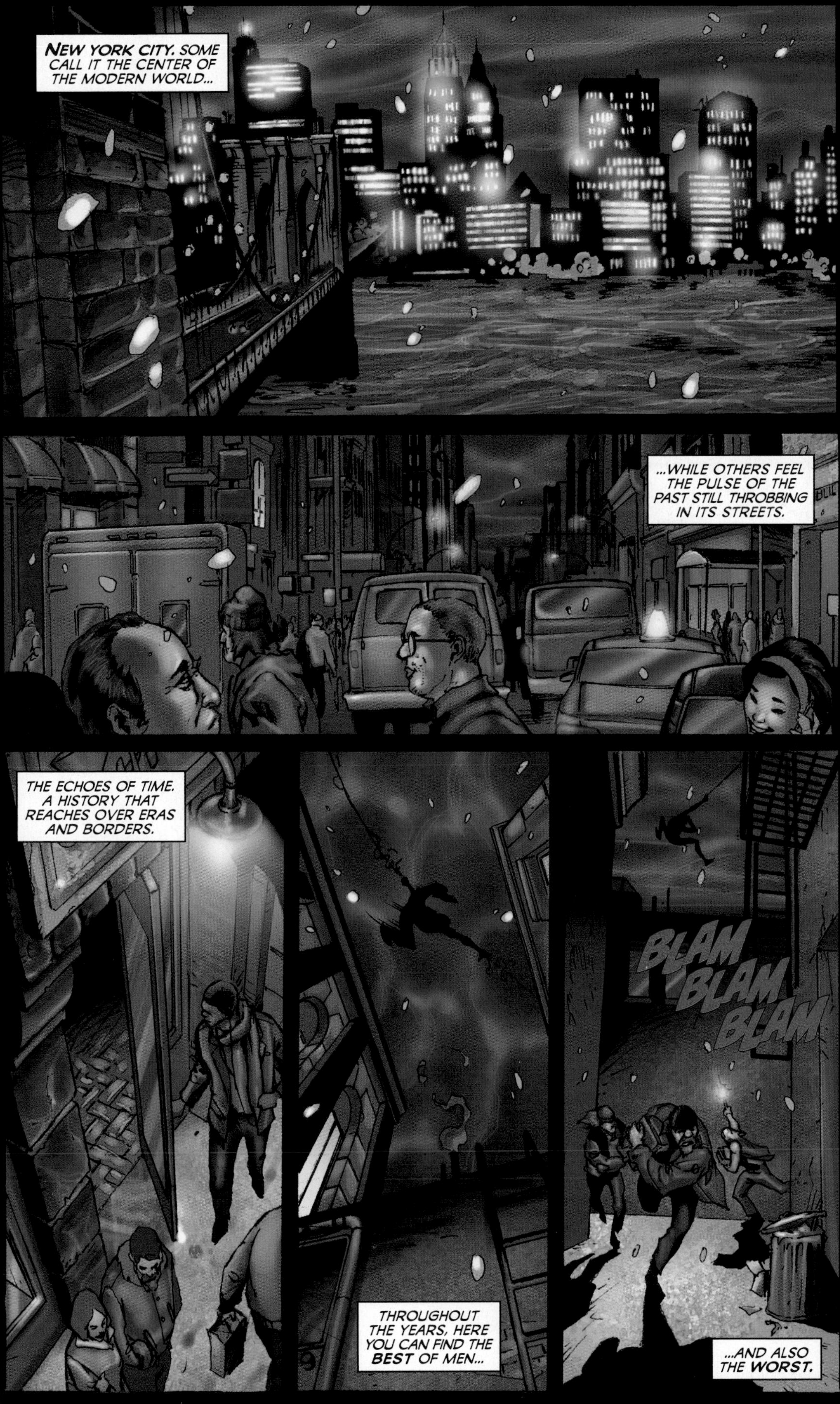
NEW YORK CITY. SOME CALL IT THE CENTER OF THE MODERN WORLD...
...WHILE OTHERS FEEL THE PULSE OF THE PAST STILL THROBBING IN ITS STREETS.
THE ECHOES OF TIME. A HISTORY THAT REACHES OVER ERAS AND BORDERS.
THROUGHOUT THE YEARS, HERE YOU CAN FIND THE BEST OF MEN...
BLAM
BLAM
BLAM
...AND ALSO THE WORST.

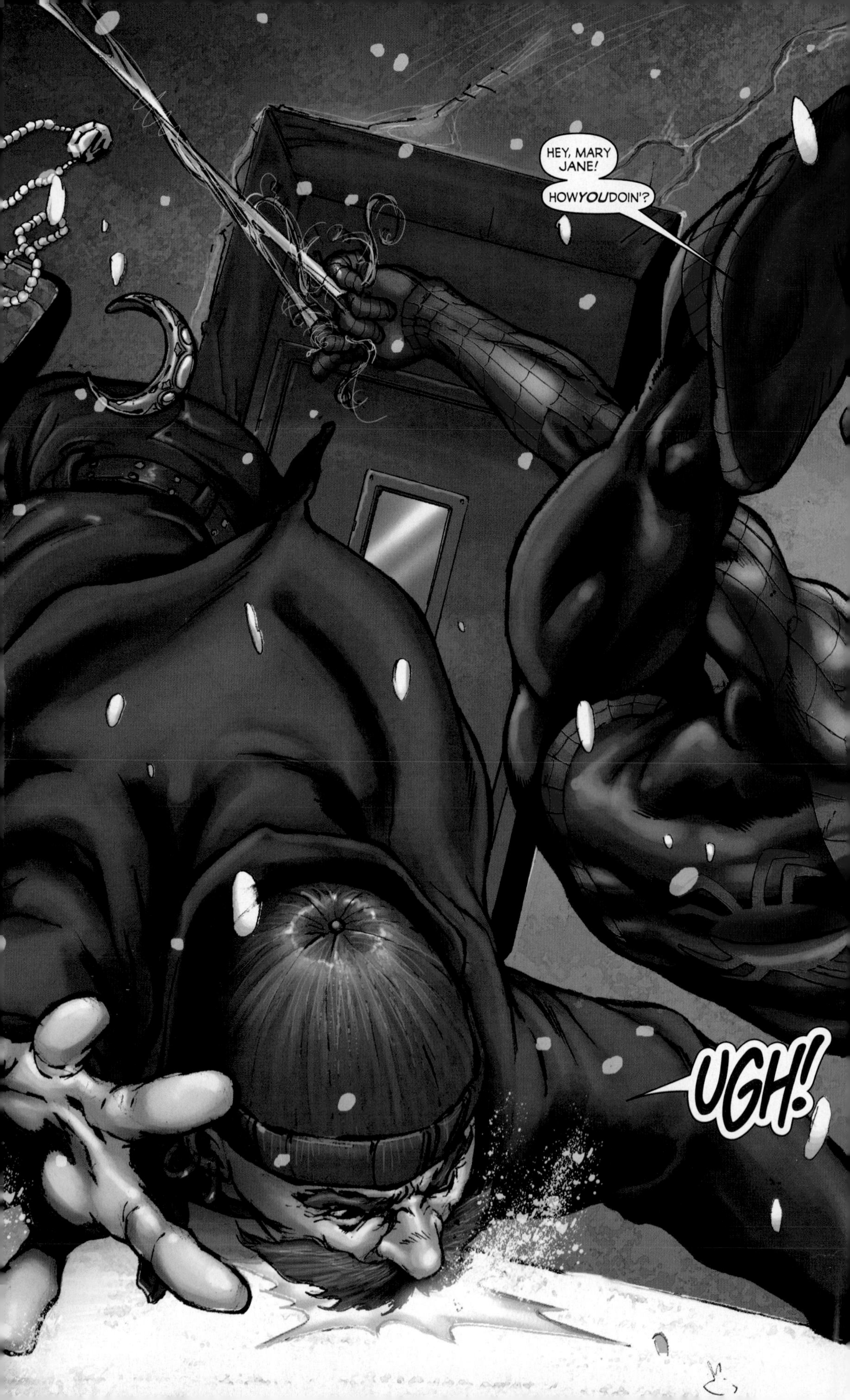
HEY, MARY JANE!
HOW *YOU* DOIN'?
UGH!

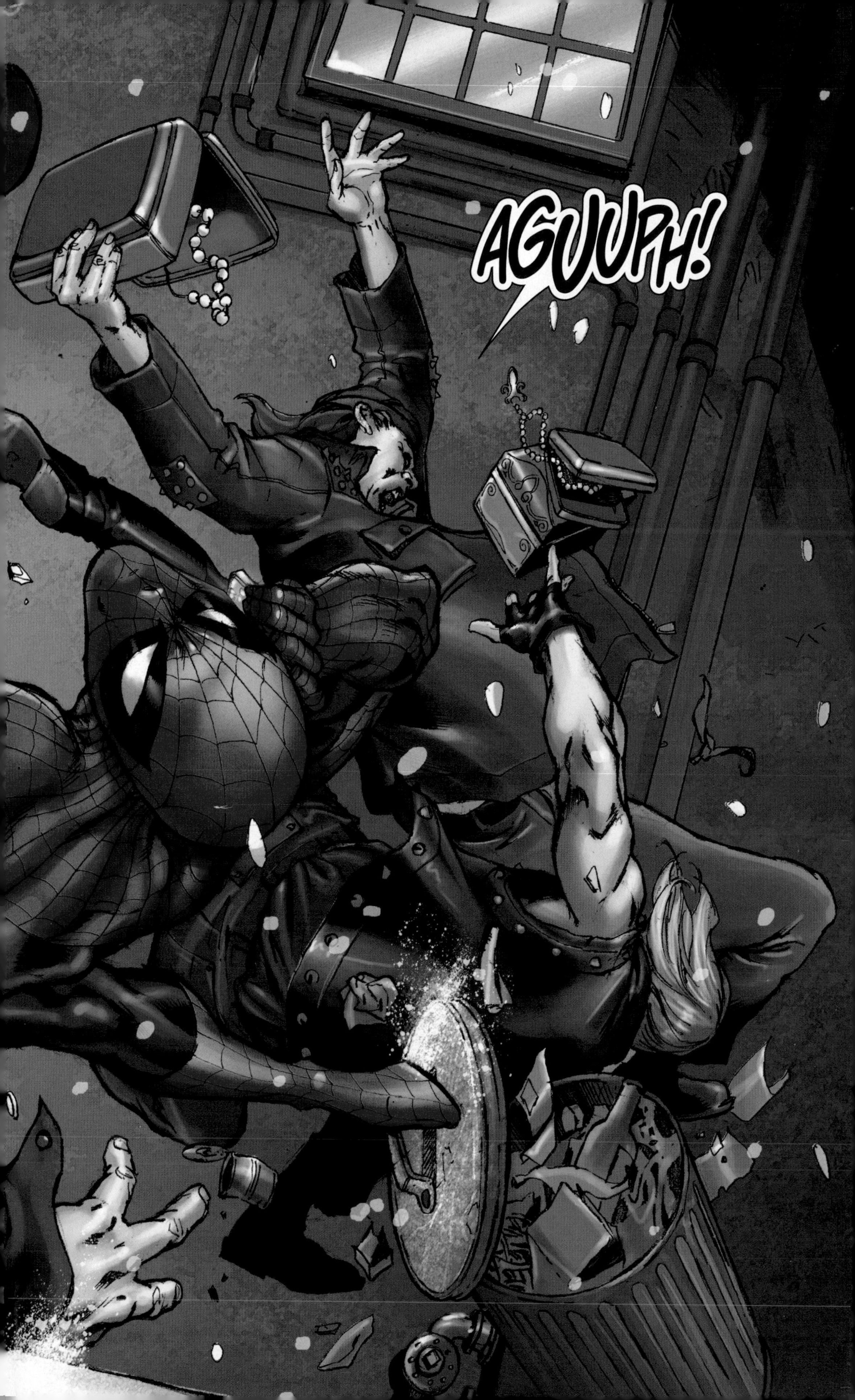
AGUUPH!

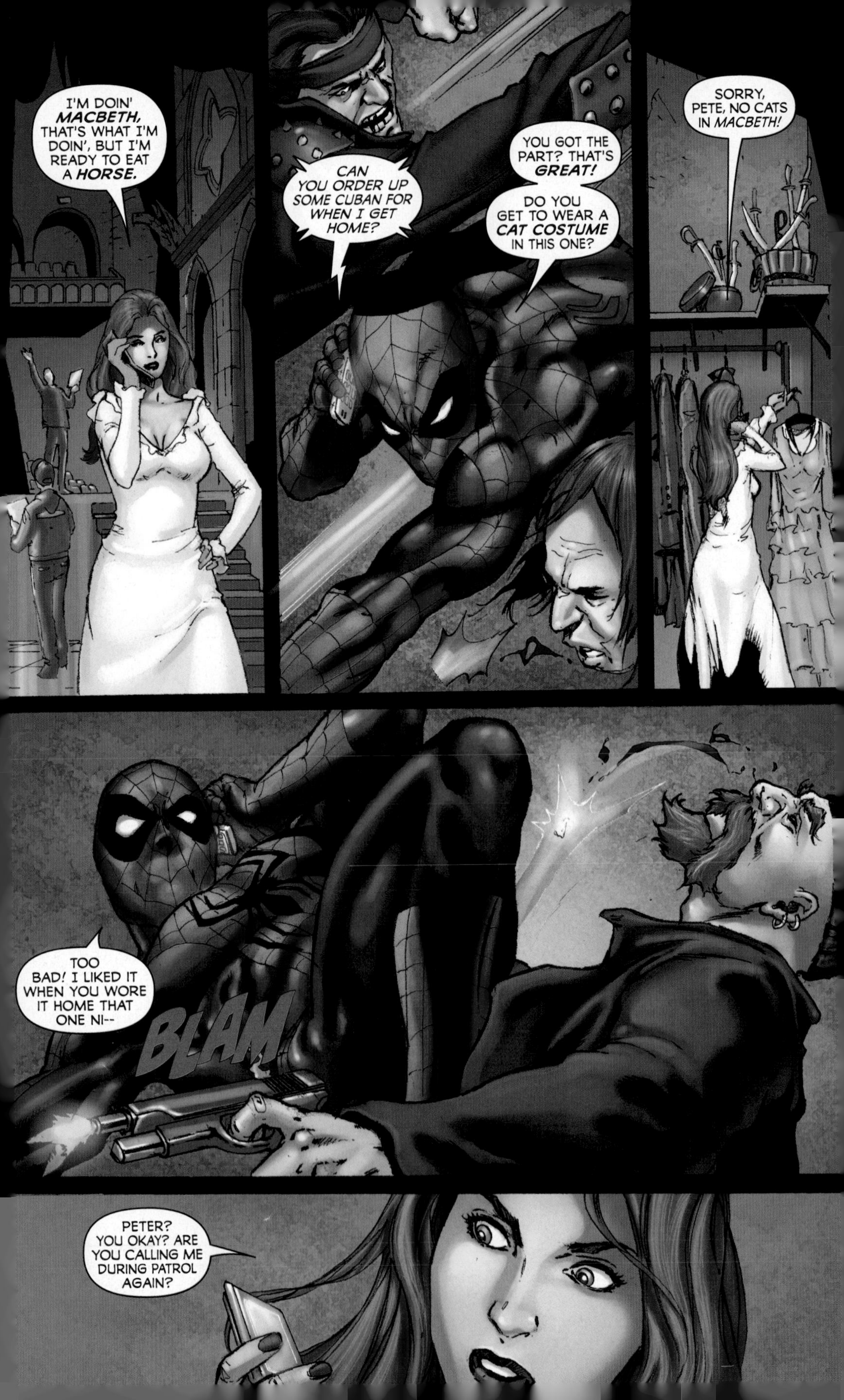
I'M DOIN' MACBETH, THAT'S WHAT I'M DOIN', BUT I'M READY TO EAT A HORSE.
CAN YOU ORDER UP SOME CUBAN FOR WHEN I GET HOME?
YOU GOT THE PART? THAT'S GREAT!
DO YOU GET TO WEAR A CAT COSTUME IN THIS ONE?
SORRY, PETE, NO CATS IN MACBETH!
TOO BAD! I LIKED IT WHEN YOU WORE IT HOME THAT ONE NI--
BLAM
PETER? YOU OKAY? ARE YOU CALLING ME DURING PATROL AGAIN?

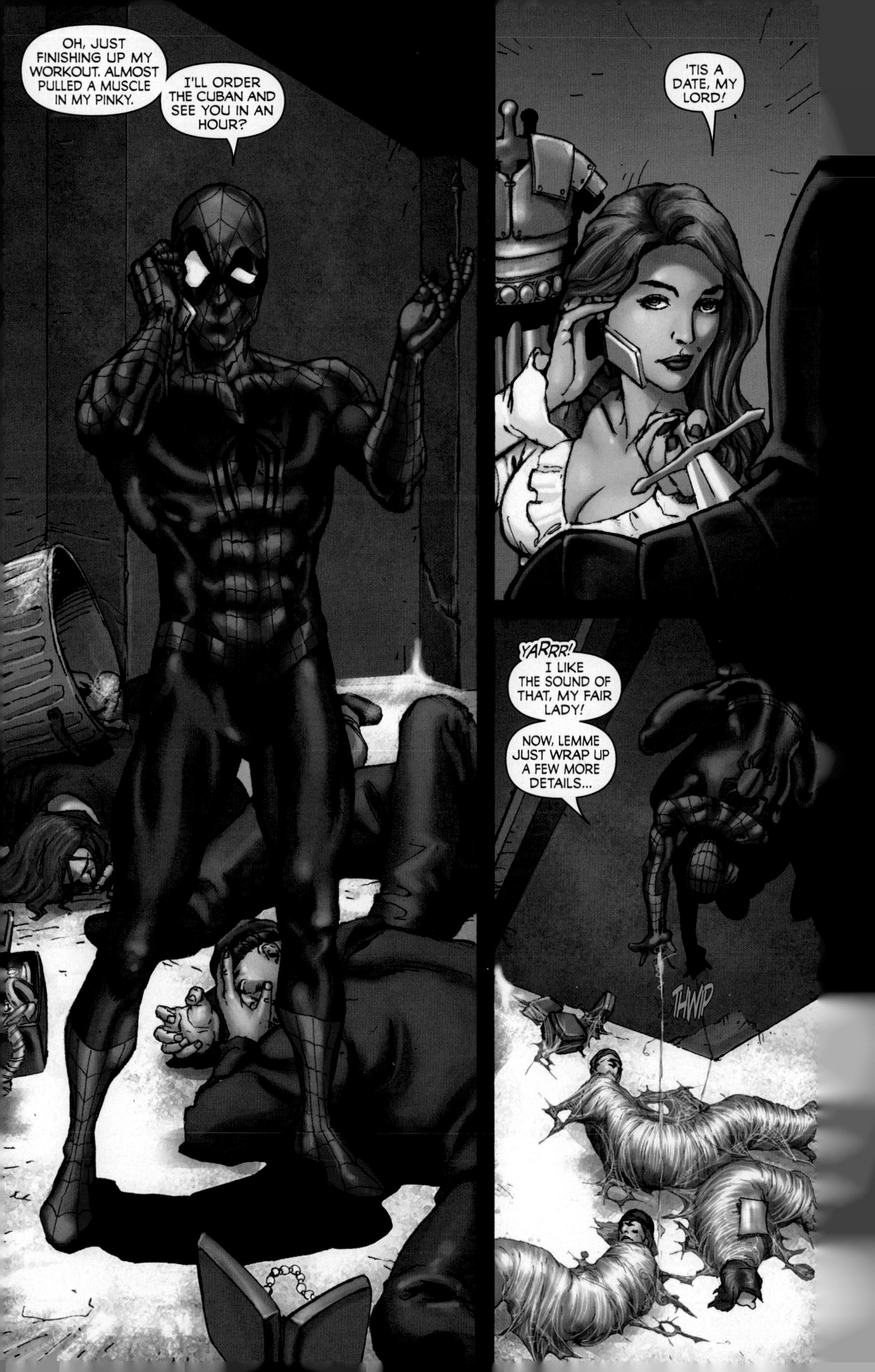
OH, JUST FINISHING UP MY WORKOUT. ALMOST PULLED A MUSCLE IN MY PINKY.
I'LL ORDER THE CUBAN AND SEE YOU IN AN HOUR?
'TIS A DATE, MY LORD!
YARRR! I LIKE THE SOUND OF THAT, MY FAIR LADY!
NOW, LEMME JUST WRAP UP A FEW MORE DETAILS...
THWIP

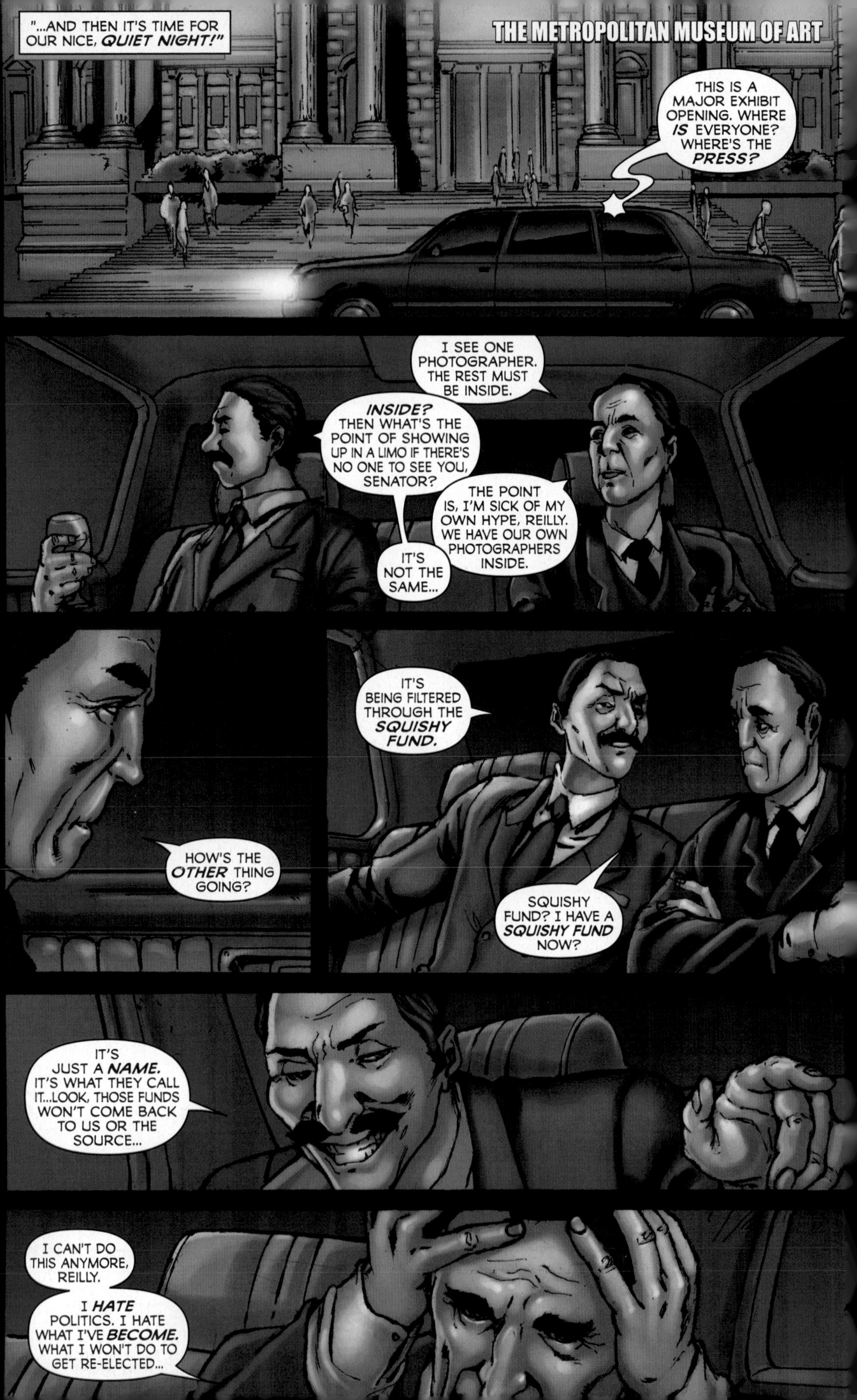
"...AND THEN IT'S TIME FOR OUR NICE, QUIET NIGHT!"
THE METROPOLITAN MUSEUM OF ART
THIS IS A MAJOR EXHIBIT OPENING. WHERE IS EVERYONE? WHERE'S THE PRESS?
I SEE ONE PHOTOGRAPHER. THE REST MUST BE INSIDE.
INSIDE? THEN WHAT'S THE POINT OF SHOWING UP IN A LIMO IF THERE'S NO ONE TO SEE YOU, SENATOR?
THE POINT IS, I'M SICK OF MY OWN HYPE, REILLY. WE HAVE OUR OWN PHOTOGRAPHERS INSIDE.
IT'S NOT THE SAME...
HOW'S THE OTHER THING GOING?
IT'S BEING FILTERED THROUGH THE SQUISHY FUND.
SQUISHY FUND? I HAVE A SQUISHY FUND NOW?
IT'S JUST A NAME. IT'S WHAT THEY CALL IT...LOOK, THOSE FUNDS WON'T COME BACK TO US OR THE SOURCE...
I CAN'T DO THIS ANYMORE, REILLY.
I HATE POLITICS. I HATE WHAT I'VE BECOME. WHAT I WON'T DO TO GET RE-ELECTED...

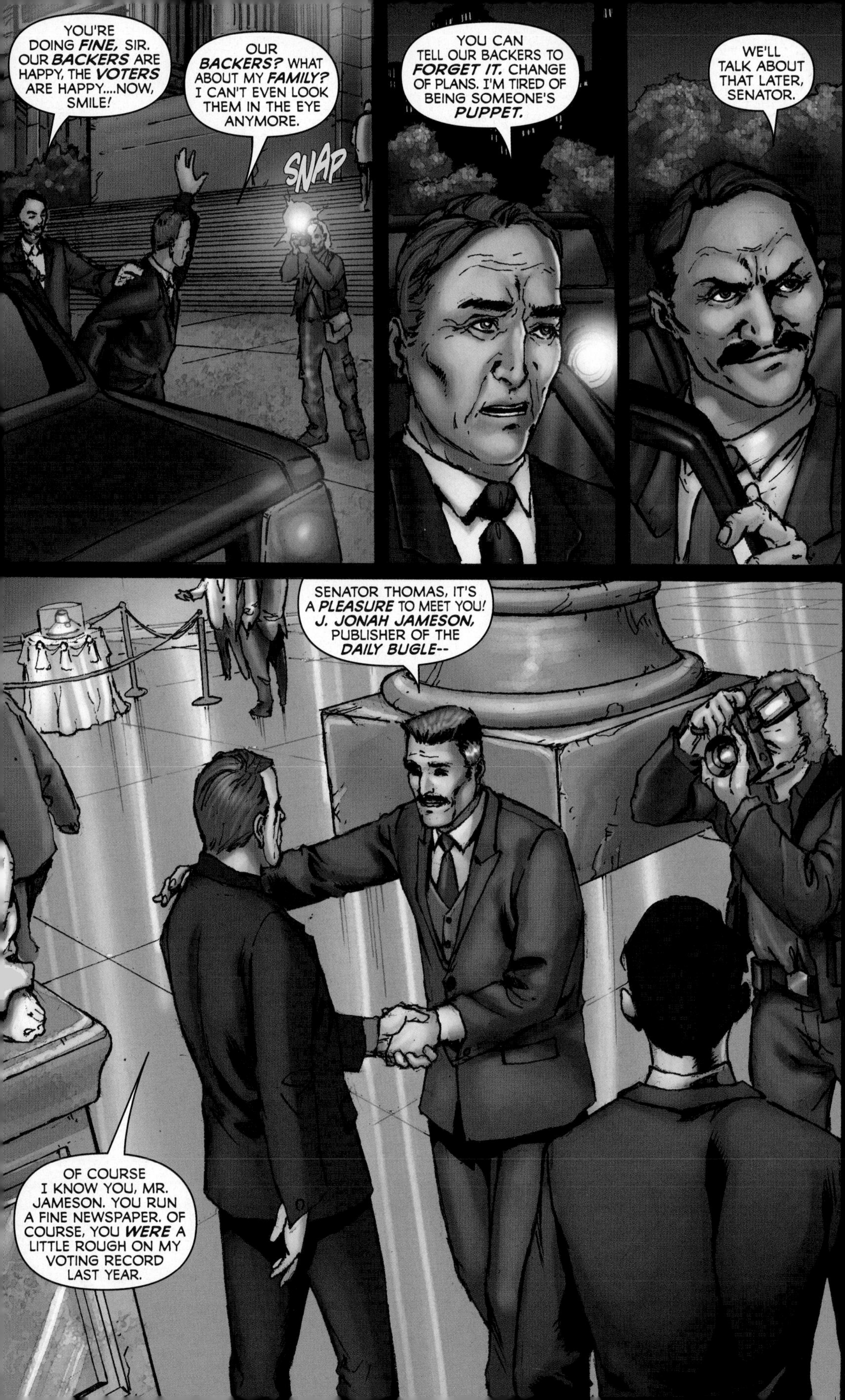
YOU'RE DOING FINE, SIR. OUR BACKERS ARE HAPPY, THE VOTERS ARE HAPPY....NOW, SMILE!
OUR BACKERS? WHAT ABOUT MY FAMILY? I CAN'T EVEN LOOK THEM IN THE EYE ANYMORE.
SNAP
YOU CAN TELL OUR BACKERS TO FORGET IT. CHANGE OF PLANS. I'M TIRED OF BEING SOMEONE'S PUPPET.
WE'LL TALK ABOUT THAT LATER, SENATOR.
SENATOR THOMAS, IT'S A PLEASURE TO MEET YOU! J. JONAH JAMESON, PUBLISHER OF THE DAILY BUGLE--
OF COURSE I KNOW YOU, MR. JAMESON. YOU RUN A FINE NEWSPAPER. OF COURSE, YOU WERE A LITTLE ROUGH ON MY VOTING RECORD LAST YEAR.

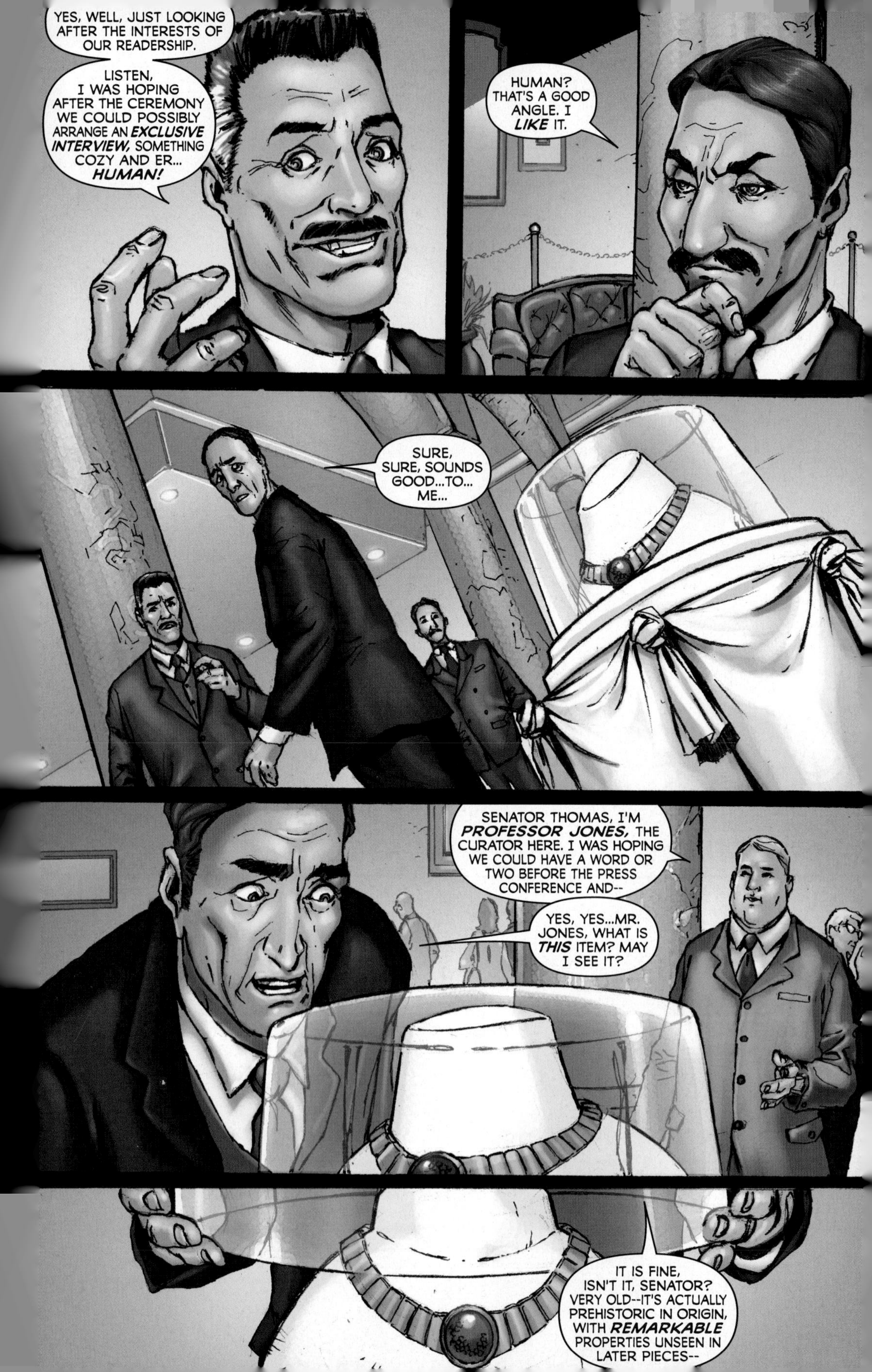
YES, WELL, JUST LOOKING AFTER THE INTERESTS OF OUR READERSHIP.
LISTEN, I WAS HOPING AFTER THE CEREMONY WE COULD POSSIBLY ARRANGE AN EXCLUSIVE INTERVIEW, SOMETHING COZY AND ER... HUMAN!
HUMAN? THAT'S A GOOD ANGLE. I LIKE IT.
SURE, SURE, SOUNDS GOOD...TO... ME...
SENATOR THOMAS, I'M PROFESSOR JONES, THE CURATOR HERE. I WAS HOPING WE COULD HAVE A WORD OR TWO BEFORE THE PRESS CONFERENCE AND--
YES, YES...MR. JONES, WHAT IS THIS ITEM? MAY I SEE IT?
IT IS FINE, ISN'T IT, SENATOR? VERY OLD--IT'S ACTUALLY PREHISTORIC IN ORIGIN, WITH REMARKABLE PROPERTIES UNSEEN IN LATER PIECES--

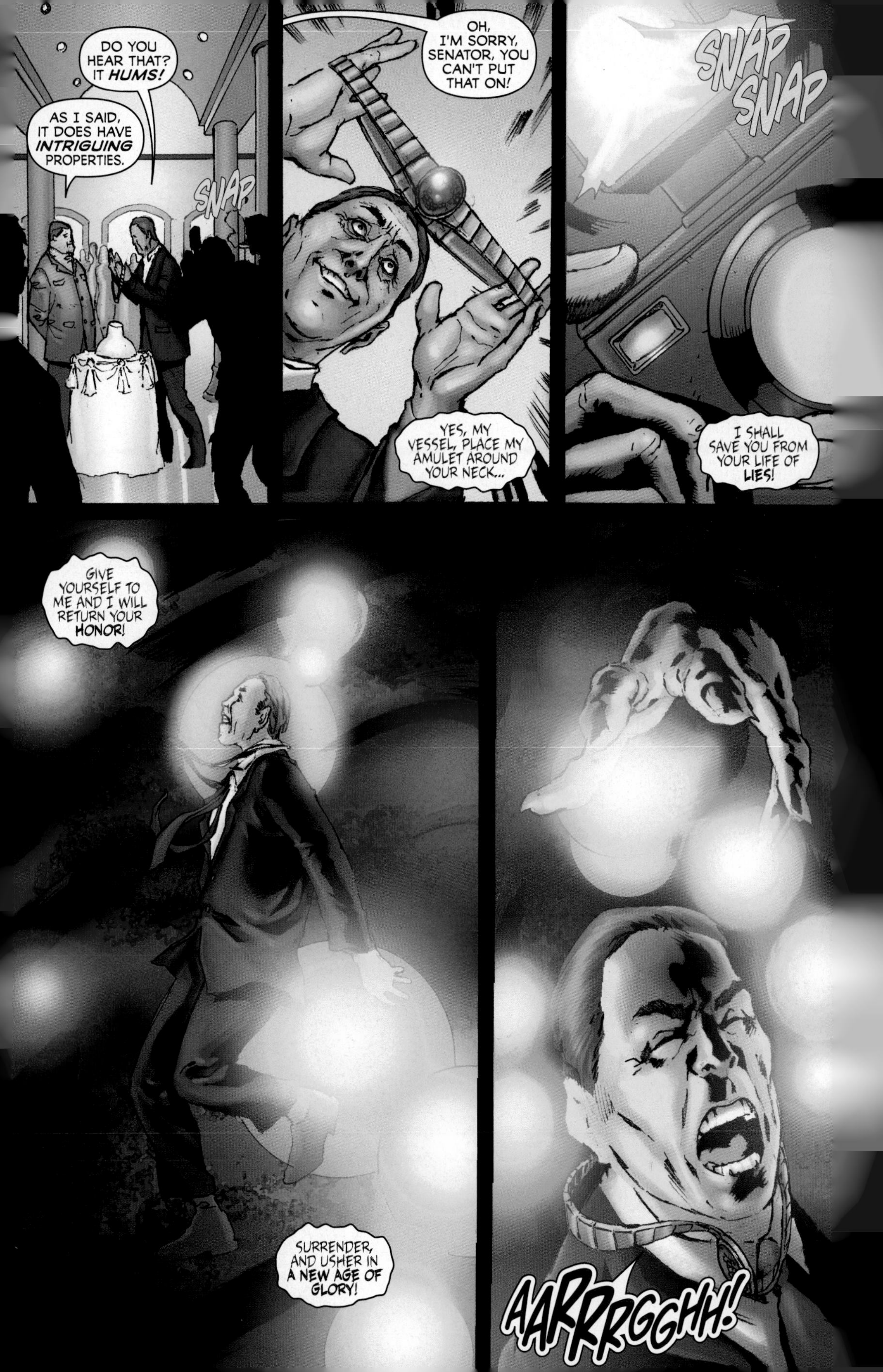

DO YOU HEAR THAT? IT HUMS!
AS I SAID, IT DOES HAVE INTRIGUING PROPERTIES.
SNAP
OH, I'M SORRY, SENATOR, YOU CAN'T PUT THAT ON!
YES, MY VESSEL, PLACE MY AMULET AROUND YOUR NECK...
SNAP SNAP
I SHALL SAVE YOU FROM YOUR LIFE OF LIES!
GIVE YOURSELF TO ME AND I WILL RETURN YOUR HONOR!
SURRENDER, AND USHER IN A NEW AGE OF GLORY!
AARRRGGHH!

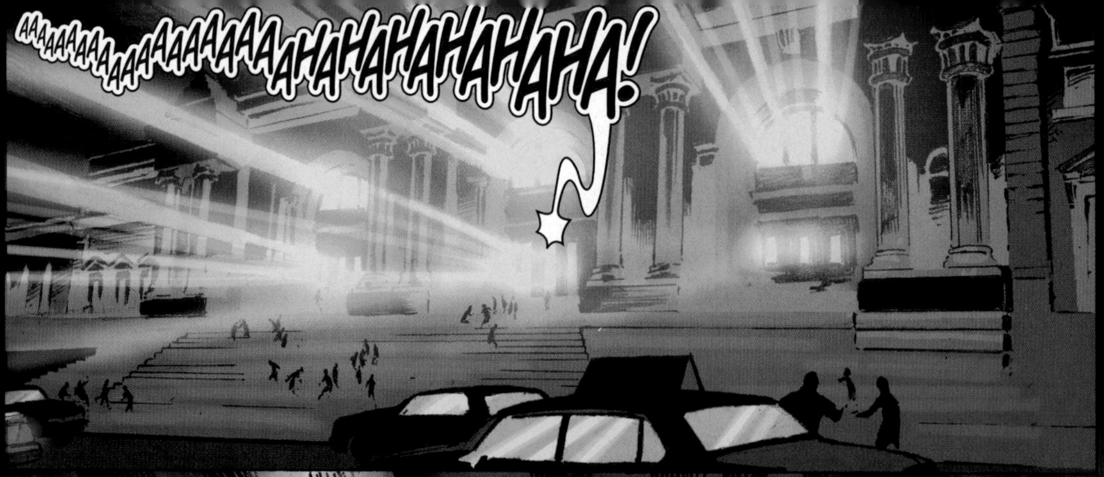
AAAAAAAAAAAAAAAAAAHAHAHAHAHAHA!

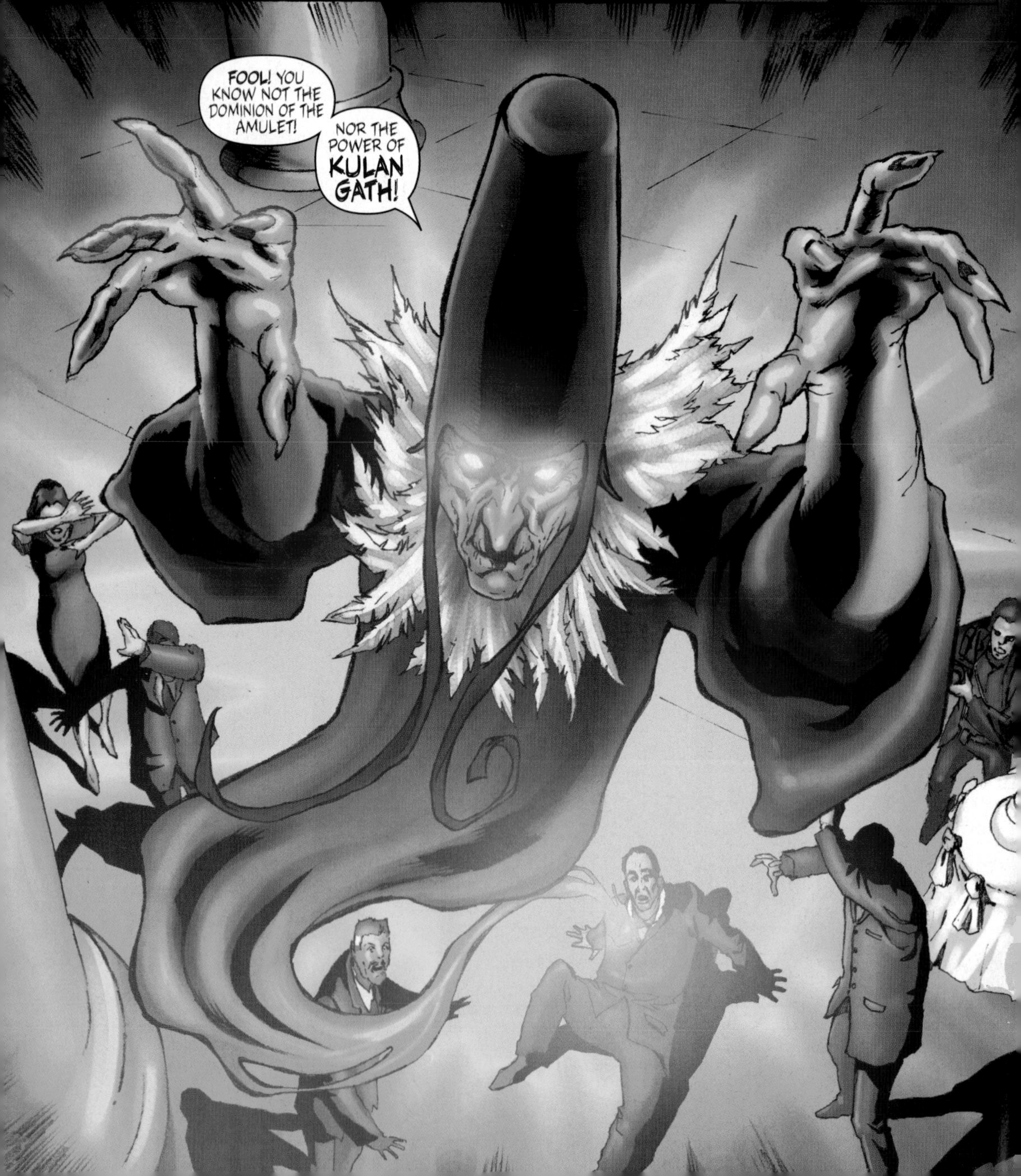
FOOL! YOU KNOW NOT THE DOMINION OF THE AMULET!
NOR THE POWER OF KULAN GATH!

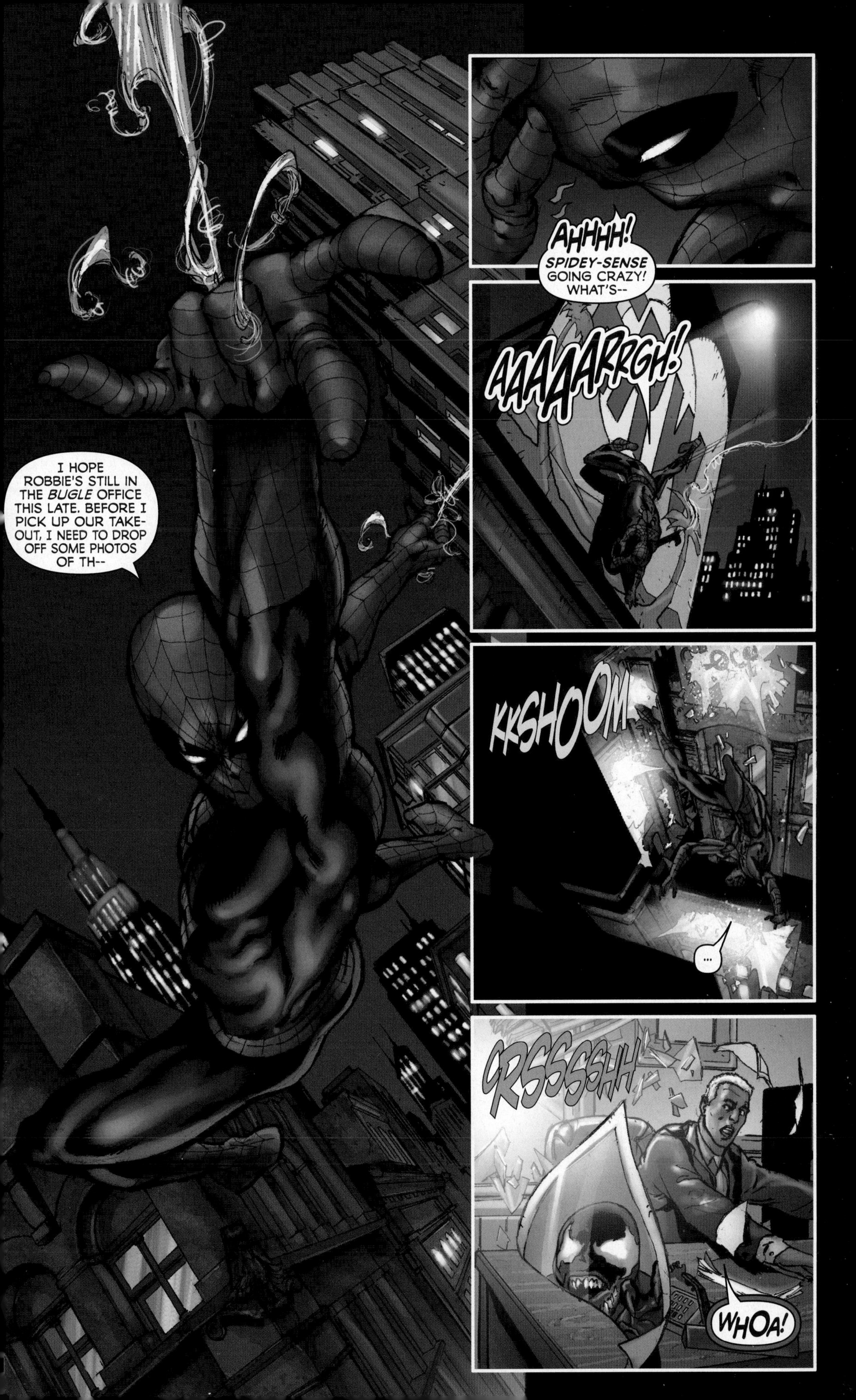
I HOPE ROBBIE'S STILL IN THE *BUGLE* OFFICE THIS LATE. BEFORE I PICK UP OUR TAKE-OUT, I NEED TO DROP OFF SOME PHOTOS OF TH--
AHHHH!
SPIDEY-SENSE GOING CRAZY! WHAT'S--
AAAAARRGH!
KKSHOOM
...
CRSSSSHH
WHOA!

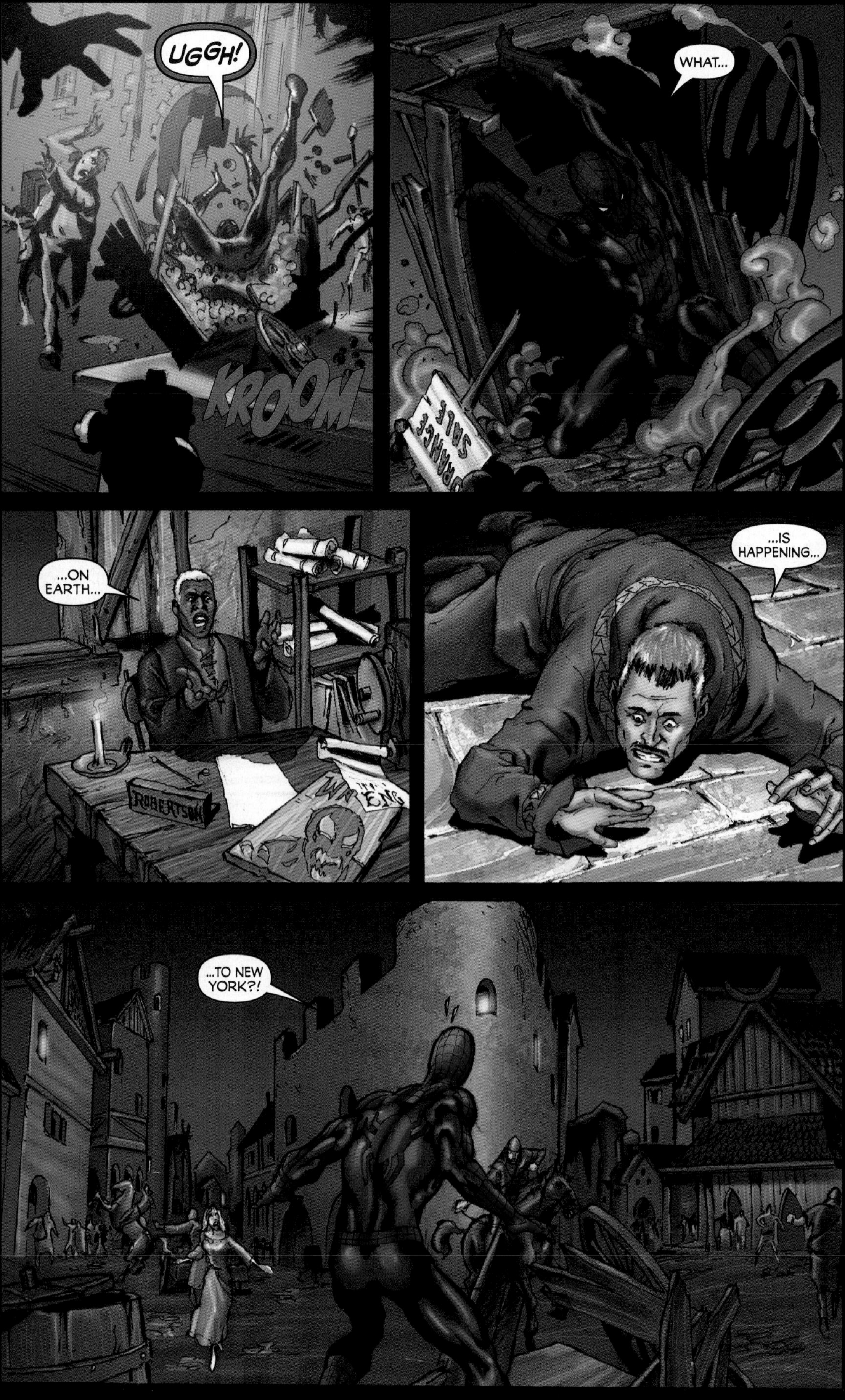
UGGH!
KROOM
WHAT...
...ON EARTH...
ROBERTSON
...IS HAPPENING...
...TO NEW YORK?!

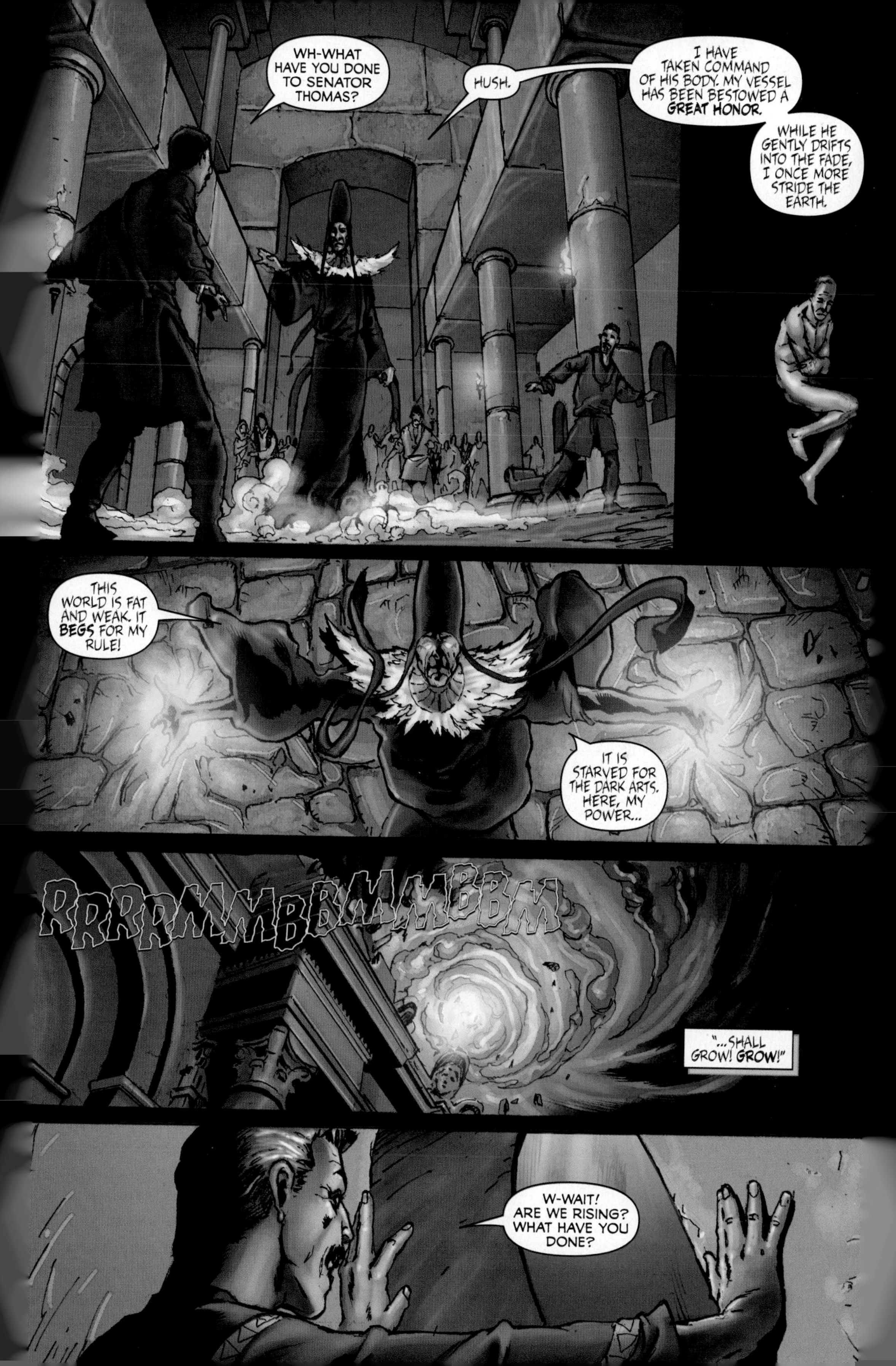
WH-WHAT HAVE YOU DONE TO SENATOR THOMAS?
HUSH.
I HAVE TAKEN COMMAND OF HIS BODY. MY VESSEL HAS BEEN BESTOWED A **GREAT HONOR**.
WHILE HE GENTLY DRIFTS INTO THE FADE, I ONCE MORE STRIDE THE EARTH.
THIS WORLD IS FAT AND WEAK. IT **BEGS** FOR MY RULE!
IT IS STARVED FOR THE DARK ARTS. HERE, MY POWER...
RRRRMMMBBMMMBBM
"...SHALL GROW! **GROW!**"
W-WAIT! ARE WE RISING? WHAT HAVE YOU DONE?

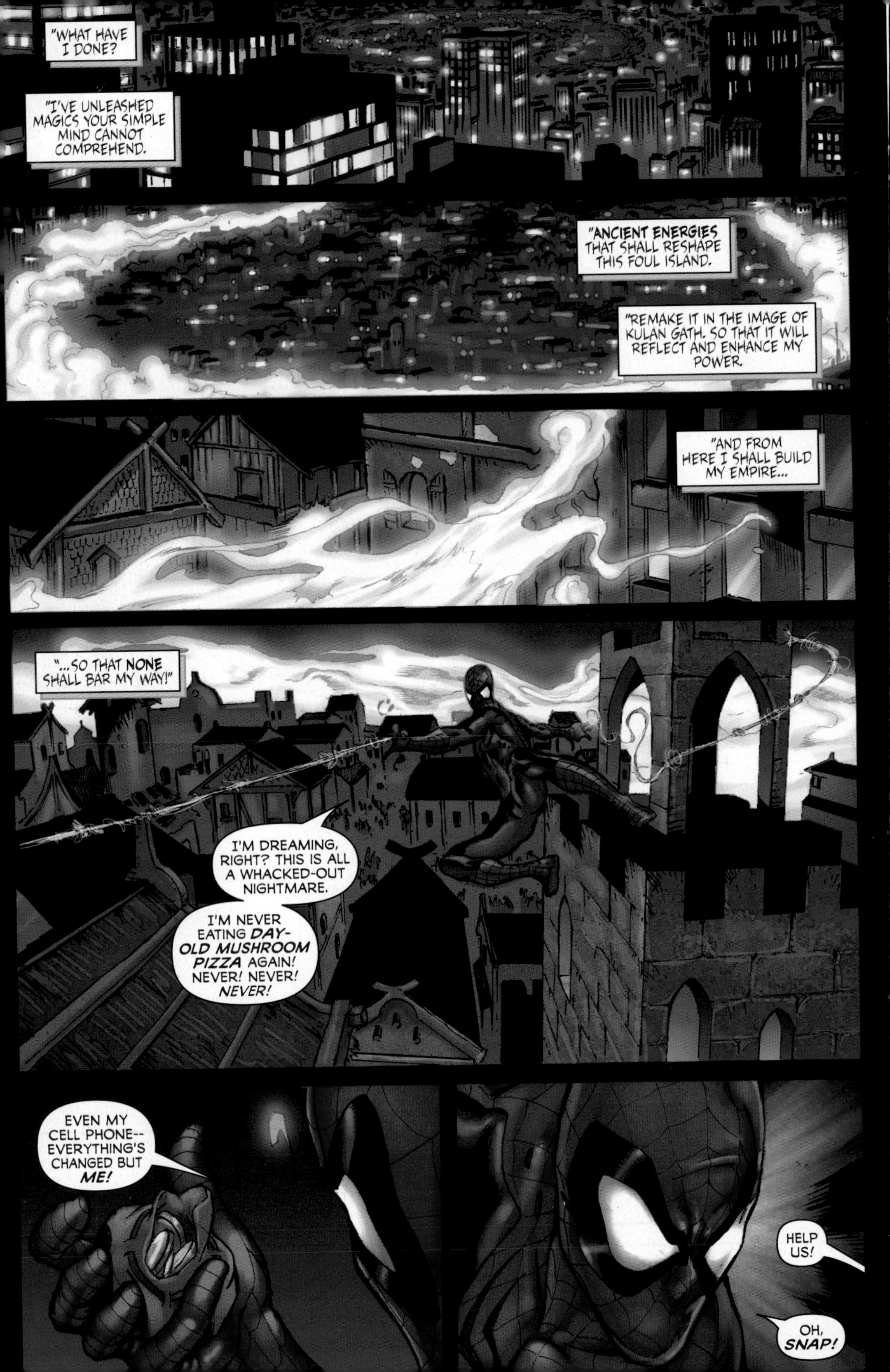

"WHAT HAVE I DONE?
"I'VE UNLEASHED MAGICS YOUR SIMPLE MIND CANNOT COMPREHEND.
"ANCIENT ENERGIES THAT SHALL RESHAPE THIS FOUL ISLAND.
"REMAKE IT IN THE IMAGE OF KULAN GATH. SO THAT IT WILL REFLECT AND ENHANCE MY POWER.
"AND FROM HERE I SHALL BUILD MY EMPIRE...
"...SO THAT NONE SHALL BAR MY WAY!"
I'M DREAMING, RIGHT? THIS IS ALL A WHACKED-OUT NIGHTMARE.
I'M NEVER EATING DAY-OLD MUSHROOM PIZZA AGAIN! NEVER! NEVER! NEVER!
EVEN MY CELL PHONE--EVERYTHING'S CHANGED BUT ME!
HELP US!
OH, SNAP!

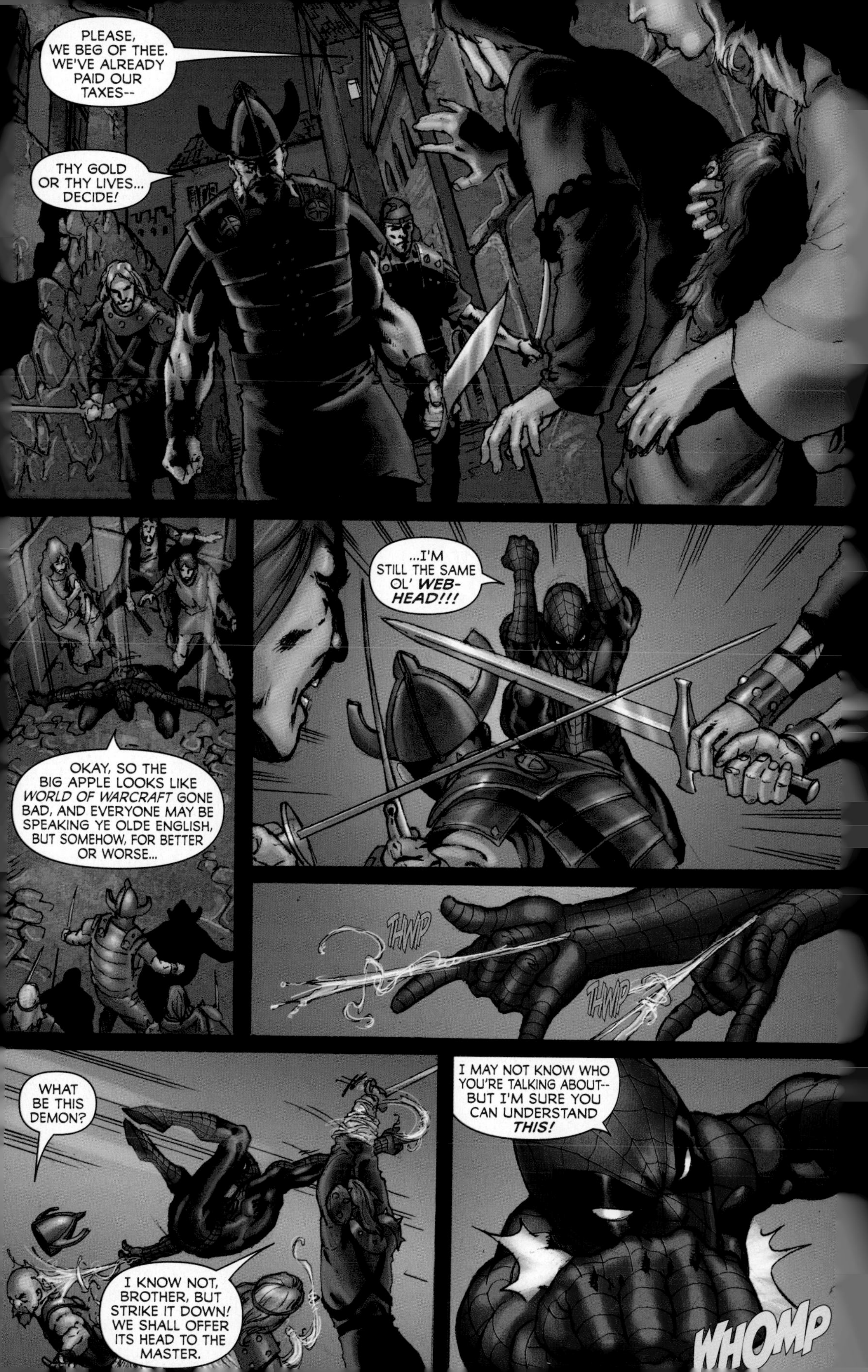
PLEASE, WE BEG OF THEE. WE'VE ALREADY PAID OUR TAXES--
THY GOLD OR THY LIVES... DECIDE!
OKAY, SO THE BIG APPLE LOOKS LIKE *WORLD OF WARCRAFT* GONE BAD, AND EVERYONE MAY BE SPEAKING YE OLDE ENGLISH, BUT SOMEHOW, FOR BETTER OR WORSE...
...I'M STILL THE SAME OL' *WEB-HEAD!!!*
THWIP
THWIP
WHAT BE THIS DEMON?
I KNOW NOT, BROTHER, BUT STRIKE IT DOWN! WE SHALL OFFER ITS HEAD TO THE MASTER.
I MAY NOT KNOW WHO YOU'RE TALKING ABOUT-- BUT I'M SURE YOU CAN UNDERSTAND *THIS!*
WHOMP

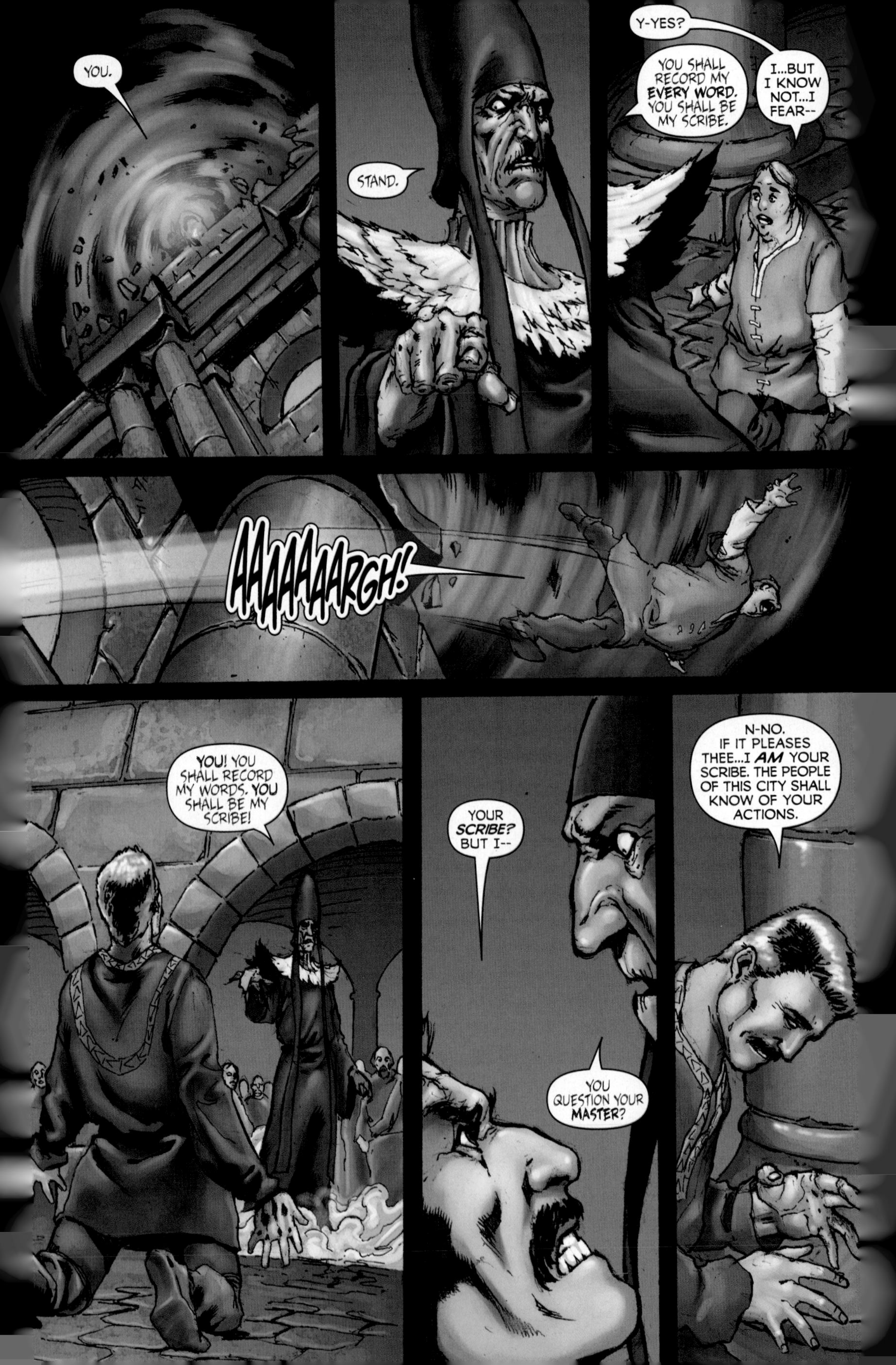
YOU.
STAND.
Y-YES?
YOU SHALL RECORD MY **EVERY WORD.** YOU SHALL BE MY SCRIBE.
I...BUT I KNOW NOT...I FEAR--
AAAAAAARGH!
**YOU!** YOU SHALL RECORD MY WORDS. **YOU** SHALL BE MY SCRIBE!
YOUR ***SCRIBE?*** BUT I--
YOU QUESTION YOUR **MASTER?**
N-NO. IF IT PLEASES THEE...I ***AM*** YOUR SCRIBE. THE PEOPLE OF THIS CITY SHALL KNOW OF YOUR ACTIONS.

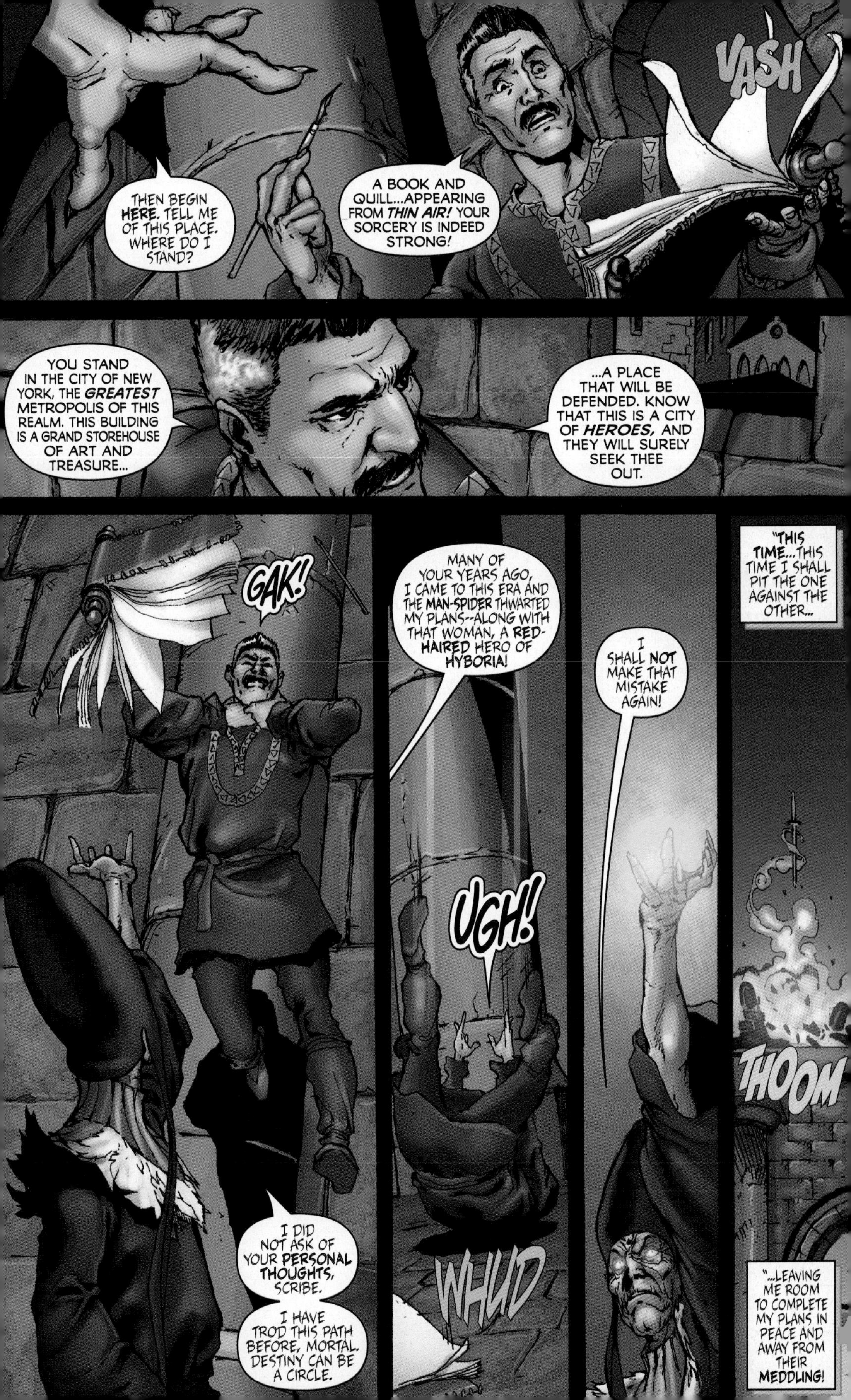
THEN BEGIN HERE. TELL ME OF THIS PLACE. WHERE DO I STAND?
A BOOK AND QUILL...APPEARING FROM THIN AIR! YOUR SORCERY IS INDEED STRONG!
VASH
YOU STAND IN THE CITY OF NEW YORK, THE GREATEST METROPOLIS OF THIS REALM. THIS BUILDING IS A GRAND STOREHOUSE OF ART AND TREASURE...
...A PLACE THAT WILL BE DEFENDED. KNOW THAT THIS IS A CITY OF HEROES, AND THEY WILL SURELY SEEK THEE OUT.
GAK!
I DID NOT ASK OF YOUR PERSONAL THOUGHTS, SCRIBE.
I HAVE TROD THIS PATH BEFORE, MORTAL. DESTINY CAN BE A CIRCLE.
MANY OF YOUR YEARS AGO, I CAME TO THIS ERA AND THE MAN-SPIDER THWARTED MY PLANS--ALONG WITH THAT WOMAN, A RED-HAIRED HERO OF HYBORIA!
UGH!
WHUD
I SHALL NOT MAKE THAT MISTAKE AGAIN!
"THIS TIME...THIS TIME I SHALL PIT THE ONE AGAINST THE OTHER...
THOOM
"...LEAVING ME ROOM TO COMPLETE MY PLANS IN PEACE AND AWAY FROM THEIR MEDDLING!

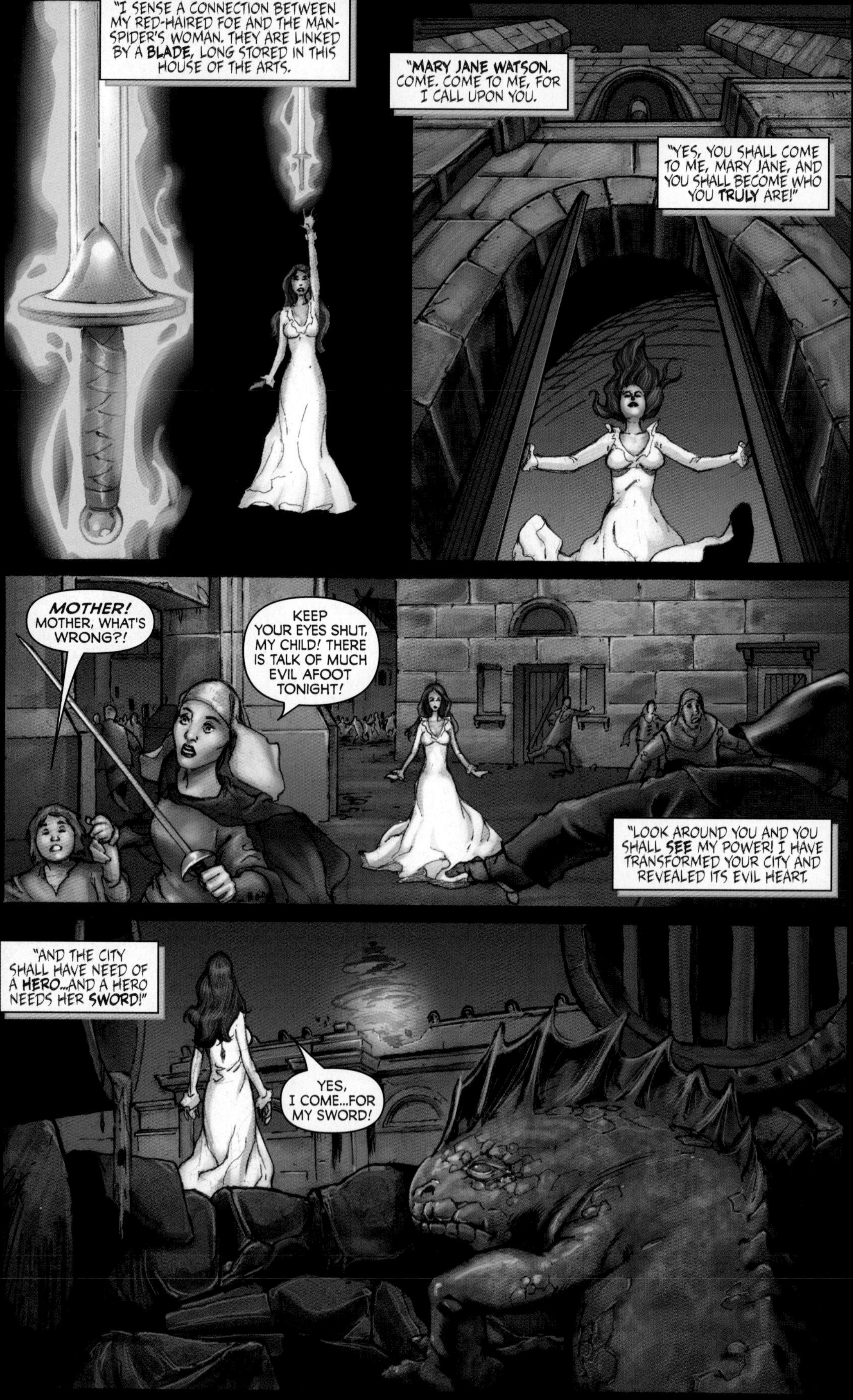
"I SENSE A CONNECTION BETWEEN MY RED-HAIRED FOE AND THE MAN-SPIDER'S WOMAN. THEY ARE LINKED BY A **BLADE**, LONG STORED IN THIS HOUSE OF THE ARTS.
"**MARY JANE WATSON**. COME. COME TO ME, FOR I CALL UPON YOU.
"YES, YOU SHALL COME TO ME, MARY JANE, AND YOU SHALL BECOME WHO YOU **TRULY** ARE!"
***MOTHER!*** MOTHER, WHAT'S WRONG?!
KEEP YOUR EYES SHUT, MY CHILD! THERE IS TALK OF MUCH EVIL AFOOT TONIGHT!
"LOOK AROUND YOU AND YOU SHALL **SEE** MY POWER! I HAVE TRANSFORMED YOUR CITY AND REVEALED ITS EVIL HEART.
"AND THE CITY SHALL HAVE NEED OF A **HERO**...AND A HERO NEEDS HER **SWORD**!"
YES, I COME...FOR MY SWORD!

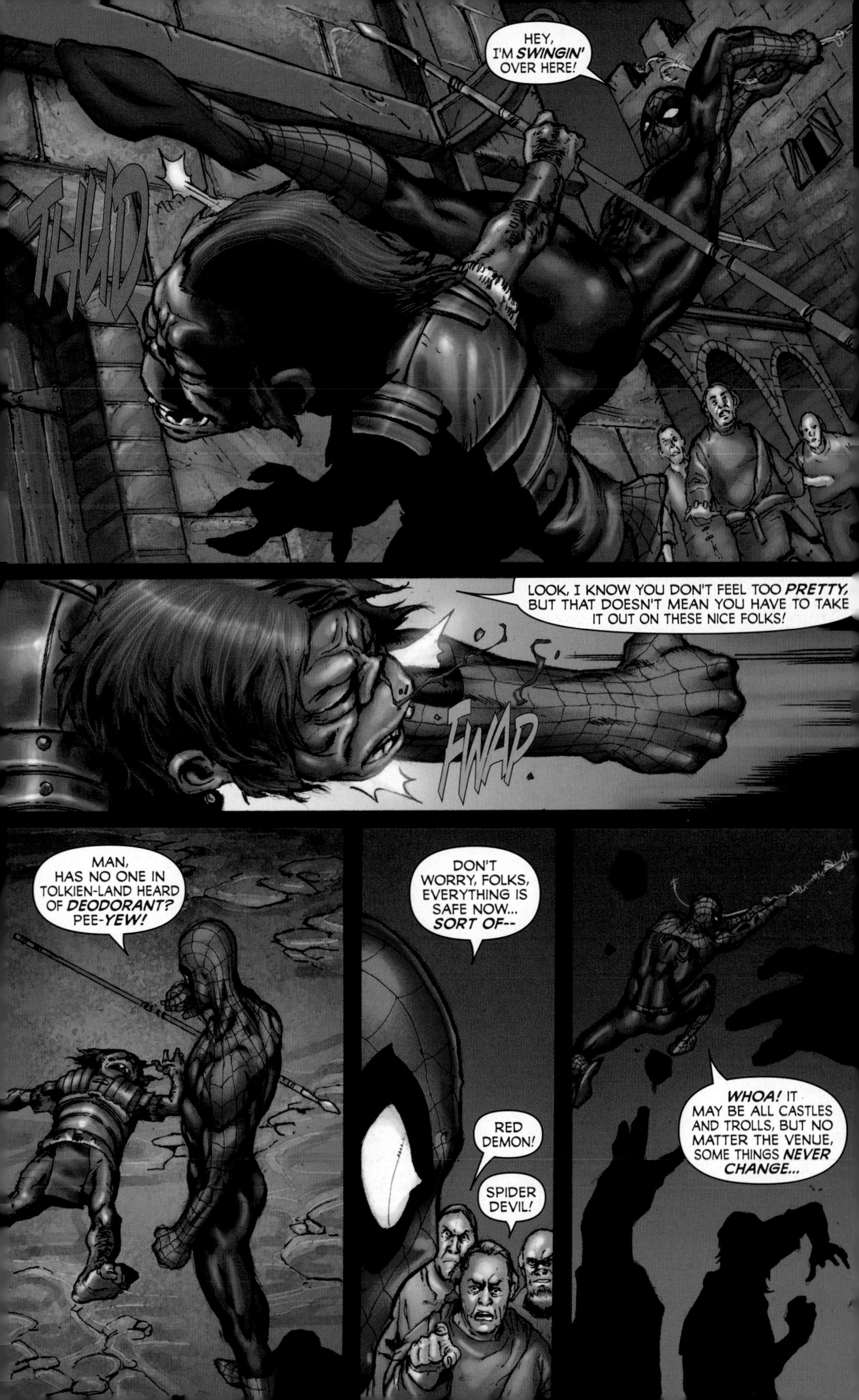
HEY, I'M SWINGIN' OVER HERE!
THUD
LOOK, I KNOW YOU DON'T FEEL TOO PRETTY, BUT THAT DOESN'T MEAN YOU HAVE TO TAKE IT OUT ON THESE NICE FOLKS!
FWAP
MAN, HAS NO ONE IN TOLKIEN-LAND HEARD OF DEODORANT? PEE-YEW!
DON'T WORRY, FOLKS, EVERYTHING IS SAFE NOW... SORT OF--
RED DEMON!
SPIDER DEVIL!
WHOA! IT MAY BE ALL CASTLES AND TROLLS, BUT NO MATTER THE VENUE, SOME THINGS NEVER CHANGE...

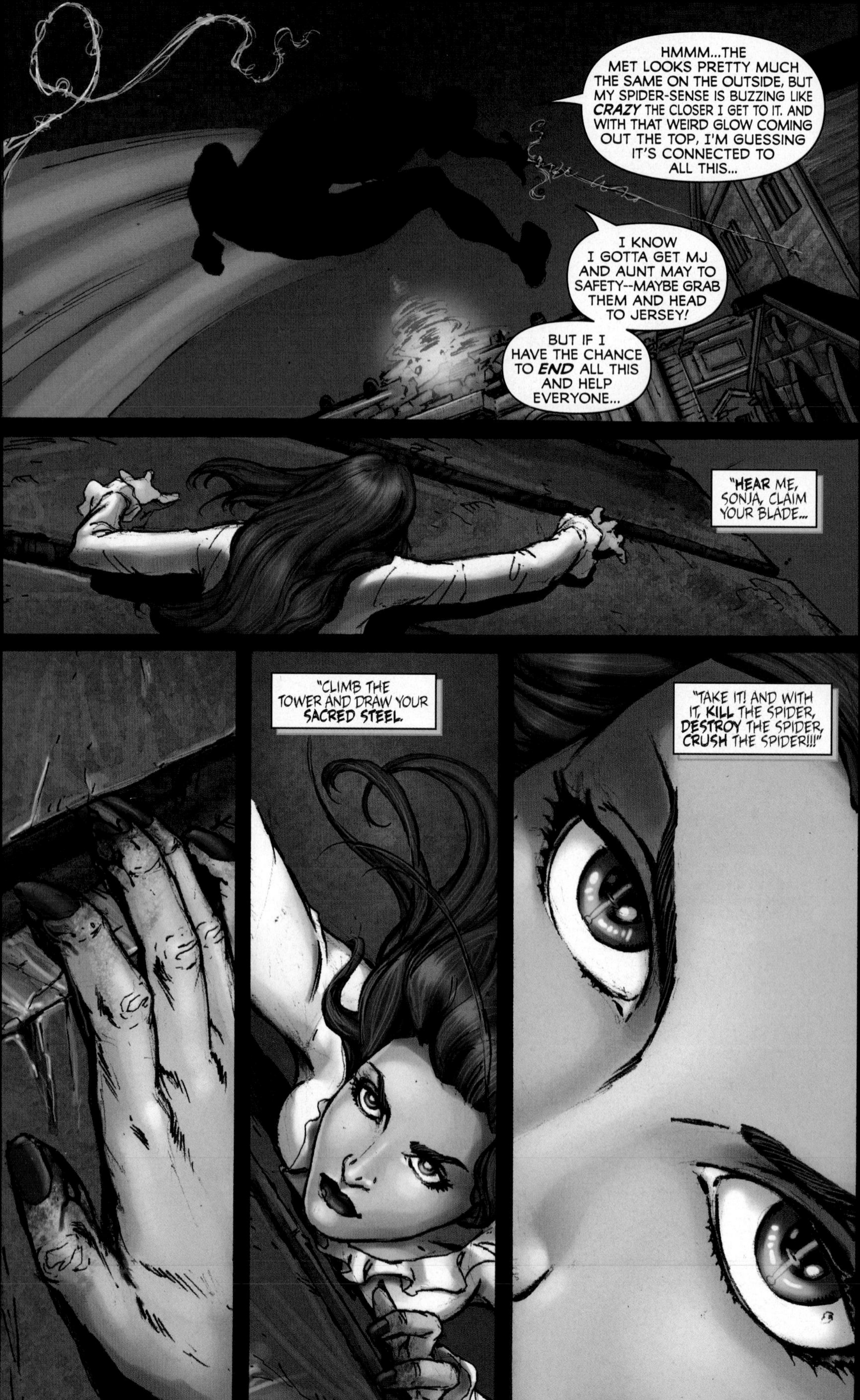
HMMM...THE MET LOOKS PRETTY MUCH THE SAME ON THE OUTSIDE, BUT MY SPIDER-SENSE IS BUZZING LIKE *CRAZY* THE CLOSER I GET TO IT. AND WITH THAT WEIRD GLOW COMING OUT THE TOP, I'M GUESSING IT'S CONNECTED TO ALL THIS...
I KNOW I GOTTA GET MJ AND AUNT MAY TO SAFETY--MAYBE GRAB THEM AND HEAD TO JERSEY!
BUT IF I HAVE THE CHANCE TO *END* ALL THIS AND HELP EVERYONE...
"**HEAR** ME, SONJA, CLAIM YOUR BLADE...
"CLIMB THE TOWER AND DRAW YOUR **SACRED STEEL**.
"TAKE IT! AND WITH IT, **KILL** THE SPIDER, **DESTROY** THE SPIDER, **CRUSH** THE SPIDER!!!"

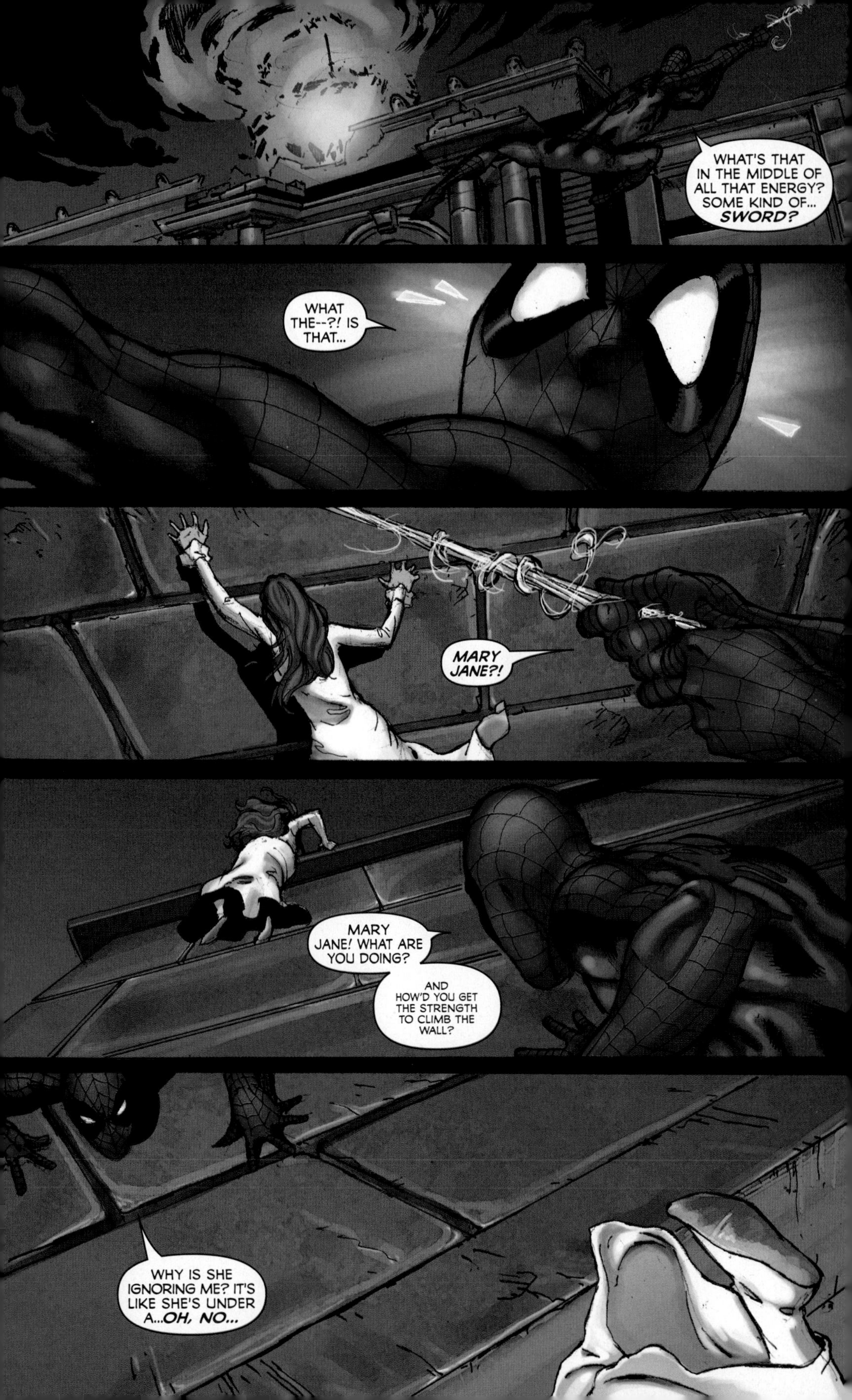
WHAT'S THAT IN THE MIDDLE OF ALL THAT ENERGY? SOME KIND OF... SWORD?
WHAT THE--?! IS THAT...
MARY JANE?!
MARY JANE! WHAT ARE YOU DOING?
AND HOW'D YOU GET THE STRENGTH TO CLIMB THE WALL?
WHY IS SHE IGNORING ME? IT'S LIKE SHE'S UNDER A...OH, NO...

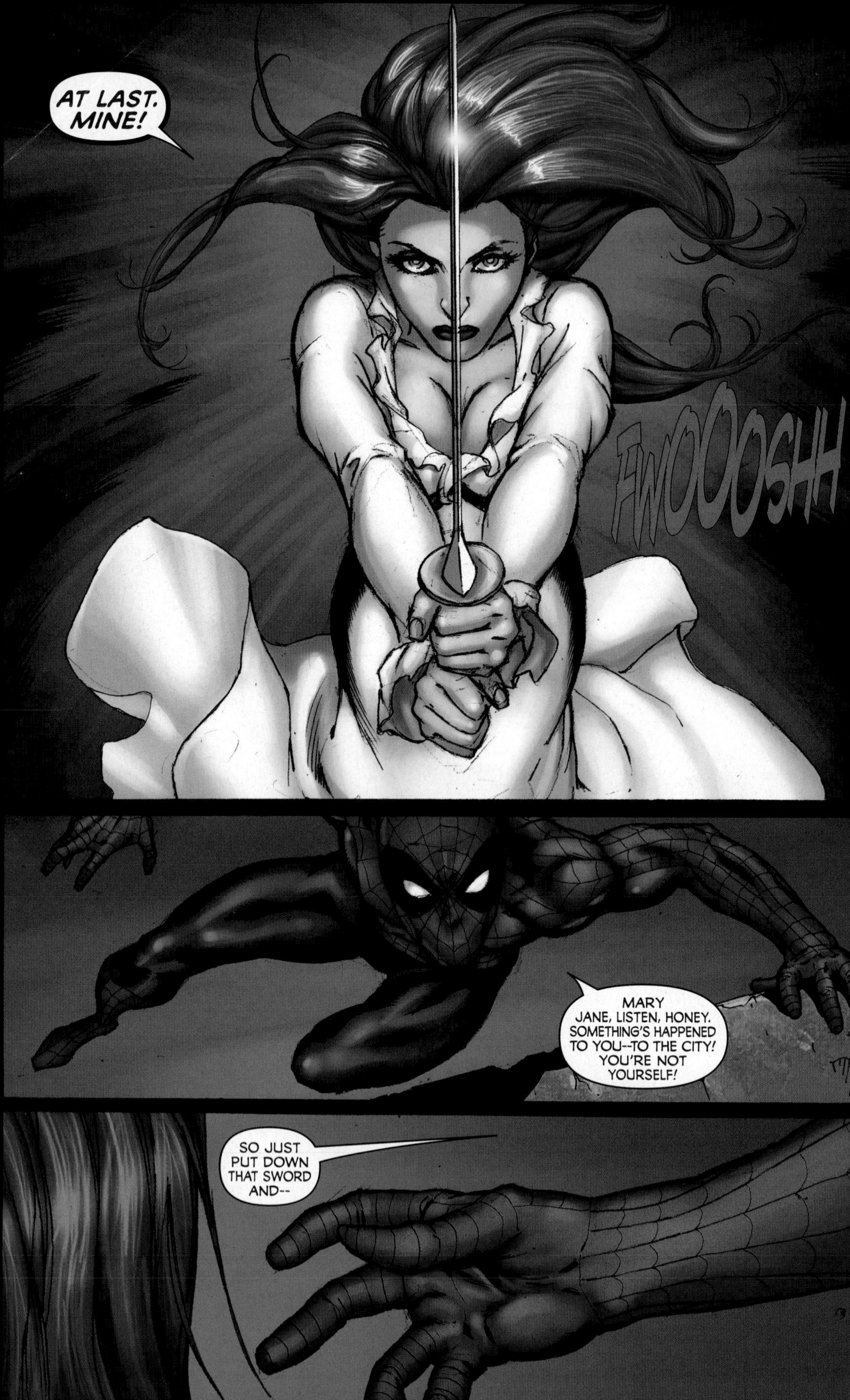
AT LAST. MINE!
FWOOOOSHH
MARY JANE, LISTEN, HONEY. SOMETHING'S HAPPENED TO YOU--TO THE CITY! YOU'RE NOT YOURSELF!
SO JUST PUT DOWN THAT SWORD AND--

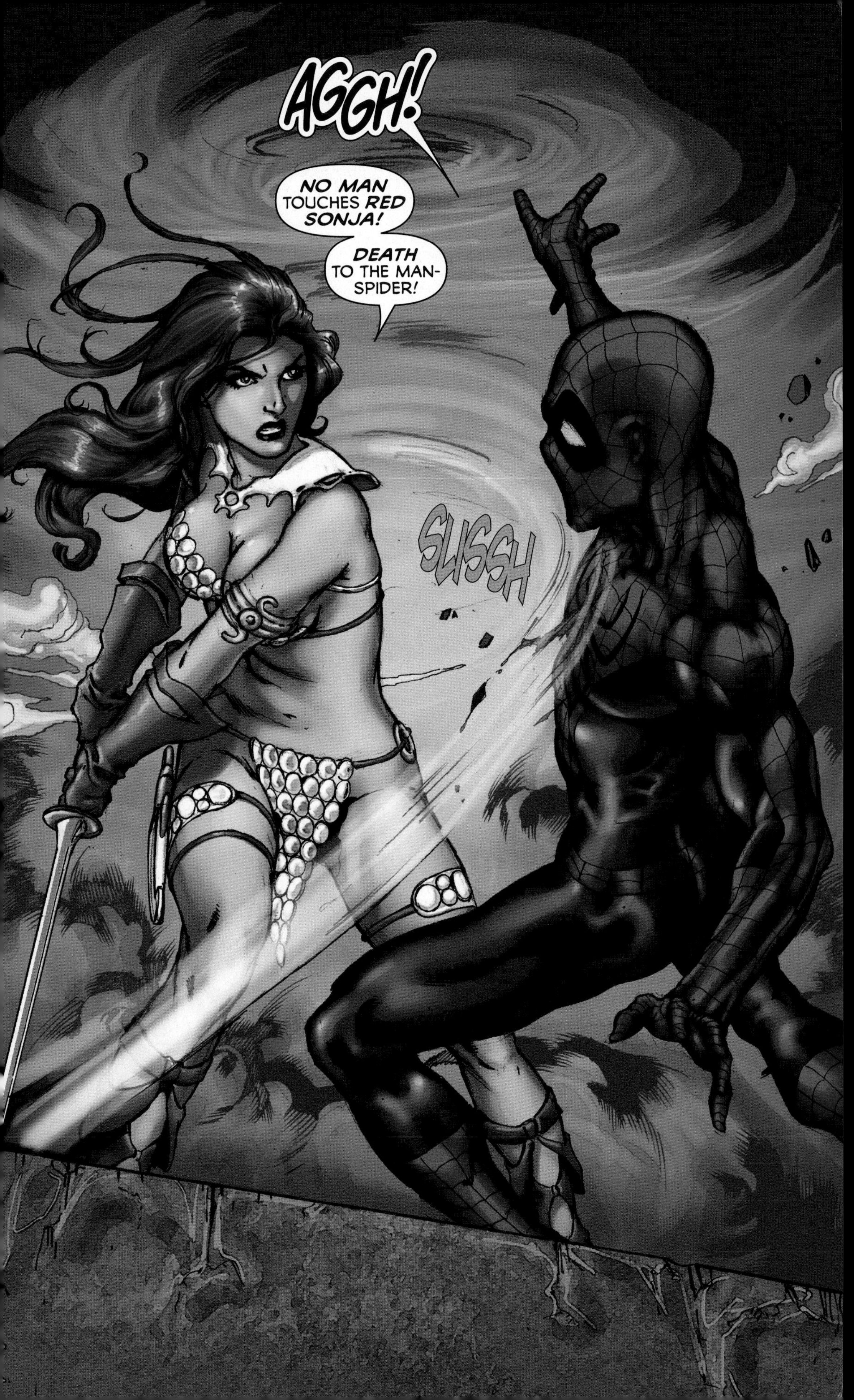
AGGH!
NO MAN TOUCHES RED SONJA!
DEATH TO THE MAN-SPIDER!
SLISSH

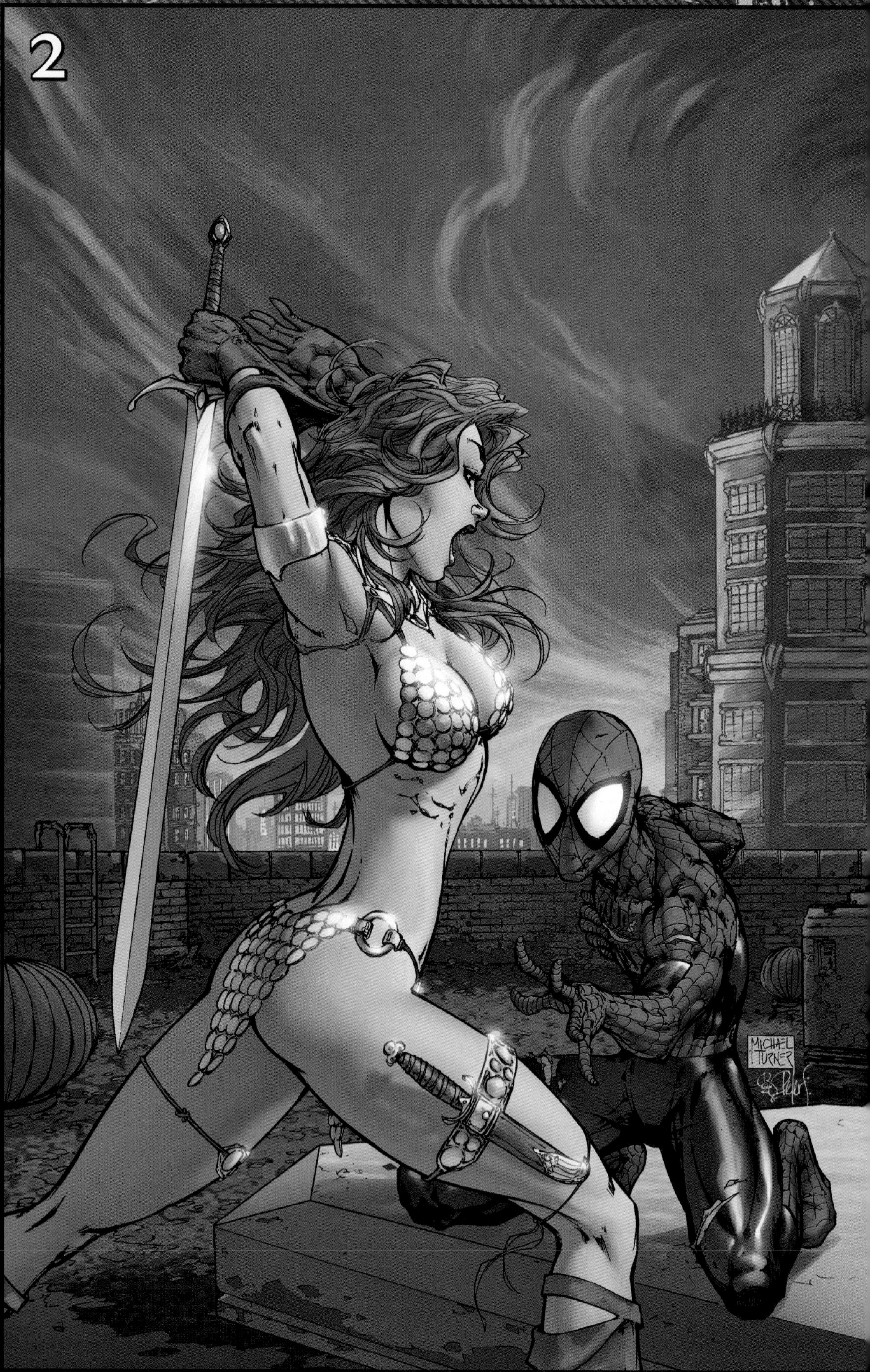
2
MICHAEL TURNER

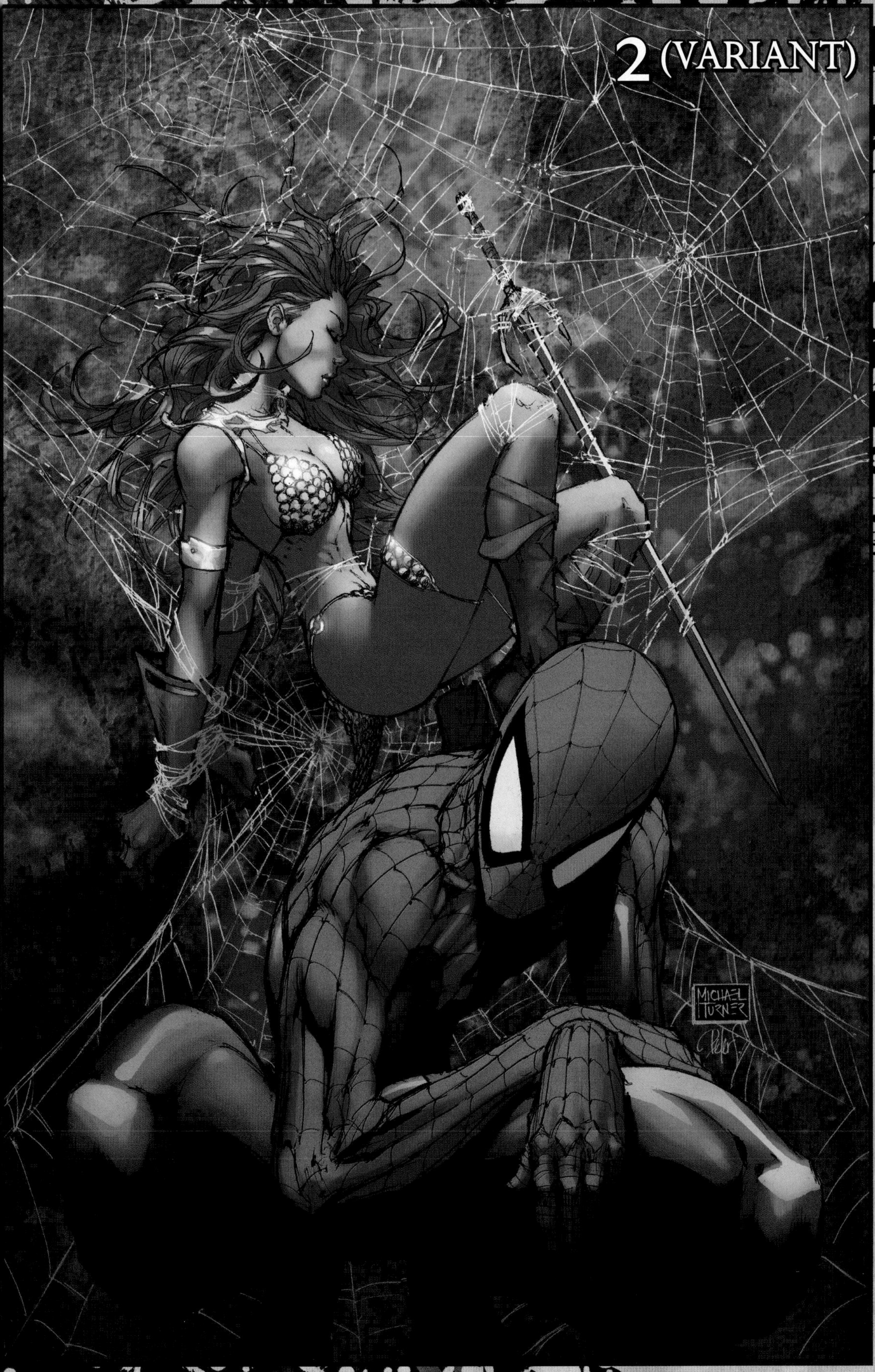
2 (VARIANT)
MICHAEL TURNER

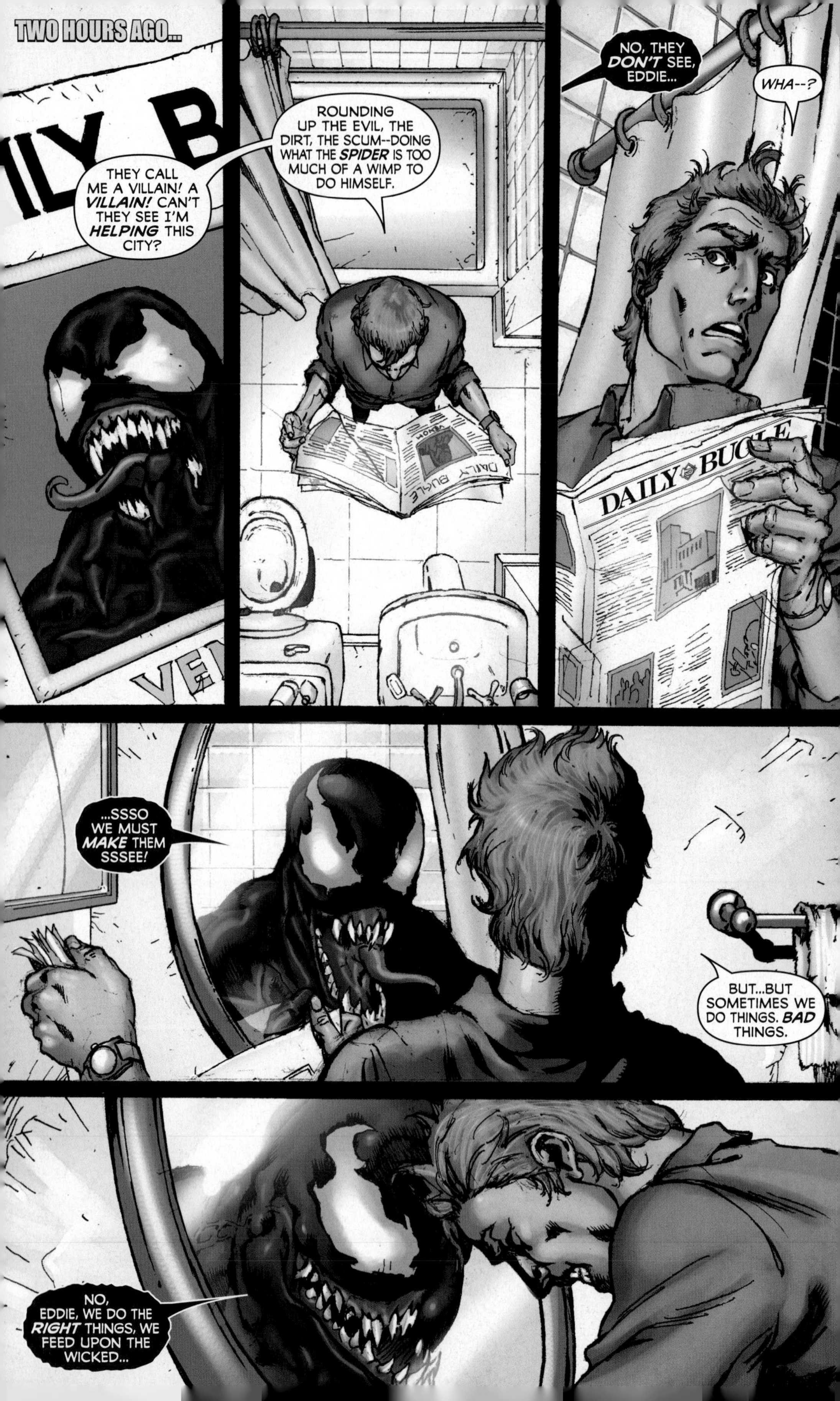
TWO HOURS AGO...
THEY CALL ME A VILLAIN! A VILLAIN! CAN'T THEY SEE I'M HELPING THIS CITY?
ROUNDING UP THE EVIL, THE DIRT, THE SCUM--DOING WHAT THE SPIDER IS TOO MUCH OF A WIMP TO DO HIMSELF.
NO, THEY DON'T SEE, EDDIE...
WHA--?
DAILY BUGLE
...SSSO WE MUST MAKE THEM SSSEE!
BUT...BUT SOMETIMES WE DO THINGS. BAD THINGS.
NO, EDDIE, WE DO THE RIGHT THINGS, WE FEED UPON THE WICKED...

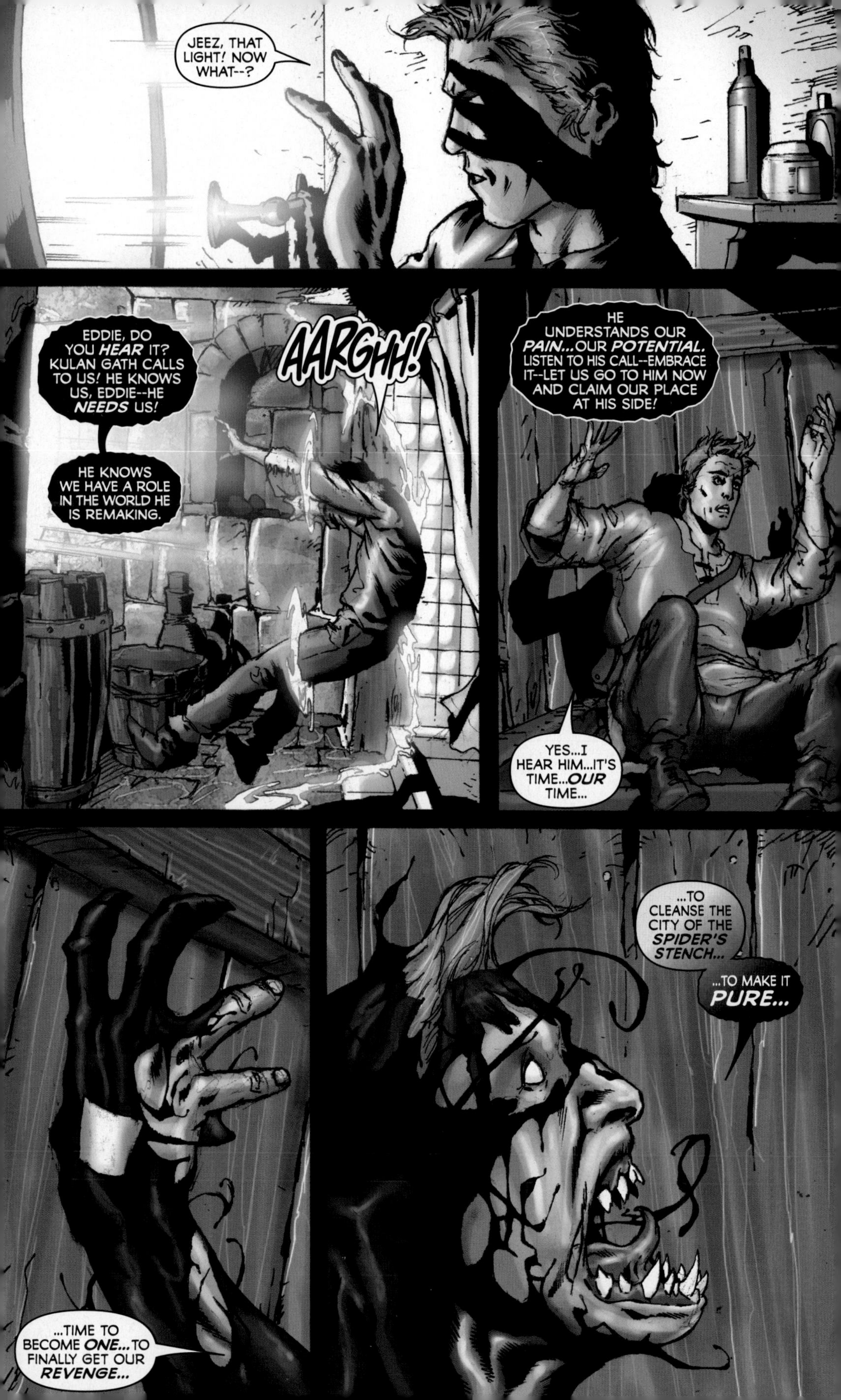
JEEZ, THAT LIGHT! NOW WHAT--?
AARGHH!
EDDIE, DO YOU HEAR IT? KULAN GATH CALLS TO US! HE KNOWS US, EDDIE--HE NEEDS US!
HE KNOWS WE HAVE A ROLE IN THE WORLD HE IS REMAKING.
HE UNDERSTANDS OUR PAIN...OUR POTENTIAL. LISTEN TO HIS CALL--EMBRACE IT--LET US GO TO HIM NOW AND CLAIM OUR PLACE AT HIS SIDE!
YES...I HEAR HIM...IT'S TIME...OUR TIME...
...TIME TO BECOME ONE...TO FINALLY GET OUR REVENGE...
...TO CLEANSE THE CITY OF THE SPIDER'S STENCH...
...TO MAKE IT PURE...

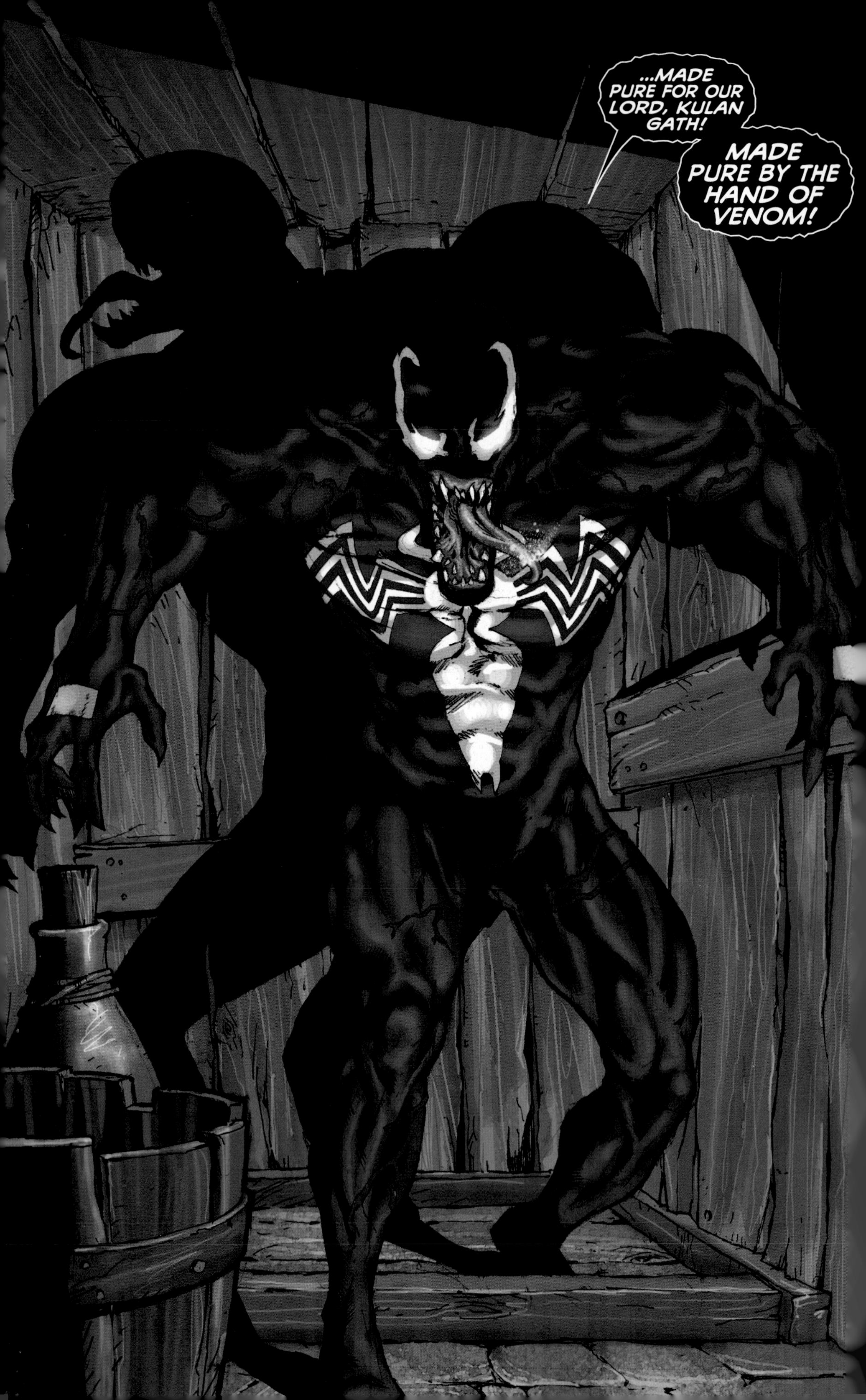
...MADE PURE FOR OUR LORD, KULAN GATH!
MADE PURE BY THE HAND OF VENOM!

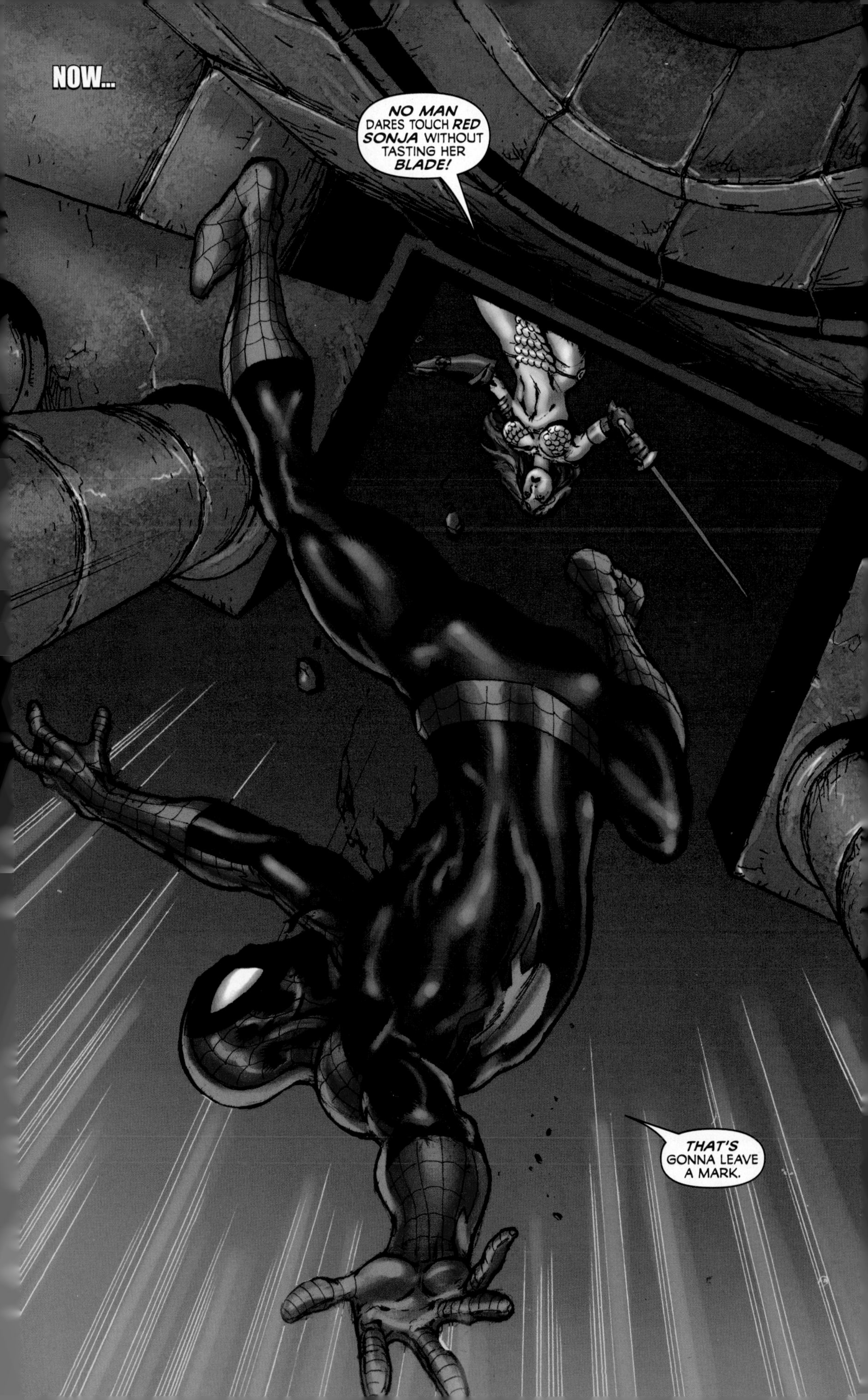
NOW...
NO MAN DARES TOUCH RED SONJA WITHOUT TASTING HER BLADE!
THAT'S GONNA LEAVE A MARK.

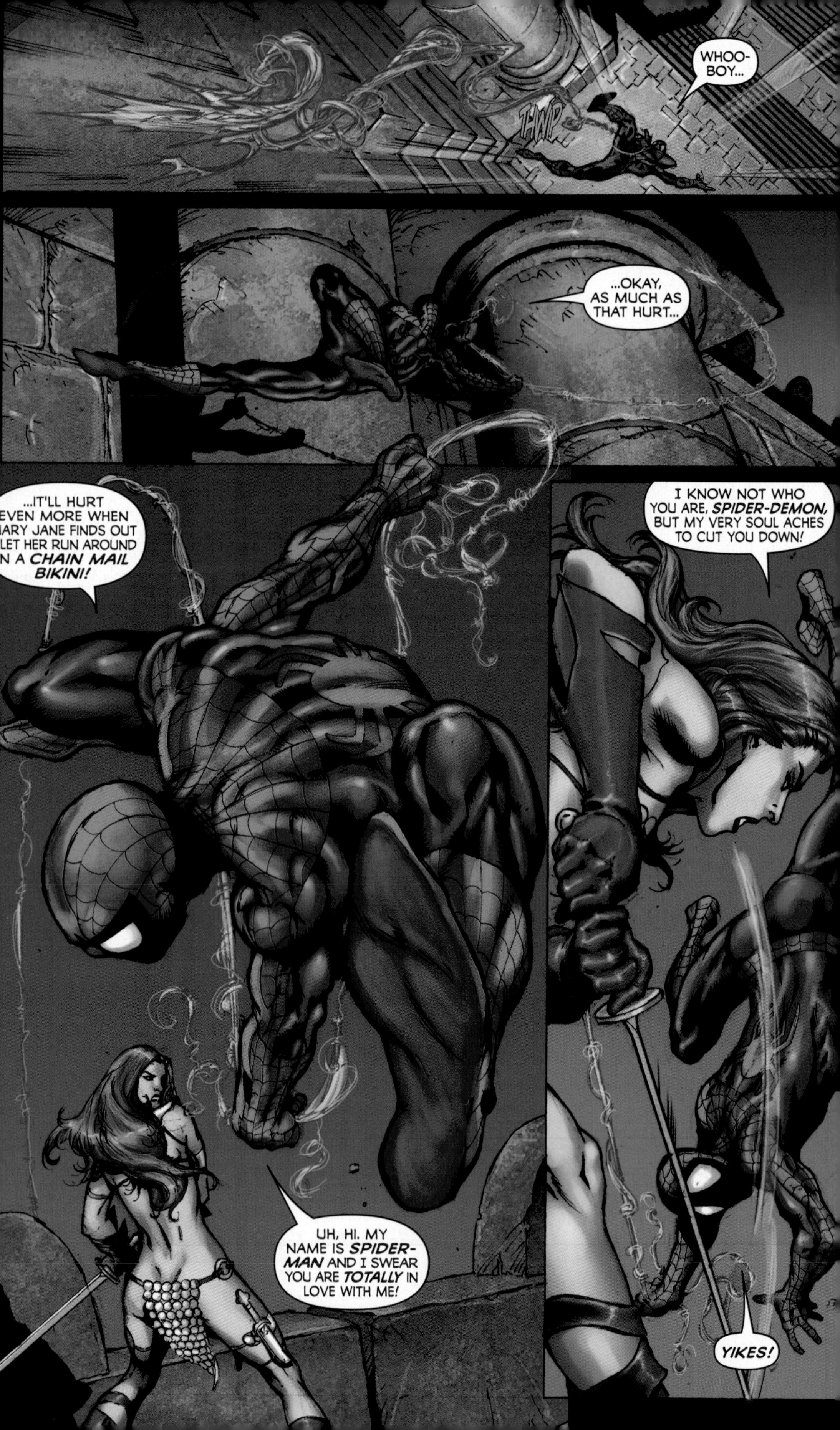
WHOO-BOY...
THWP
...OKAY, AS MUCH AS THAT HURT...
...IT'LL HURT EVEN MORE WHEN MARY JANE FINDS OUT I LET HER RUN AROUND IN A CHAIN MAIL BIKINI!
UH, HI. MY NAME IS SPIDER-MAN AND I SWEAR YOU ARE TOTALLY IN LOVE WITH ME!
I KNOW NOT WHO YOU ARE, SPIDER-DEMON, BUT MY VERY SOUL ACHES TO CUT YOU DOWN!
YIKES!

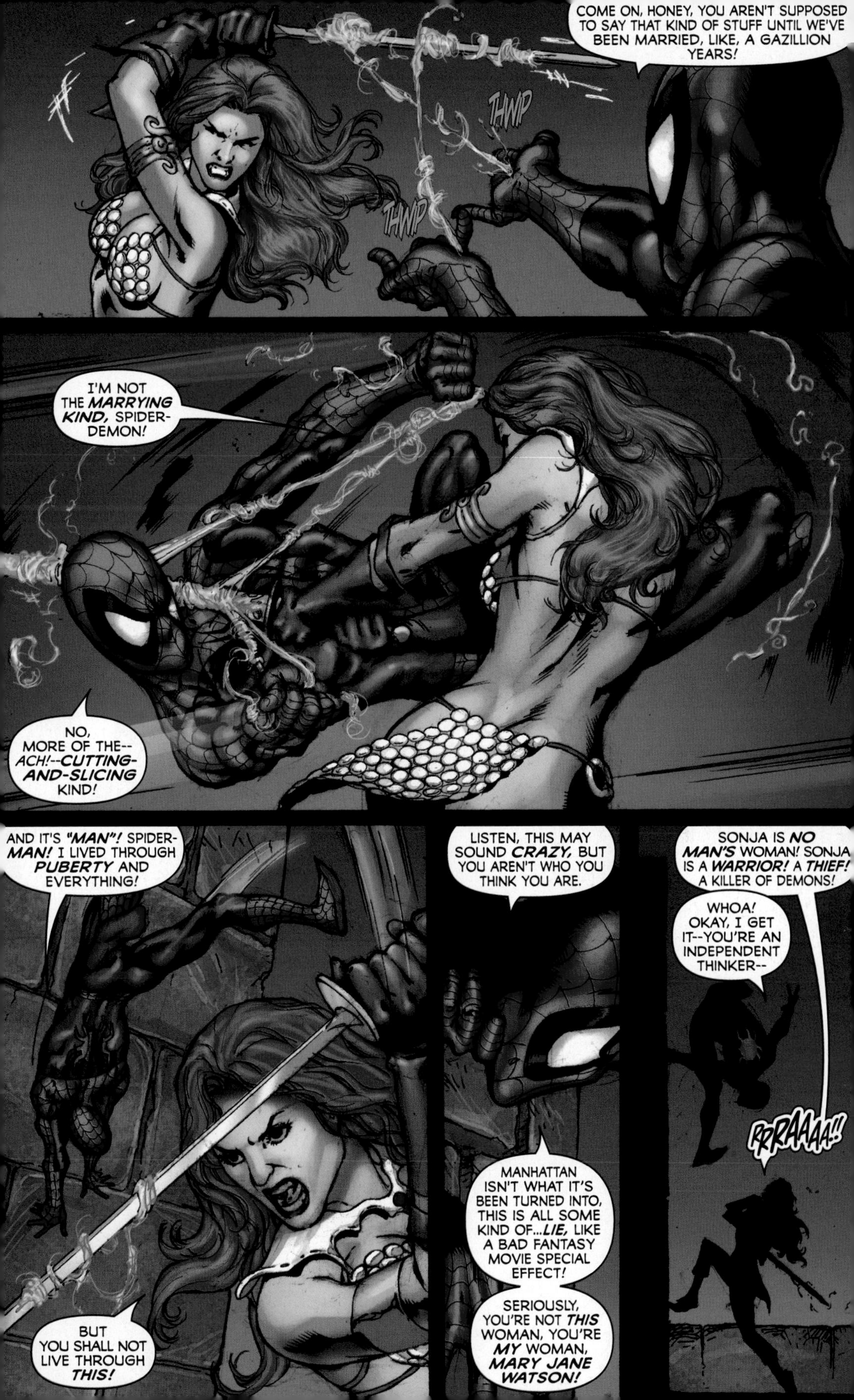
COME ON, HONEY, YOU AREN'T SUPPOSED TO SAY THAT KIND OF STUFF UNTIL WE'VE BEEN MARRIED, LIKE, A GAZILLION YEARS!
THWIP
THWIP
I'M NOT THE MARRYING KIND, SPIDER-DEMON!
NO, MORE OF THE-- ACH!--CUTTING-AND-SLICING KIND!
AND IT'S "MAN"! SPIDER-MAN! I LIVED THROUGH PUBERTY AND EVERYTHING!
BUT YOU SHALL NOT LIVE THROUGH THIS!
LISTEN, THIS MAY SOUND CRAZY, BUT YOU AREN'T WHO YOU THINK YOU ARE.
MANHATTAN ISN'T WHAT IT'S BEEN TURNED INTO, THIS IS ALL SOME KIND OF...LIE, LIKE A BAD FANTASY MOVIE SPECIAL EFFECT!
SERIOUSLY, YOU'RE NOT THIS WOMAN, YOU'RE MY WOMAN, MARY JANE WATSON!
SONJA IS NO MAN'S WOMAN! SONJA IS A WARRIOR! A THIEF! A KILLER OF DEMONS!
WHOA! OKAY, I GET IT--YOU'RE AN INDEPENDENT THINKER--
RRRAAAA!!

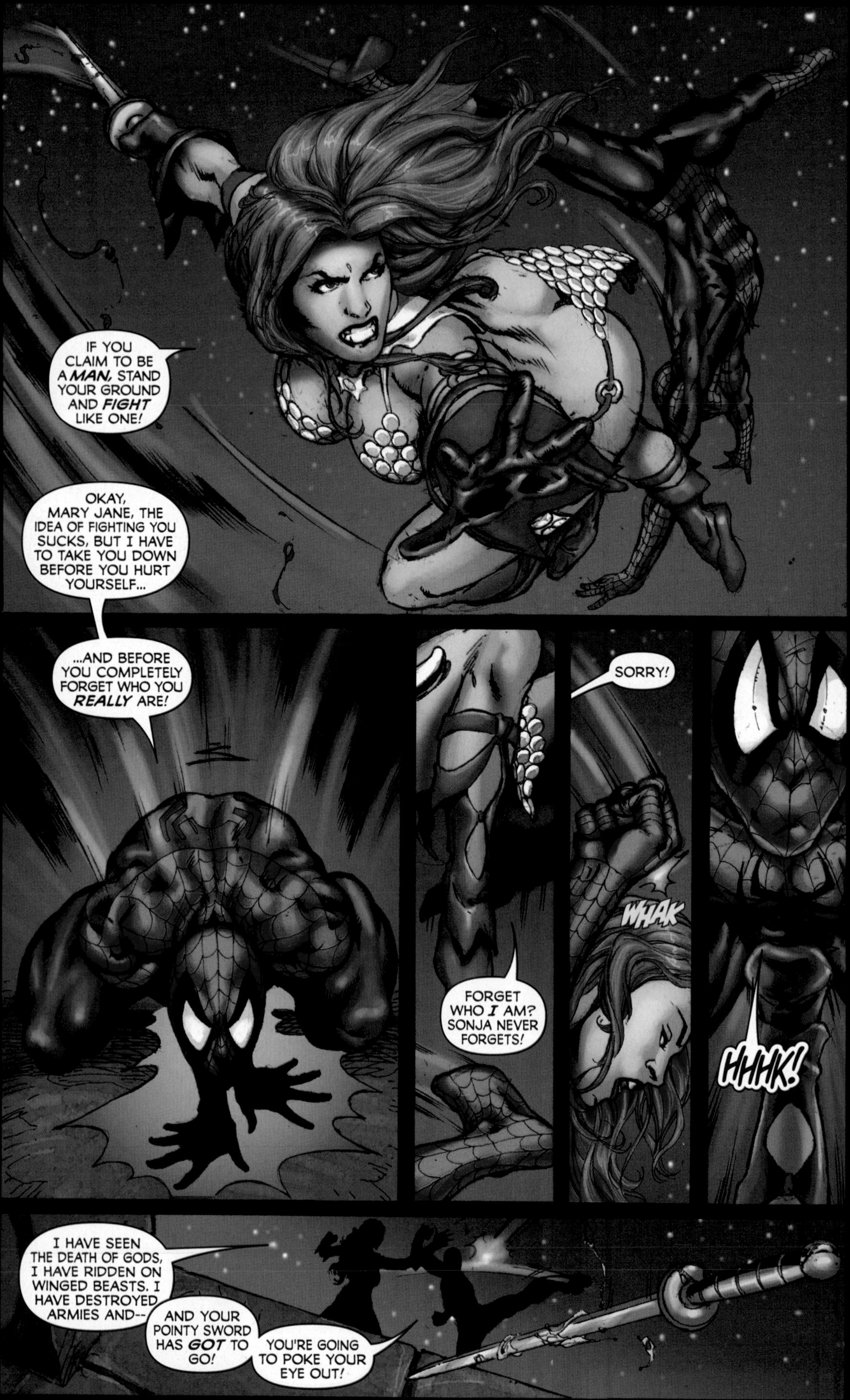
IF YOU CLAIM TO BE A MAN, STAND YOUR GROUND AND FIGHT LIKE ONE!
OKAY, MARY JANE, THE IDEA OF FIGHTING YOU SUCKS, BUT I HAVE TO TAKE YOU DOWN BEFORE YOU HURT YOURSELF...
...AND BEFORE YOU COMPLETELY FORGET WHO YOU REALLY ARE!
FORGET WHO I AM? SONJA NEVER FORGETS!
SORRY!
WHAK
HHHK!
I HAVE SEEN THE DEATH OF GODS, I HAVE RIDDEN ON WINGED BEASTS. I HAVE DESTROYED ARMIES AND--
AND YOUR POINTY SWORD HAS GOT TO GO!
YOU'RE GOING TO POKE YOUR EYE OUT!

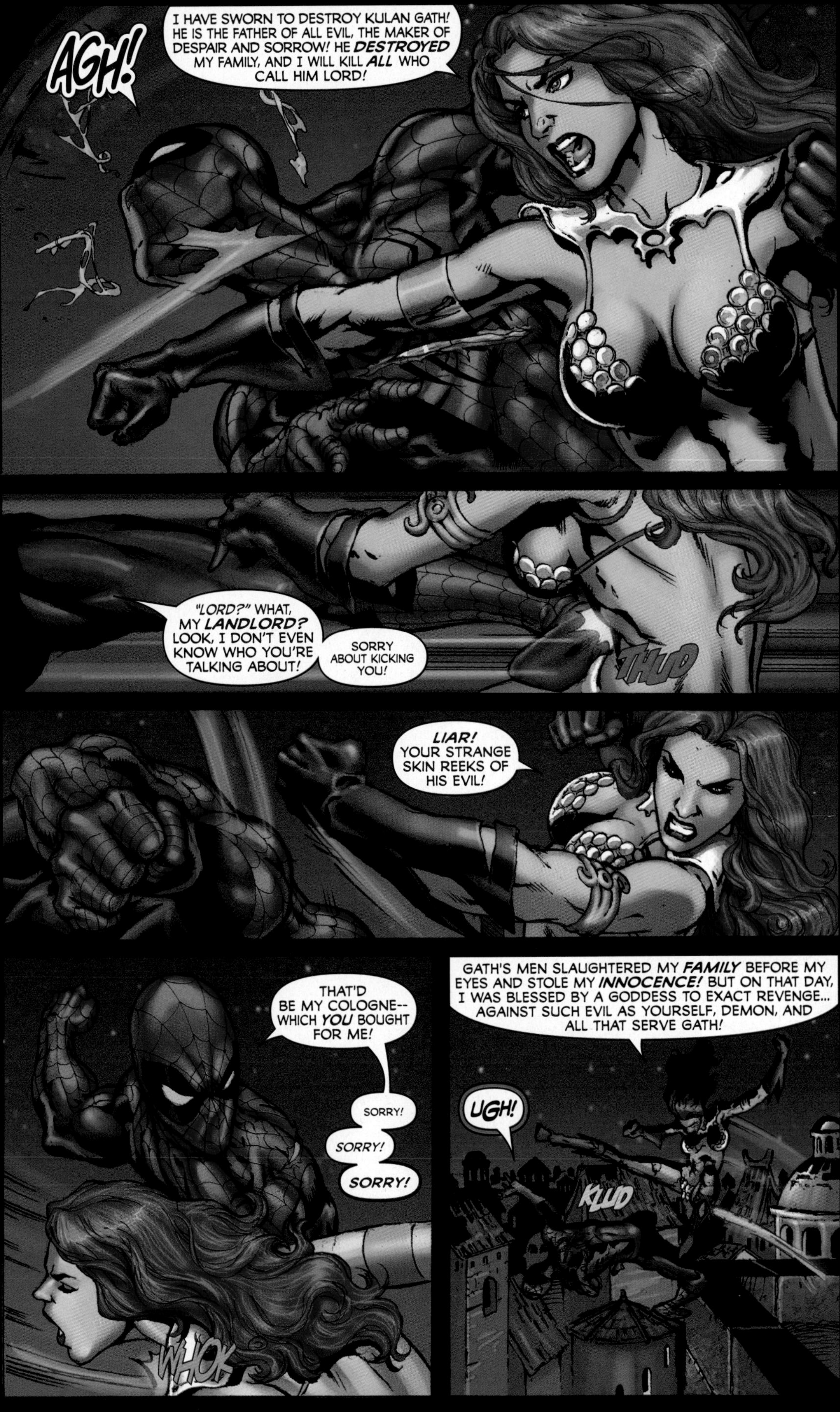
AGH!
I HAVE SWORN TO DESTROY KULAN GATH! HE IS THE FATHER OF ALL EVIL, THE MAKER OF DESPAIR AND SORROW! HE DESTROYED MY FAMILY, AND I WILL KILL ALL WHO CALL HIM LORD!
"LORD?" WHAT, MY LANDLORD? LOOK, I DON'T EVEN KNOW WHO YOU'RE TALKING ABOUT!
SORRY ABOUT KICKING YOU!
THUD
LIAR! YOUR STRANGE SKIN REEKS OF HIS EVIL!
THAT'D BE MY COLOGNE-- WHICH YOU BOUGHT FOR ME!
SORRY!
SORRY!
SORRY!
WHOK
GATH'S MEN SLAUGHTERED MY FAMILY BEFORE MY EYES AND STOLE MY INNOCENCE! BUT ON THAT DAY, I WAS BLESSED BY A GODDESS TO EXACT REVENGE... AGAINST SUCH EVIL AS YOURSELF, DEMON, AND ALL THAT SERVE GATH!
UGH!
KLUD

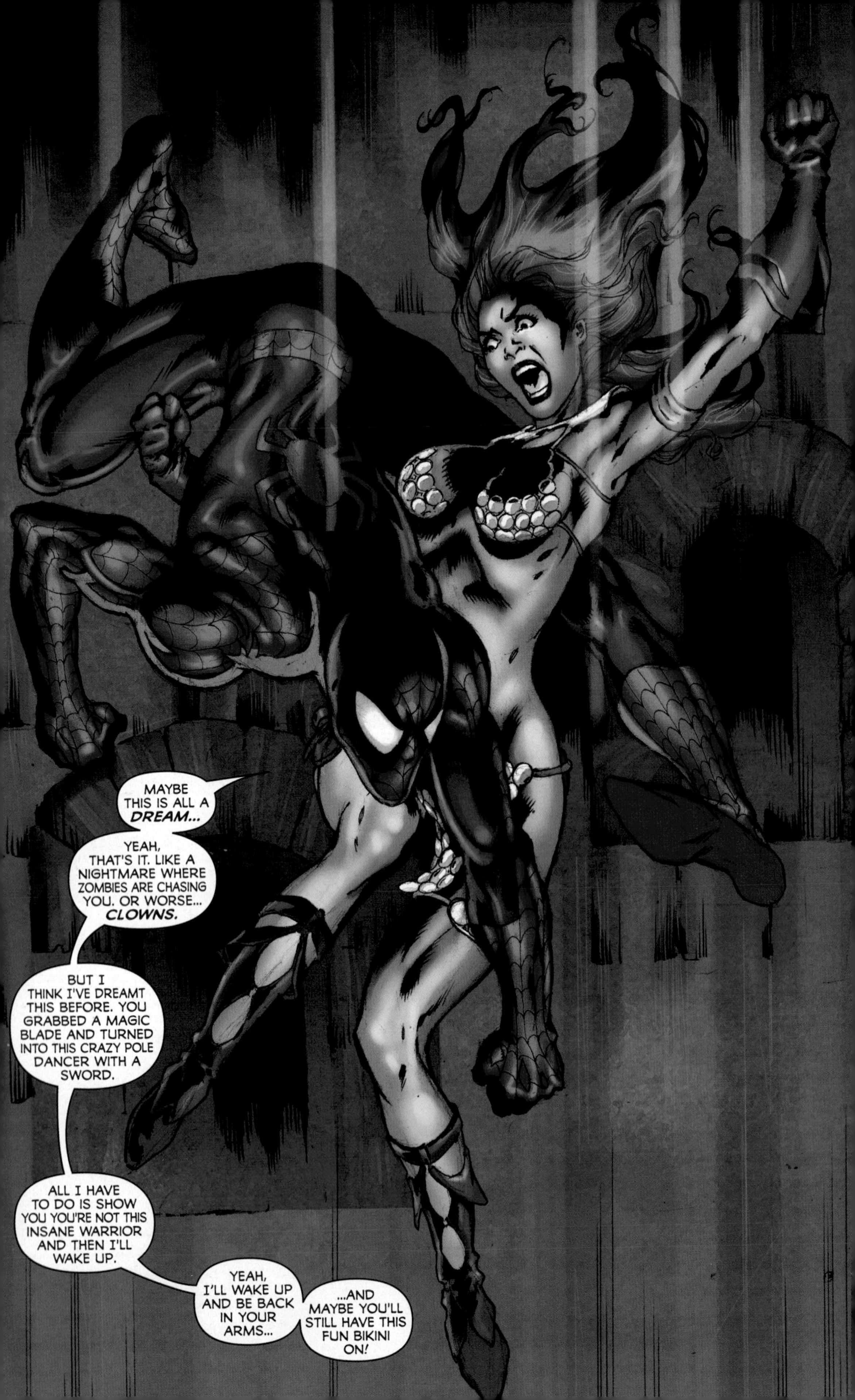
MAYBE THIS IS ALL A *DREAM...*
YEAH, THAT'S IT. LIKE A NIGHTMARE WHERE ZOMBIES ARE CHASING YOU. OR WORSE... *CLOWNS.*
BUT I THINK I'VE DREAMT THIS BEFORE. YOU GRABBED A MAGIC BLADE AND TURNED INTO THIS CRAZY POLE DANCER WITH A SWORD.
ALL I HAVE TO DO IS SHOW YOU YOU'RE NOT THIS INSANE WARRIOR AND THEN I'LL WAKE UP.
YEAH, I'LL WAKE UP AND BE BACK IN YOUR ARMS...
...AND MAYBE YOU'LL STILL HAVE THIS FUN BIKINI ON!

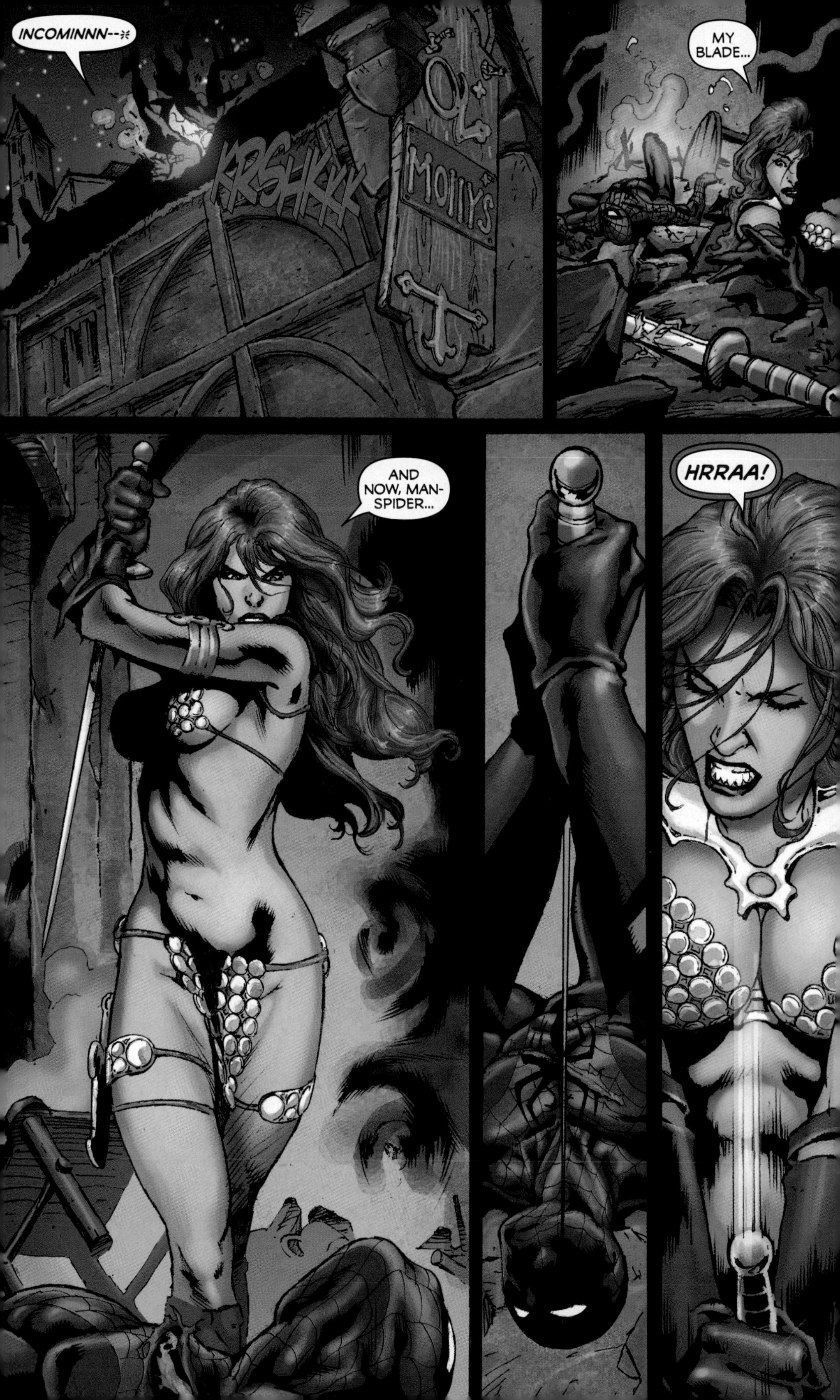
INCOMINNN--
KRSHKK
OL' MOLLY'S
MY BLADE...
AND NOW, MAN-SPIDER...
HRRAA!

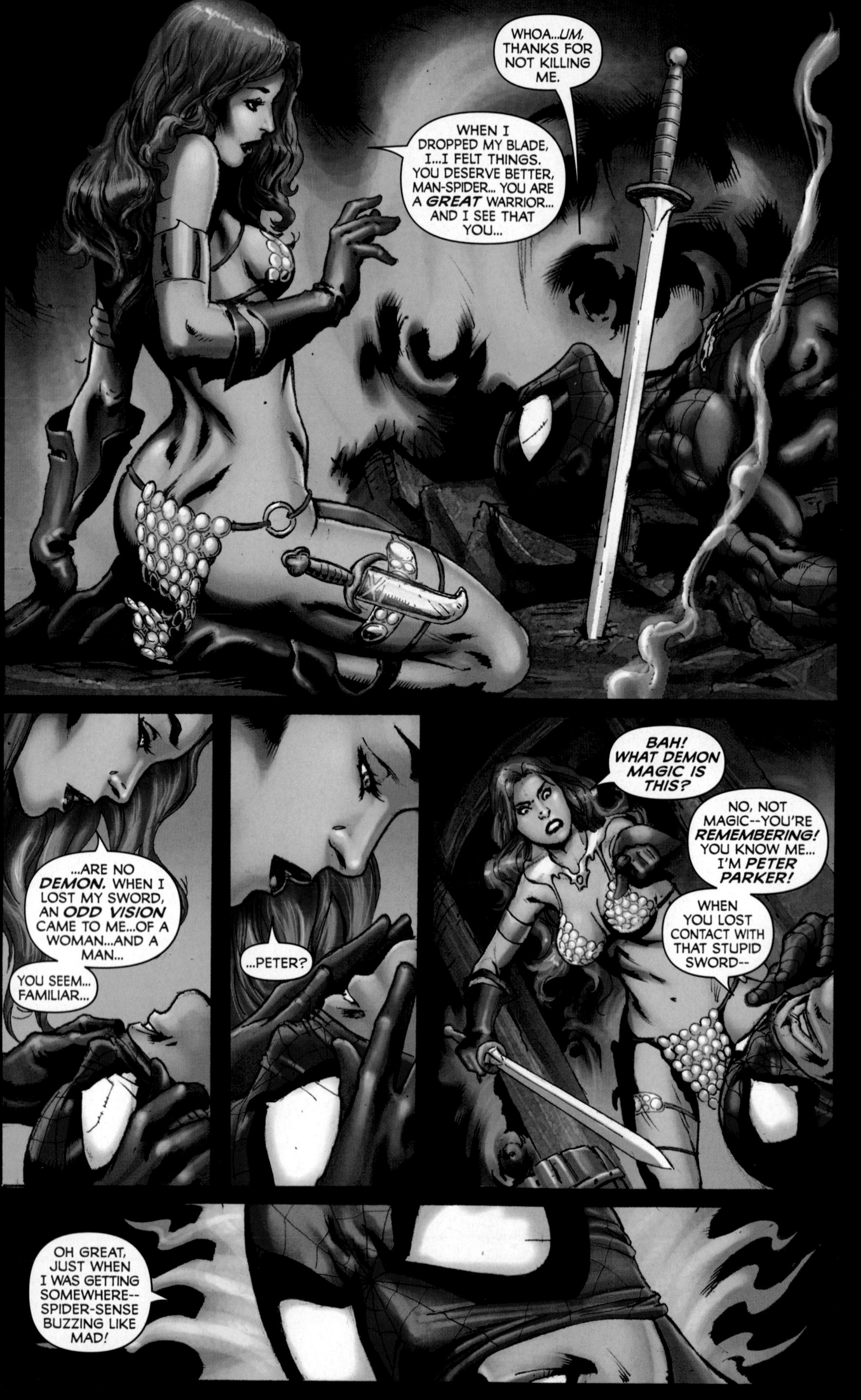
WHOA...UM, THANKS FOR NOT KILLING ME.
WHEN I DROPPED MY BLADE, I...I FELT THINGS. YOU DESERVE BETTER, MAN-SPIDER... YOU ARE A GREAT WARRIOR... AND I SEE THAT YOU...
...ARE NO DEMON. WHEN I LOST MY SWORD, AN ODD VISION CAME TO ME...OF A WOMAN...AND A MAN...
YOU SEEM... FAMILIAR...
...PETER?
BAH! WHAT DEMON MAGIC IS THIS?
NO, NOT MAGIC--YOU'RE REMEMBERING! YOU KNOW ME... I'M PETER PARKER!
WHEN YOU LOST CONTACT WITH THAT STUPID SWORD--
OH GREAT, JUST WHEN I WAS GETTING SOMEWHERE-- SPIDER-SENSE BUZZING LIKE MAD!

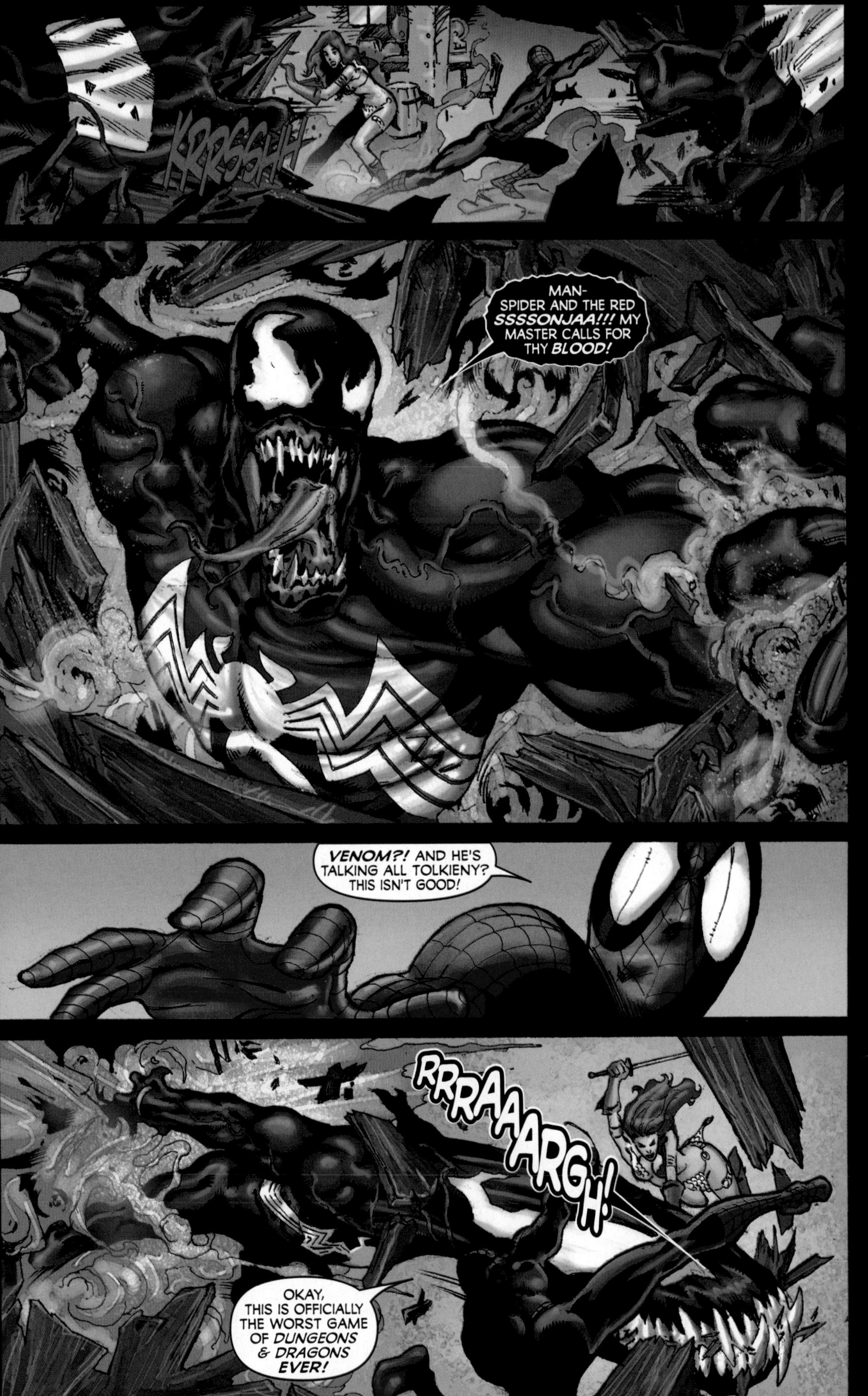
KRRSSHH
MAN-SPIDER AND THE RED SSSSONJAA!!! MY MASTER CALLS FOR THY BLOOD!
VENOM?! AND HE'S TALKING ALL TOLKIENY? THIS ISN'T GOOD!
RRRAAAARGH!
OKAY, THIS IS OFFICIALLY THE WORST GAME OF DUNGEONS & DRAGONS EVER!

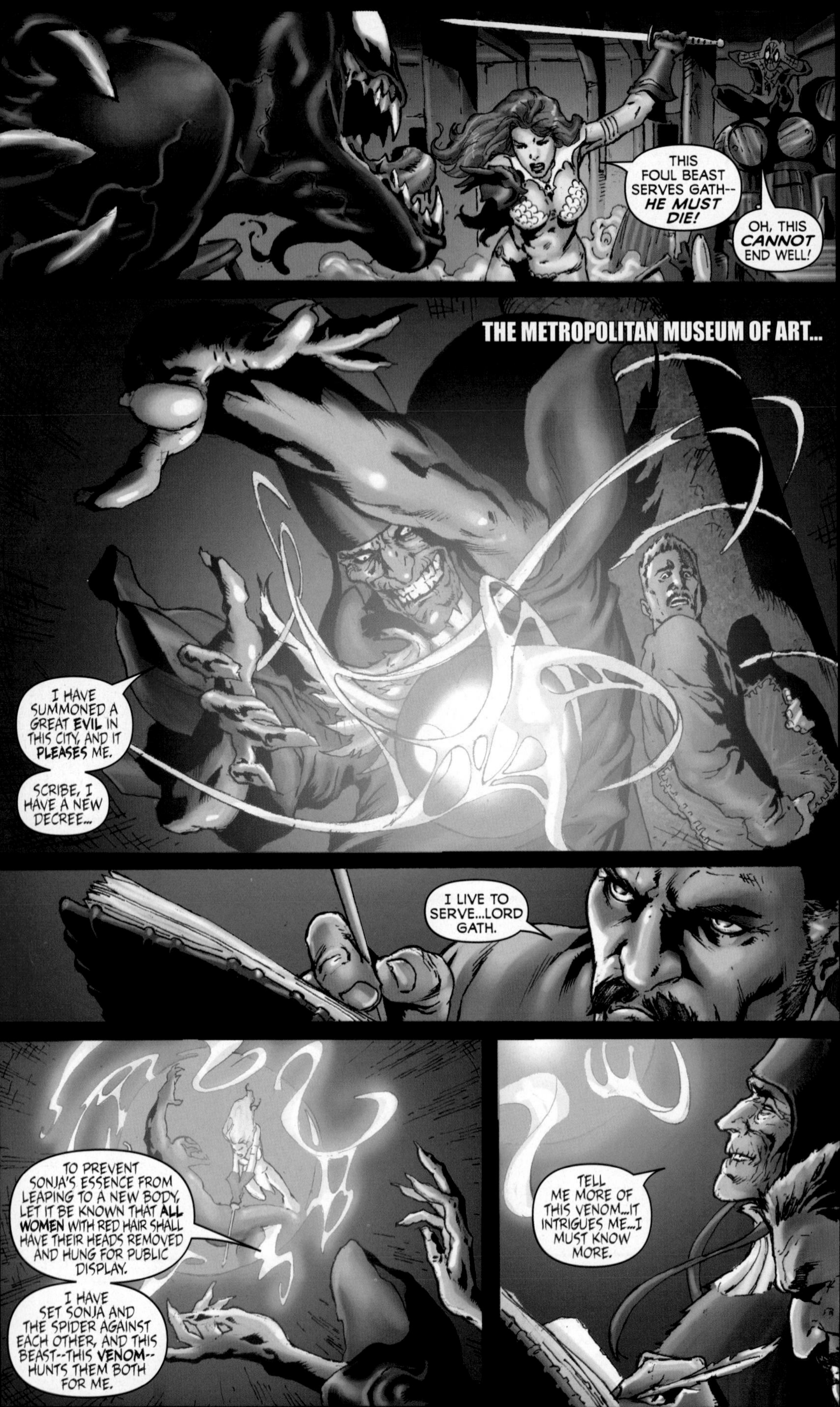
THIS FOUL BEAST SERVES GATH-- HE MUST DIE!
OH, THIS CANNOT END WELL!
THE METROPOLITAN MUSEUM OF ART...
I HAVE SUMMONED A GREAT EVIL IN THIS CITY, AND IT PLEASES ME.
SCRIBE, I HAVE A NEW DECREE...
I LIVE TO SERVE...LORD GATH.
TO PREVENT SONJA'S ESSENCE FROM LEAPING TO A NEW BODY, LET IT BE KNOWN THAT ALL WOMEN WITH RED HAIR SHALL HAVE THEIR HEADS REMOVED AND HUNG FOR PUBLIC DISPLAY.
I HAVE SET SONJA AND THE SPIDER AGAINST EACH OTHER, AND THIS BEAST--THIS VENOM--HUNTS THEM BOTH FOR ME.
TELL ME MORE OF THIS VENOM...IT INTRIGUES ME...I MUST KNOW MORE.

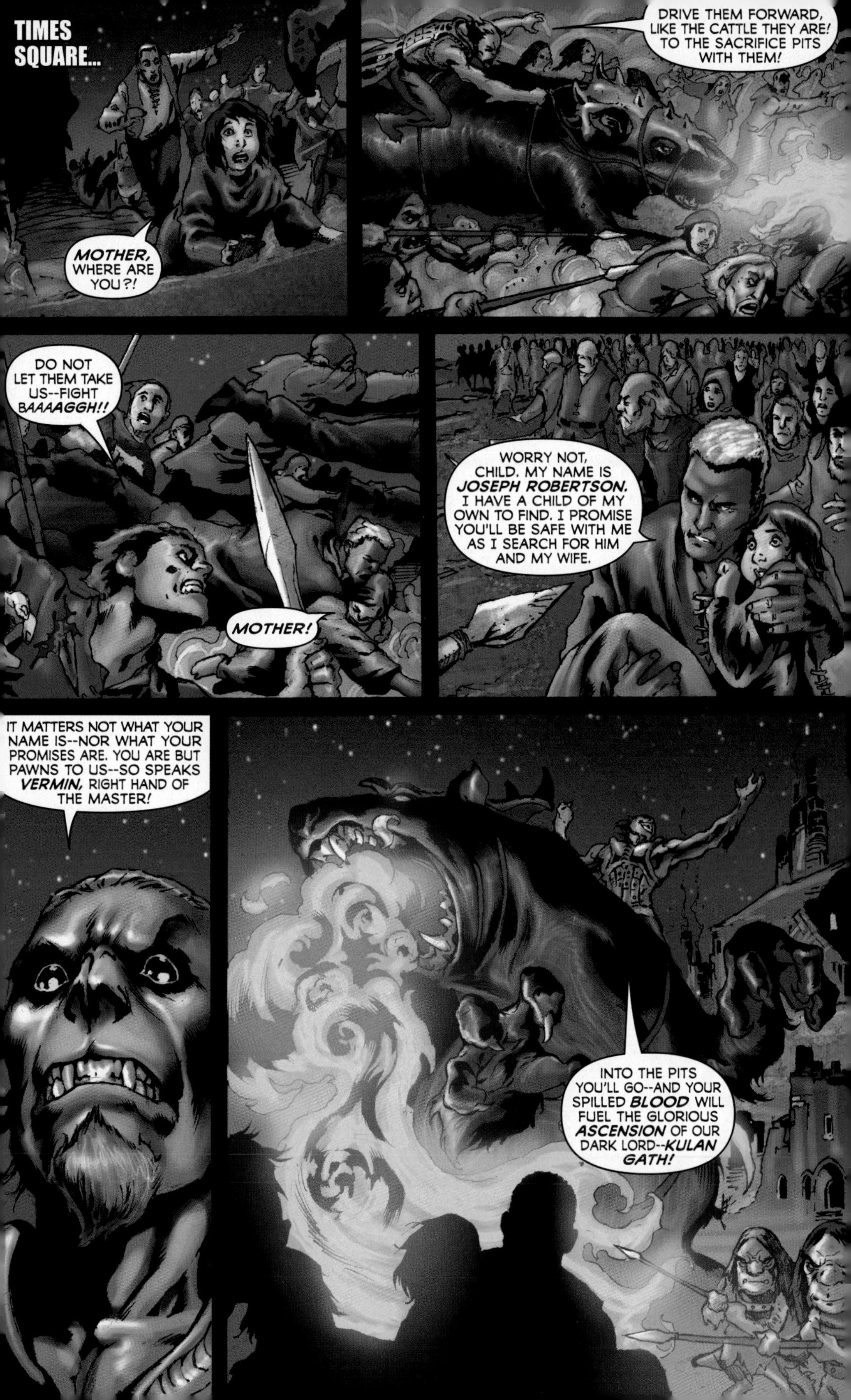

TIMES SQUARE...
MOTHER, WHERE ARE YOU?!
DRIVE THEM FORWARD, LIKE THE CATTLE THEY ARE! TO THE SACRIFICE PITS WITH THEM!
DO NOT LET THEM TAKE US--FIGHT BAAAAGGH!!
MOTHER!
WORRY NOT, CHILD. MY NAME IS JOSEPH ROBERTSON. I HAVE A CHILD OF MY OWN TO FIND. I PROMISE YOU'LL BE SAFE WITH ME AS I SEARCH FOR HIM AND MY WIFE.
IT MATTERS NOT WHAT YOUR NAME IS--NOR WHAT YOUR PROMISES ARE. YOU ARE BUT PAWNS TO US--SO SPEAKS VERMIN, RIGHT HAND OF THE MASTER!
INTO THE PITS YOU'LL GO--AND YOUR SPILLED BLOOD WILL FUEL THE GLORIOUS ASCENSION OF OUR DARK LORD--KULAN GATH!

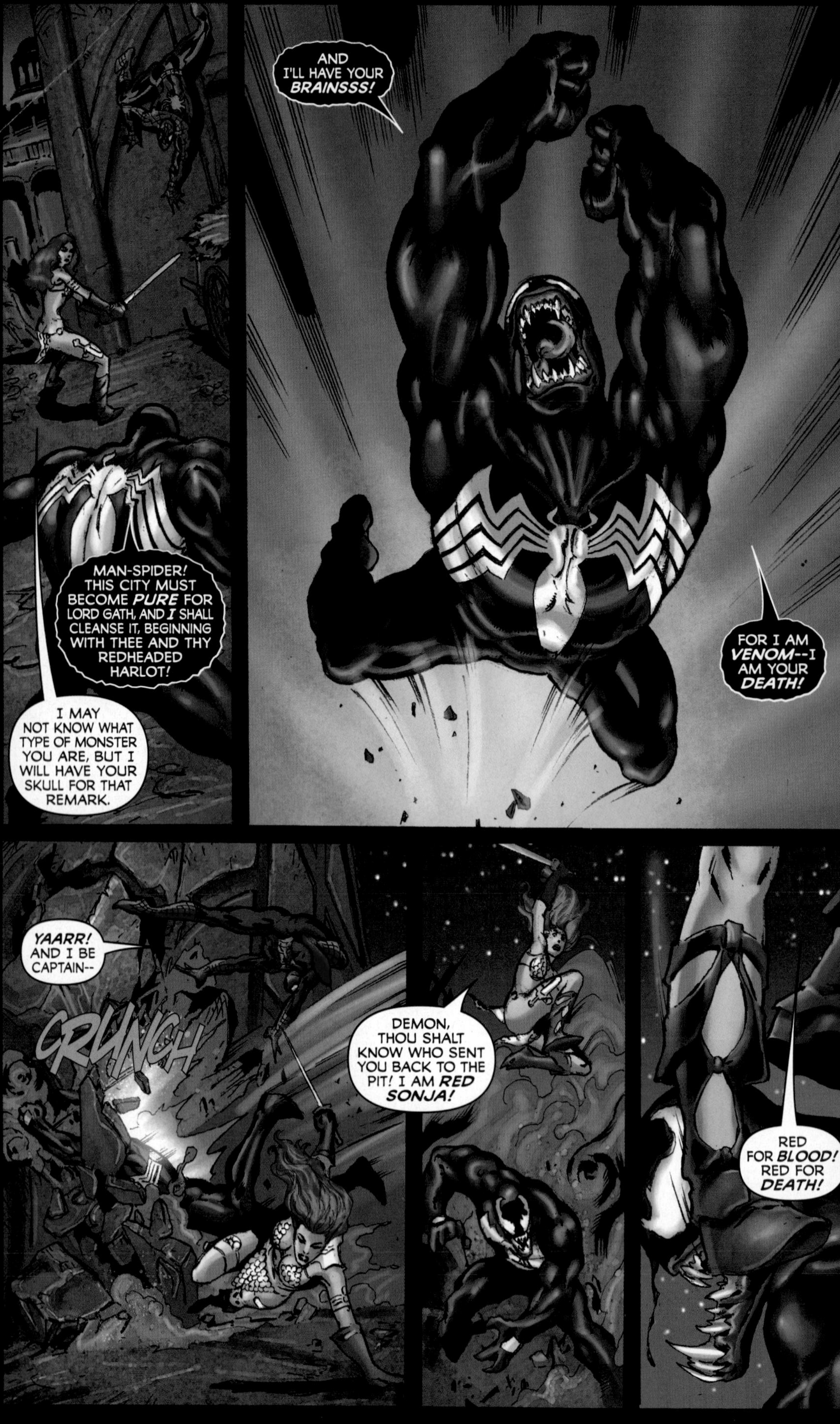
MAN-SPIDER! THIS CITY MUST BECOME PURE FOR LORD GATH, AND I SHALL CLEANSE IT, BEGINNING WITH THEE AND THY REDHEADED HARLOT!
I MAY NOT KNOW WHAT TYPE OF MONSTER YOU ARE, BUT I WILL HAVE YOUR SKULL FOR THAT REMARK.
AND I'LL HAVE YOUR BRAINSSS!
FOR I AM VENOM--I AM YOUR DEATH!
YAARR! AND I BE CAPTAIN--
CRUNCH
DEMON, THOU SHALT KNOW WHO SENT YOU BACK TO THE PIT! I AM RED SONJA!
RED FOR BLOOD! RED FOR DEATH!

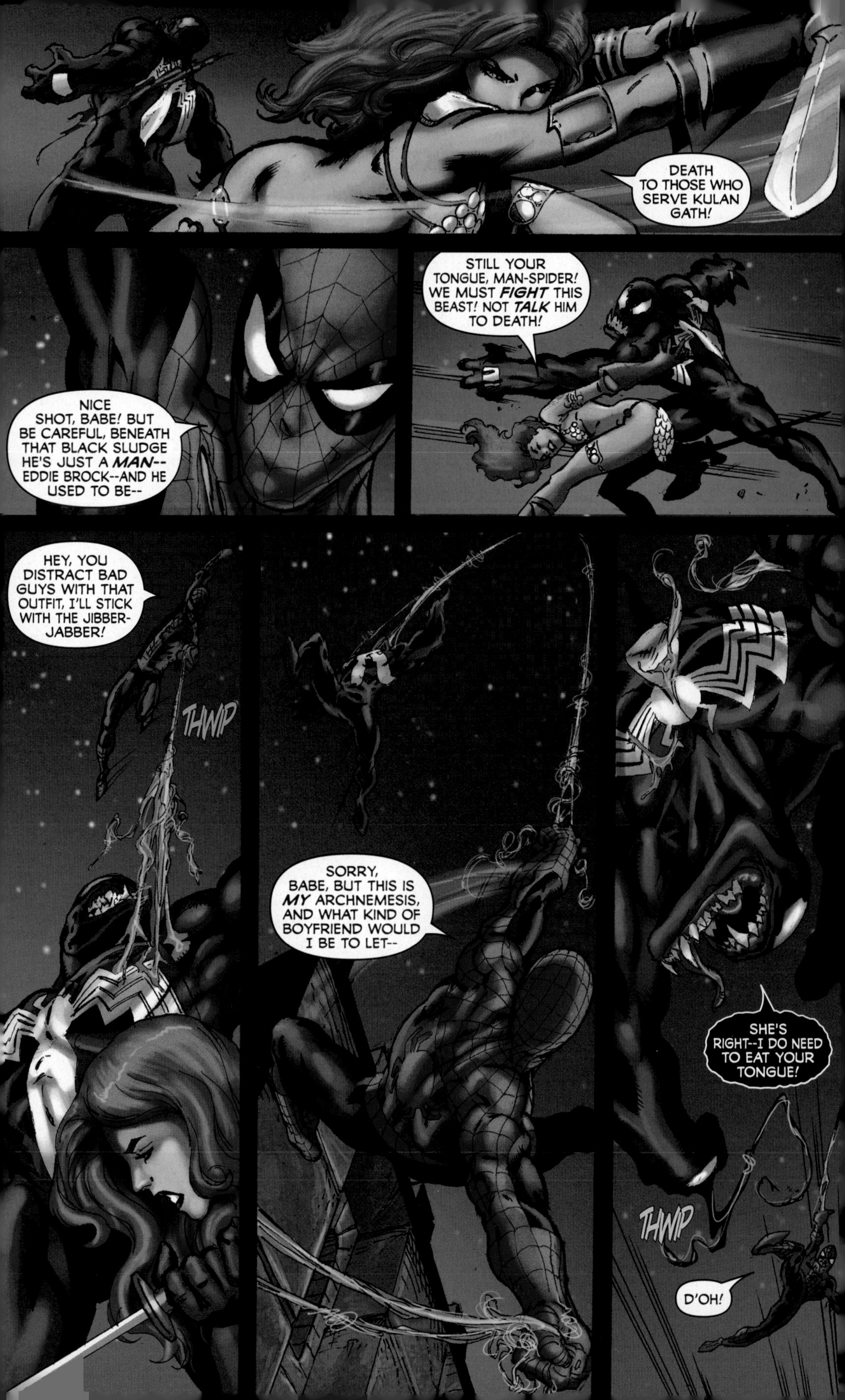
DEATH TO THOSE WHO SERVE KULAN GATH!
NICE SHOT, BABE! BUT BE CAREFUL, BENEATH THAT BLACK SLUDGE HE'S JUST A *MAN*--EDDIE BROCK--AND HE USED TO BE--
STILL YOUR TONGUE, MAN-SPIDER! WE MUST *FIGHT* THIS BEAST! NOT *TALK* HIM TO DEATH!
HEY, YOU DISTRACT BAD GUYS WITH THAT OUTFIT, I'LL STICK WITH THE JIBBER-JABBER!
THWIP
SORRY, BABE, BUT THIS IS *MY* ARCHNEMESIS, AND WHAT KIND OF BOYFRIEND WOULD I BE TO LET--
SHE'S RIGHT--I DO NEED TO EAT YOUR TONGUE!
THWIP
D'OH!

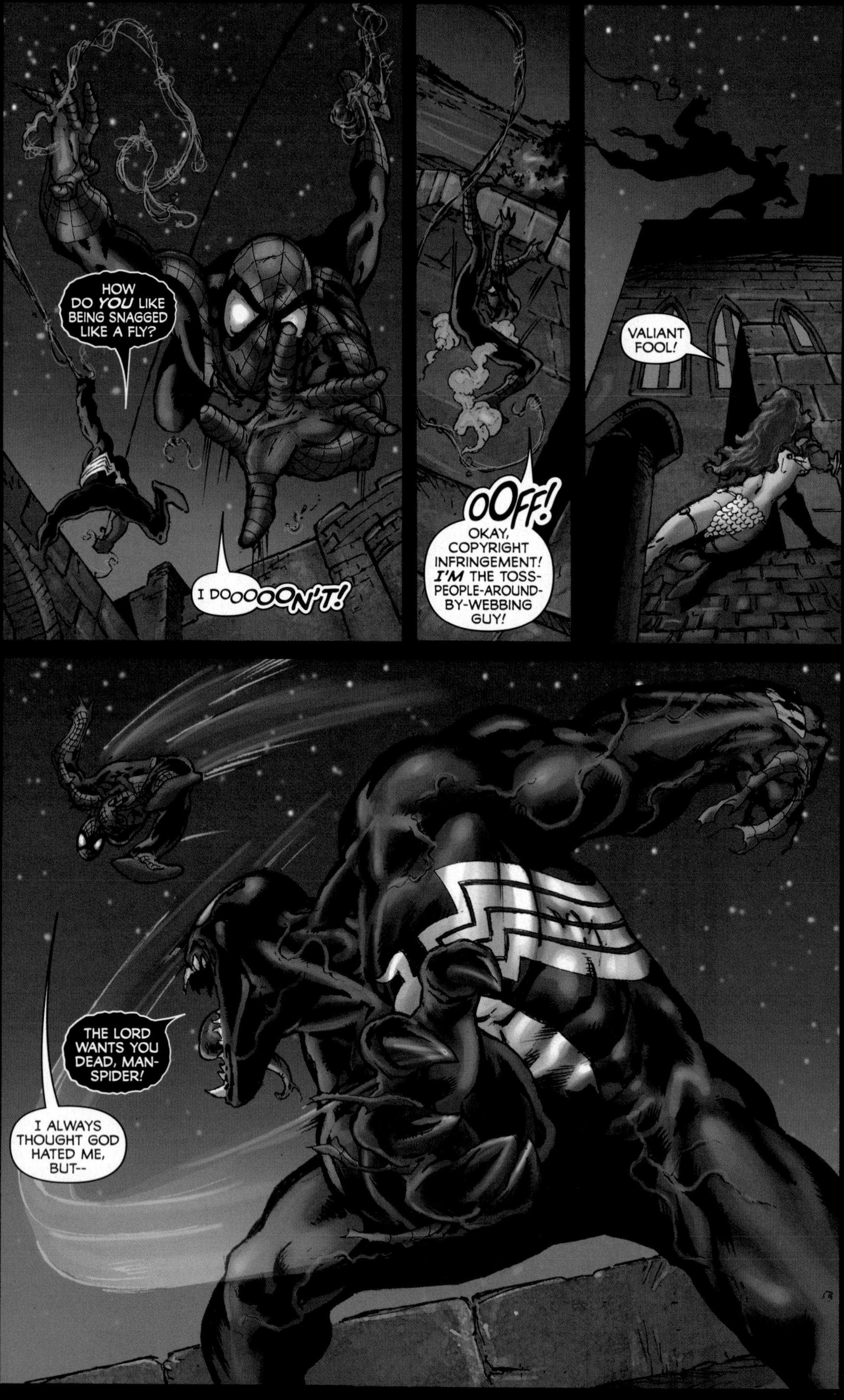
HOW DO *YOU* LIKE BEING SNAGGED LIKE A FLY?
I DOOOOOON'T!
OOFF!
OKAY, COPYRIGHT INFRINGEMENT! *I'M* THE TOSS-PEOPLE-AROUND-BY-WEBBING GUY!
VALIANT FOOL!
THE LORD WANTS YOU DEAD, MAN-SPIDER!
I ALWAYS THOUGHT GOD HATED ME, BUT--

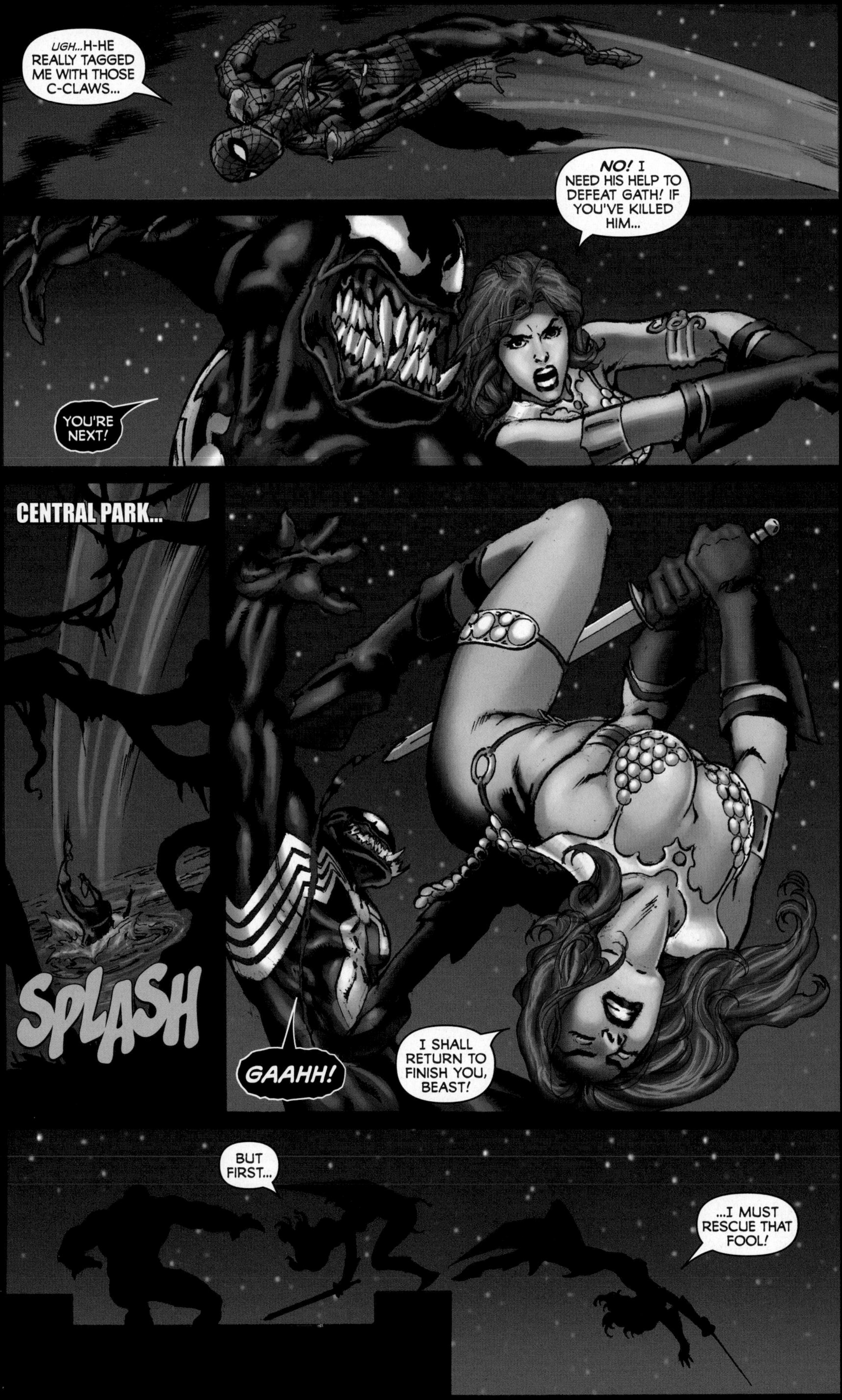
UGH...H-HE REALLY TAGGED ME WITH THOSE C-CLAWS...
NO! I NEED HIS HELP TO DEFEAT GATH! IF YOU'VE KILLED HIM...
YOU'RE NEXT!
CENTRAL PARK...
SPLASH
GAAHH!
I SHALL RETURN TO FINISH YOU, BEAST!
BUT FIRST...
...I MUST RESCUE THAT FOOL!

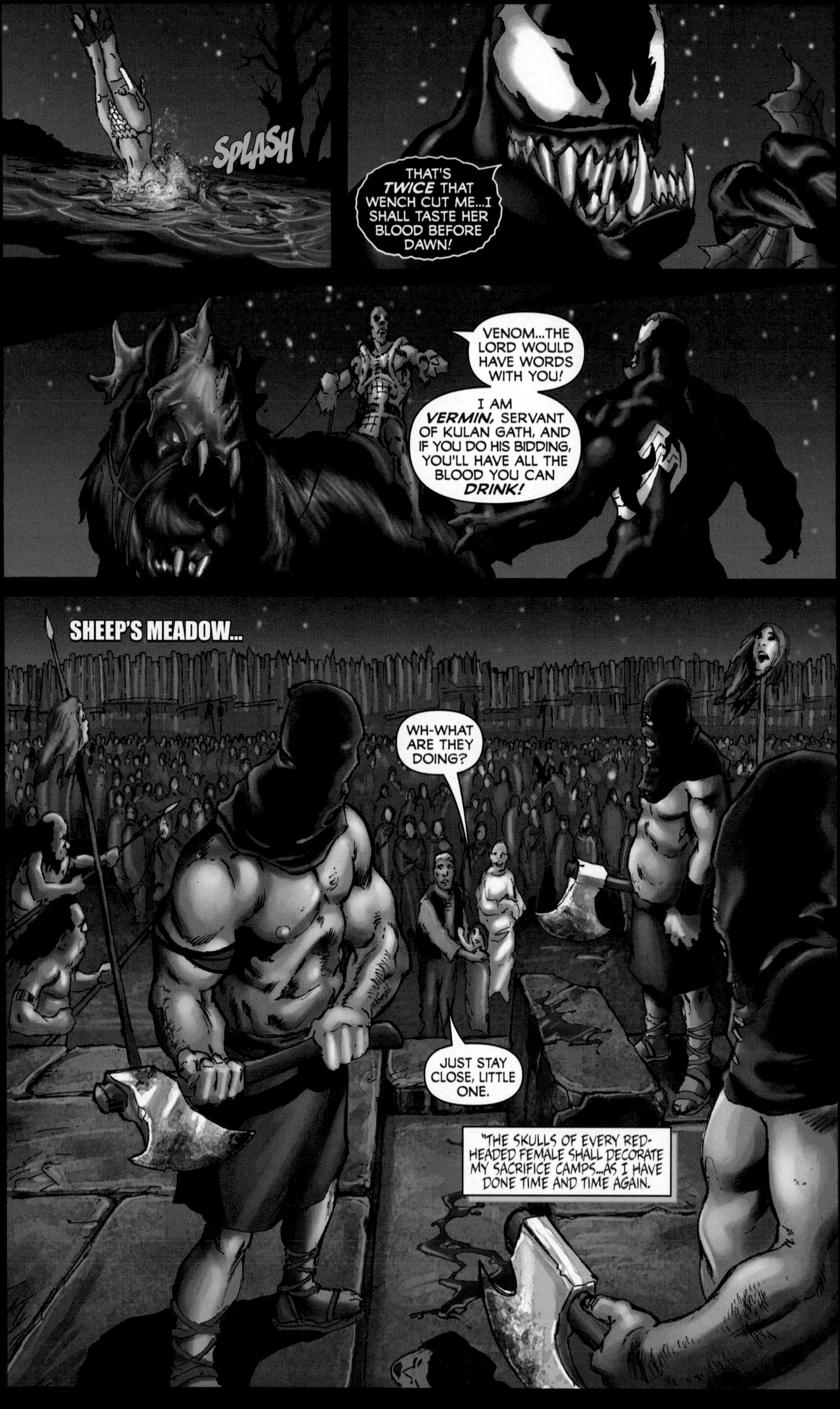
SPLASH
THAT'S TWICE THAT WENCH CUT ME...I SHALL TASTE HER BLOOD BEFORE DAWN!
VENOM...THE LORD WOULD HAVE WORDS WITH YOU!
I AM VERMIN, SERVANT OF KULAN GATH, AND IF YOU DO HIS BIDDING, YOU'LL HAVE ALL THE BLOOD YOU CAN DRINK!
SHEEP'S MEADOW...
WH-WHAT ARE THEY DOING?
JUST STAY CLOSE, LITTLE ONE.
"THE SKULLS OF EVERY RED-HEADED FEMALE SHALL DECORATE MY SACRIFICE CAMPS...AS I HAVE DONE TIME AND TIME AGAIN.

"THE CITY HAS FALLEN TO ME WITH LITTLE STRIFE, EVEN WITH SONJA HUNTING ME. IN MY HOMELAND, **SHE** IS MY CURSE, AND **HERE** IT IS THE MAN-SPIDER...

"...BUT I HAVE SET THEM AGAINST EACH OTHER AND NOW THEY ARE DEAD.

...SHALL GROW MY POWER.

AND WHEN MY MAGIC GROWS HIGH, I'LL TRANSFORM THE ENTIRE WORLD IN MY IMAGE. I SHALL LEAVE IT A ROTTED CARCASS WITH MY FACE SEARED UPON IT FOR ALL THE GODS TO SEE.

'TWAS EASY, WAS IT NOT, SCRIBE?

"THERE IS NO RESISTANCE. MY CAMPS WILL BE FULL OF SACRIFICES, AND FROM THE FLOW OF THEIR BLOOD..."

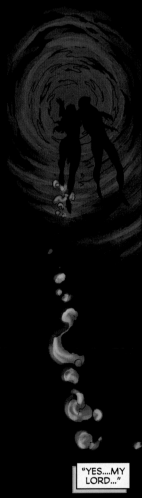

"YES....MY LORD..."

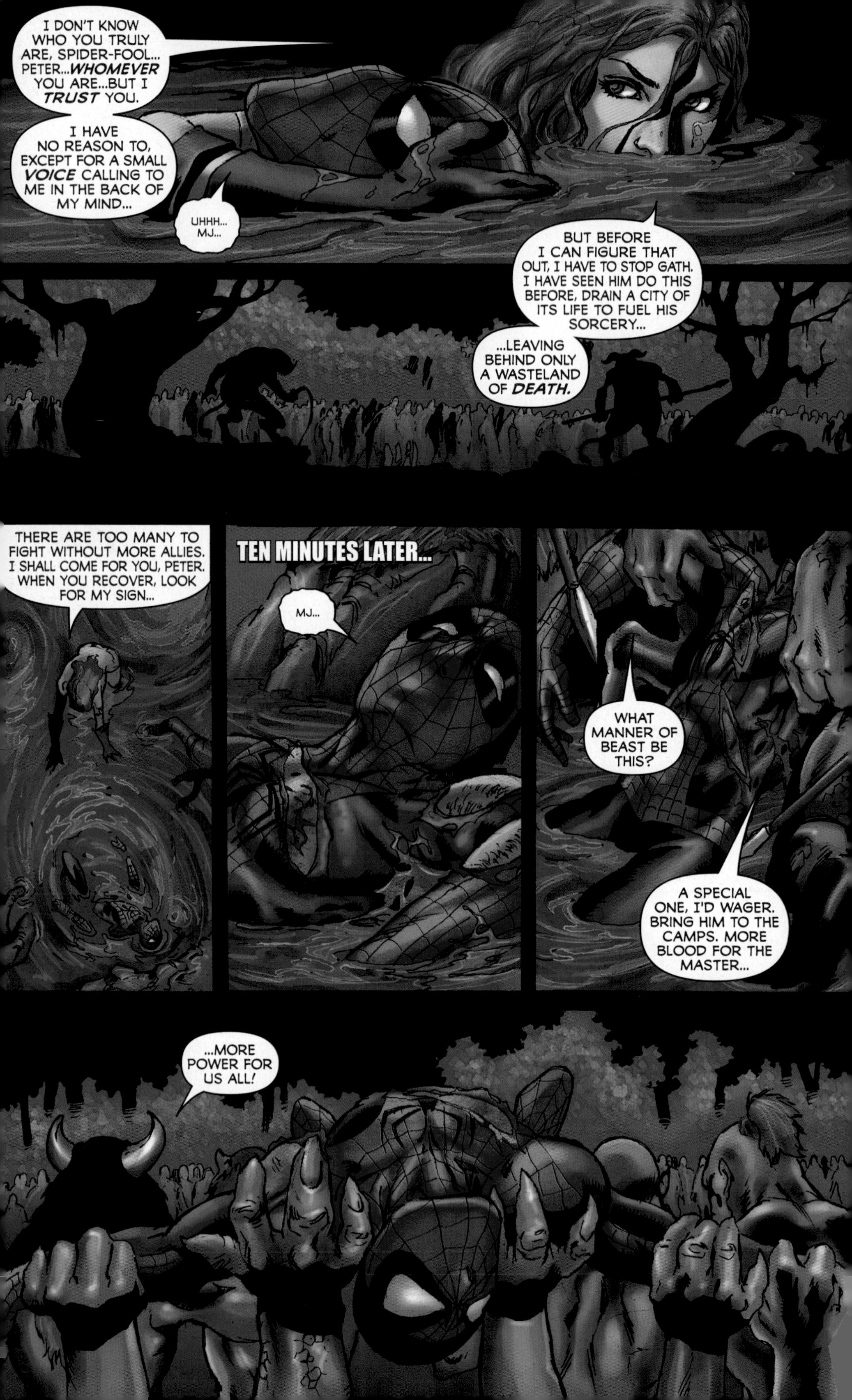
I DON'T KNOW WHO YOU TRULY ARE, SPIDER-FOOL... PETER...WHOMEVER YOU ARE...BUT I TRUST YOU.
I HAVE NO REASON TO, EXCEPT FOR A SMALL VOICE CALLING TO ME IN THE BACK OF MY MIND...
UHHH... MJ...
BUT BEFORE I CAN FIGURE THAT OUT, I HAVE TO STOP GATH. I HAVE SEEN HIM DO THIS BEFORE, DRAIN A CITY OF ITS LIFE TO FUEL HIS SORCERY...
...LEAVING BEHIND ONLY A WASTELAND OF DEATH.
THERE ARE TOO MANY TO FIGHT WITHOUT MORE ALLIES. I SHALL COME FOR YOU, PETER. WHEN YOU RECOVER, LOOK FOR MY SIGN...
TEN MINUTES LATER...
MJ...
WHAT MANNER OF BEAST BE THIS?
A SPECIAL ONE, I'D WAGER. BRING HIM TO THE CAMPS. MORE BLOOD FOR THE MASTER...
...MORE POWER FOR US ALL!

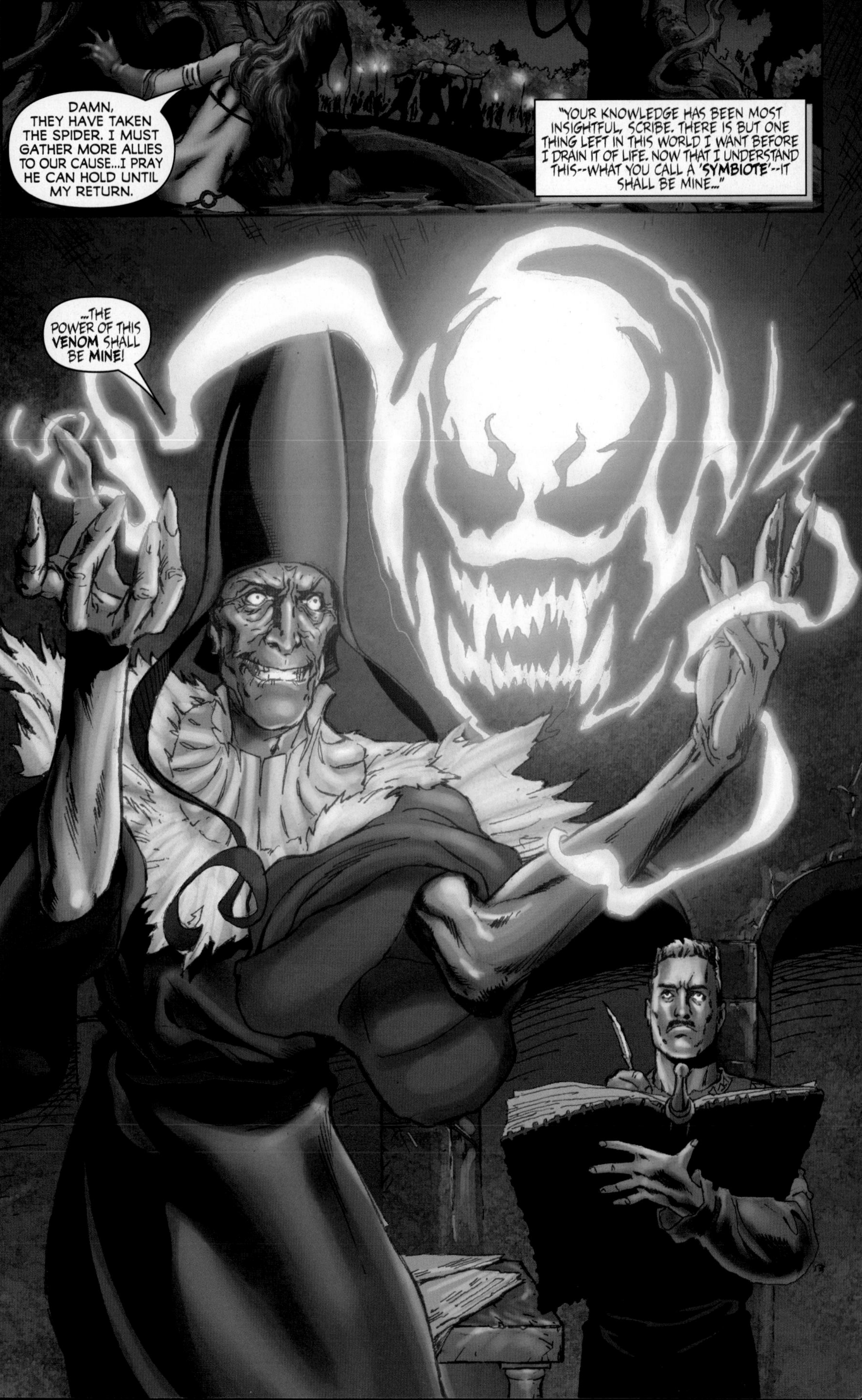
DAMN, THEY HAVE TAKEN THE SPIDER. I MUST GATHER MORE ALLIES TO OUR CAUSE...I PRAY HE CAN HOLD UNTIL MY RETURN.
"YOUR KNOWLEDGE HAS BEEN MOST INSIGHTFUL, SCRIBE. THERE IS BUT ONE THING LEFT IN THIS WORLD I WANT BEFORE I DRAIN IT OF LIFE. NOW THAT I UNDERSTAND THIS--WHAT YOU CALL A 'SYMBIOTE'--IT SHALL BE MINE..."
...THE POWER OF THIS VENOM SHALL BE MINE!

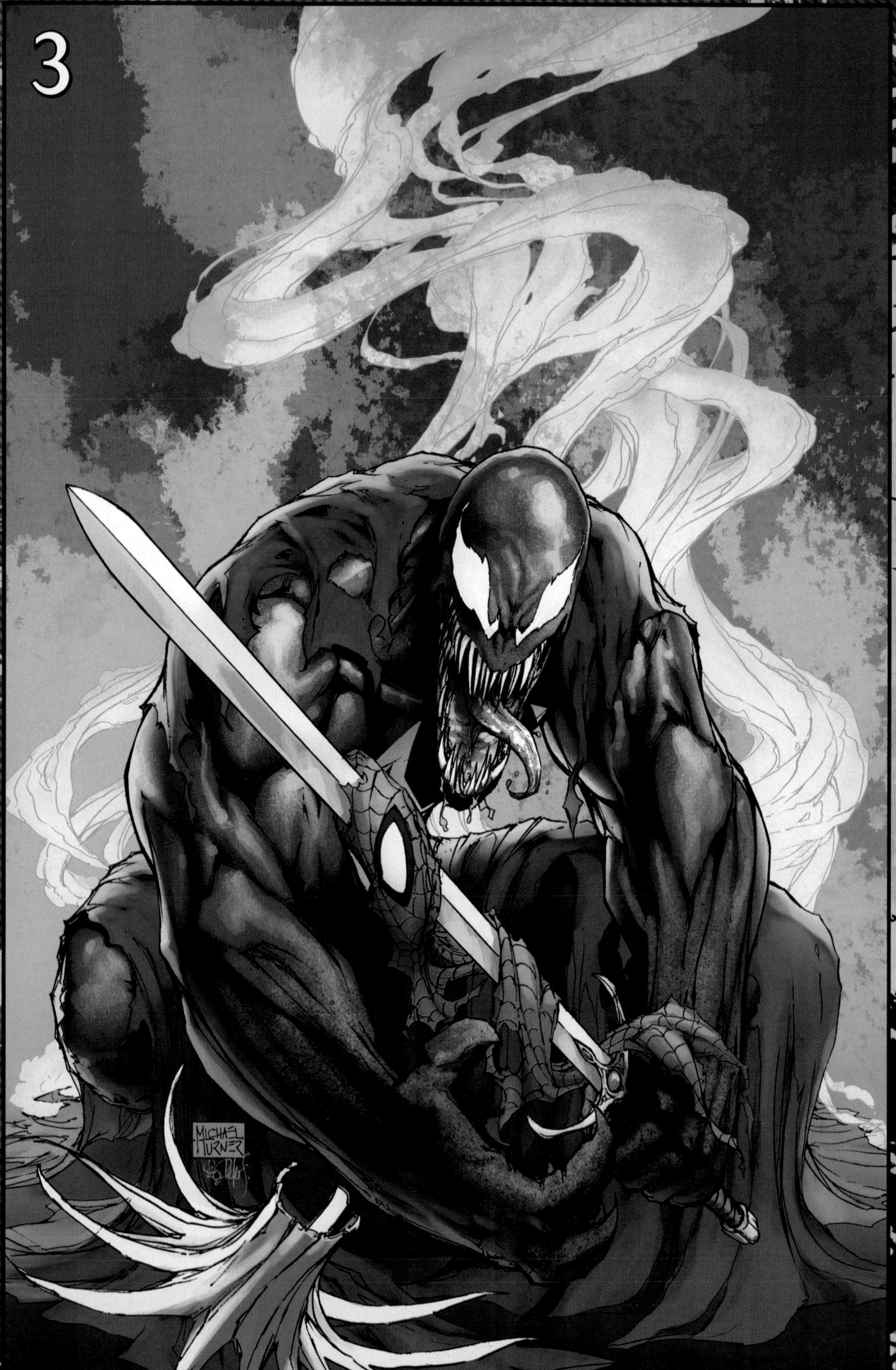
3
MICHAEL TURNER

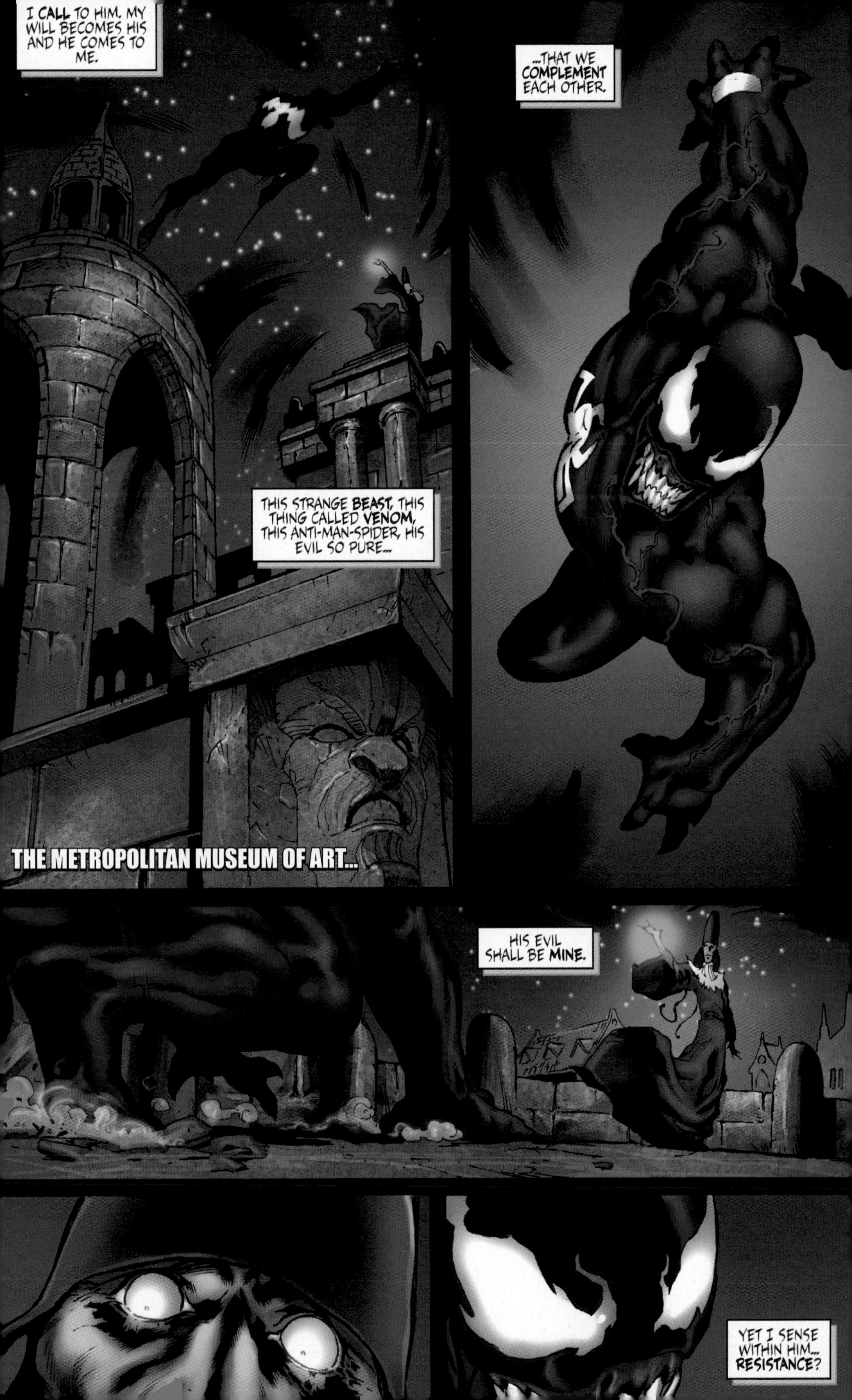
I CALL TO HIM. MY WILL BECOMES HIS AND HE COMES TO ME.
THIS STRANGE BEAST, THIS THING CALLED VENOM, THIS ANTI-MAN-SPIDER, HIS EVIL SO PURE...
THE METROPOLITAN MUSEUM OF ART...
...THAT WE COMPLEMENT EACH OTHER.
HIS EVIL SHALL BE MINE.
YET I SENSE WITHIN HIM... RESISTANCE?

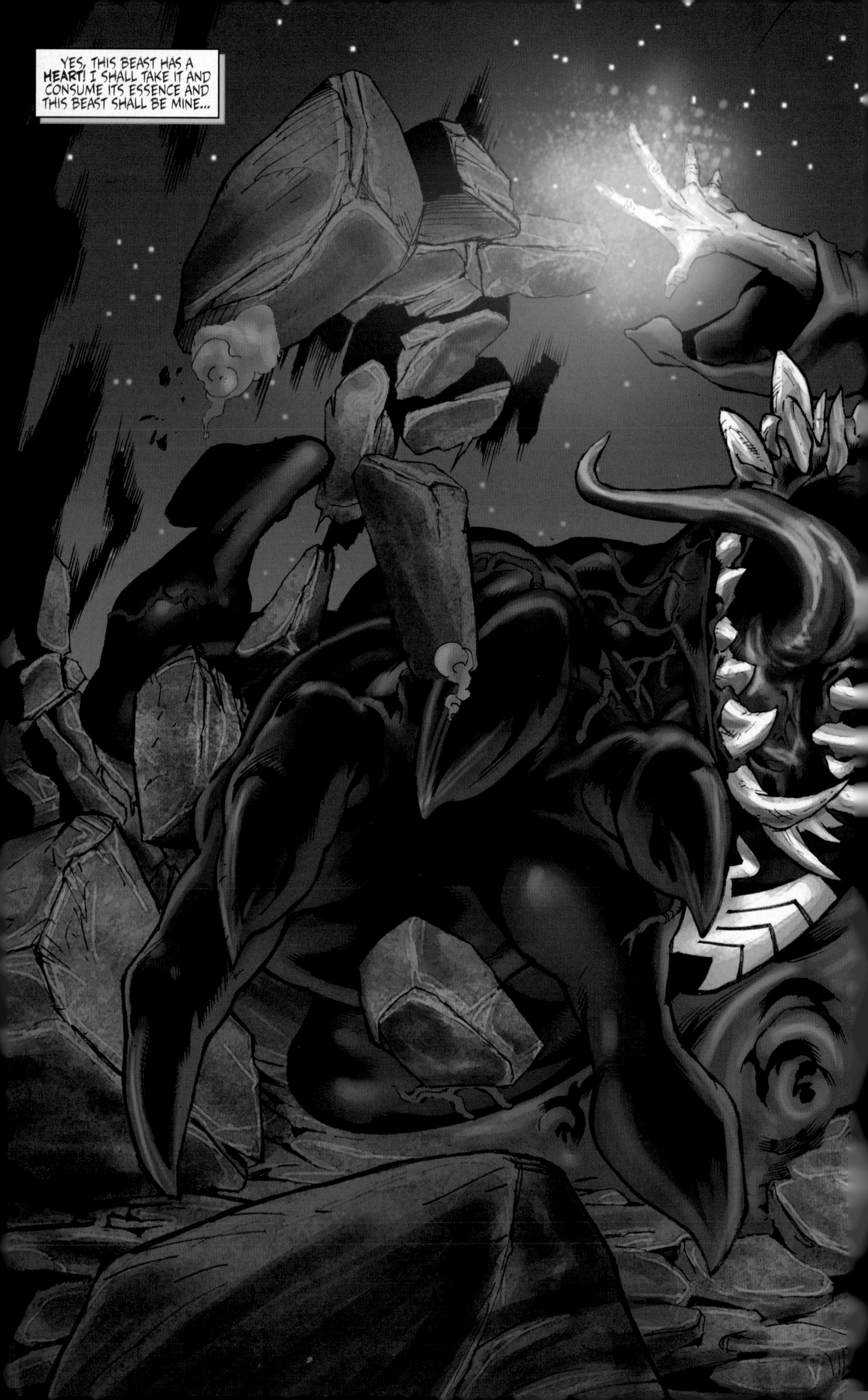
YES, THIS BEAST HAS A HEART! I SHALL TAKE IT AND CONSUME ITS ESSENCE AND THIS BEAST SHALL BE MINE...

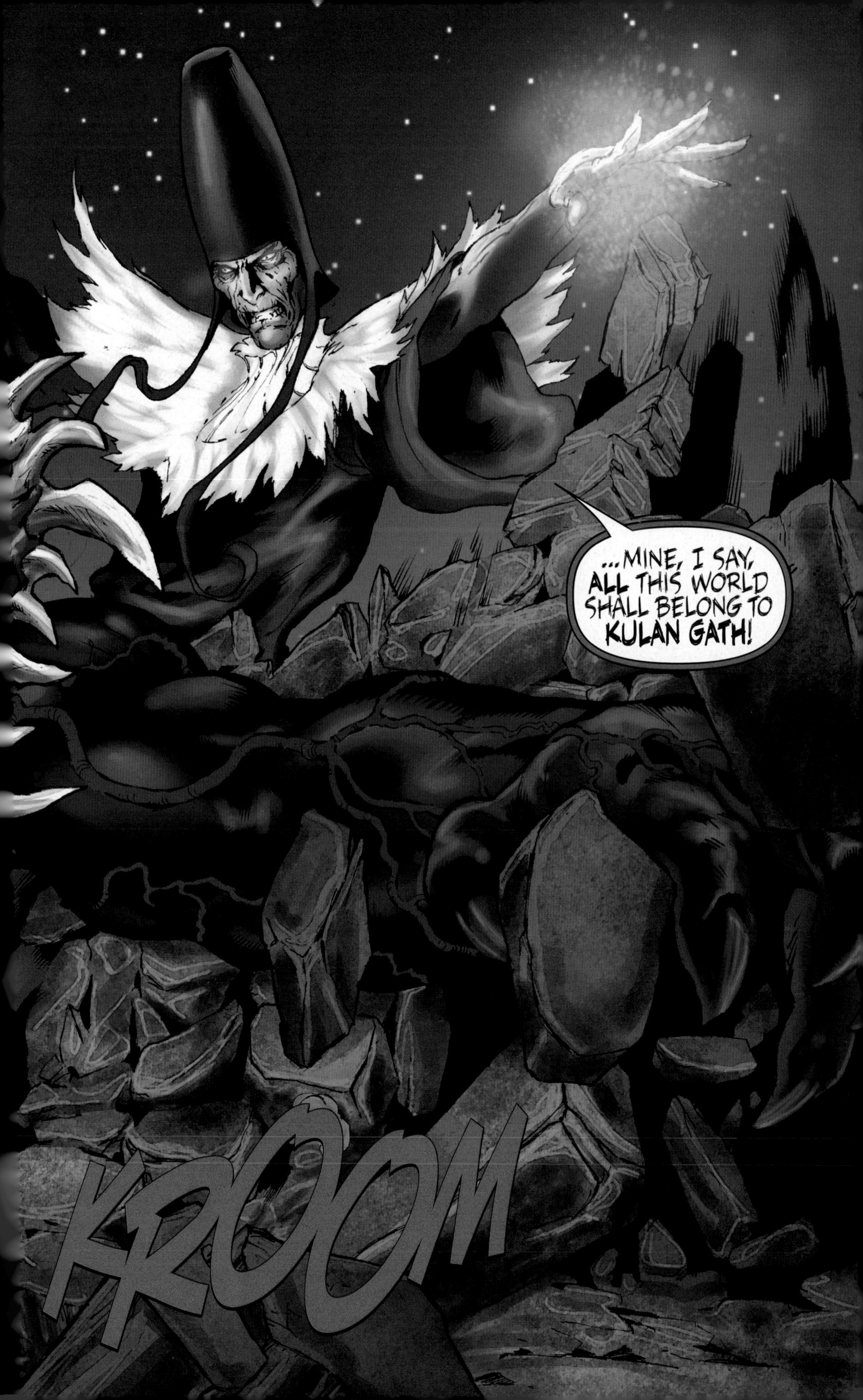
...MINE, I SAY, ALL THIS WORLD SHALL BELONG TO KULAN GATH!
KROOOM

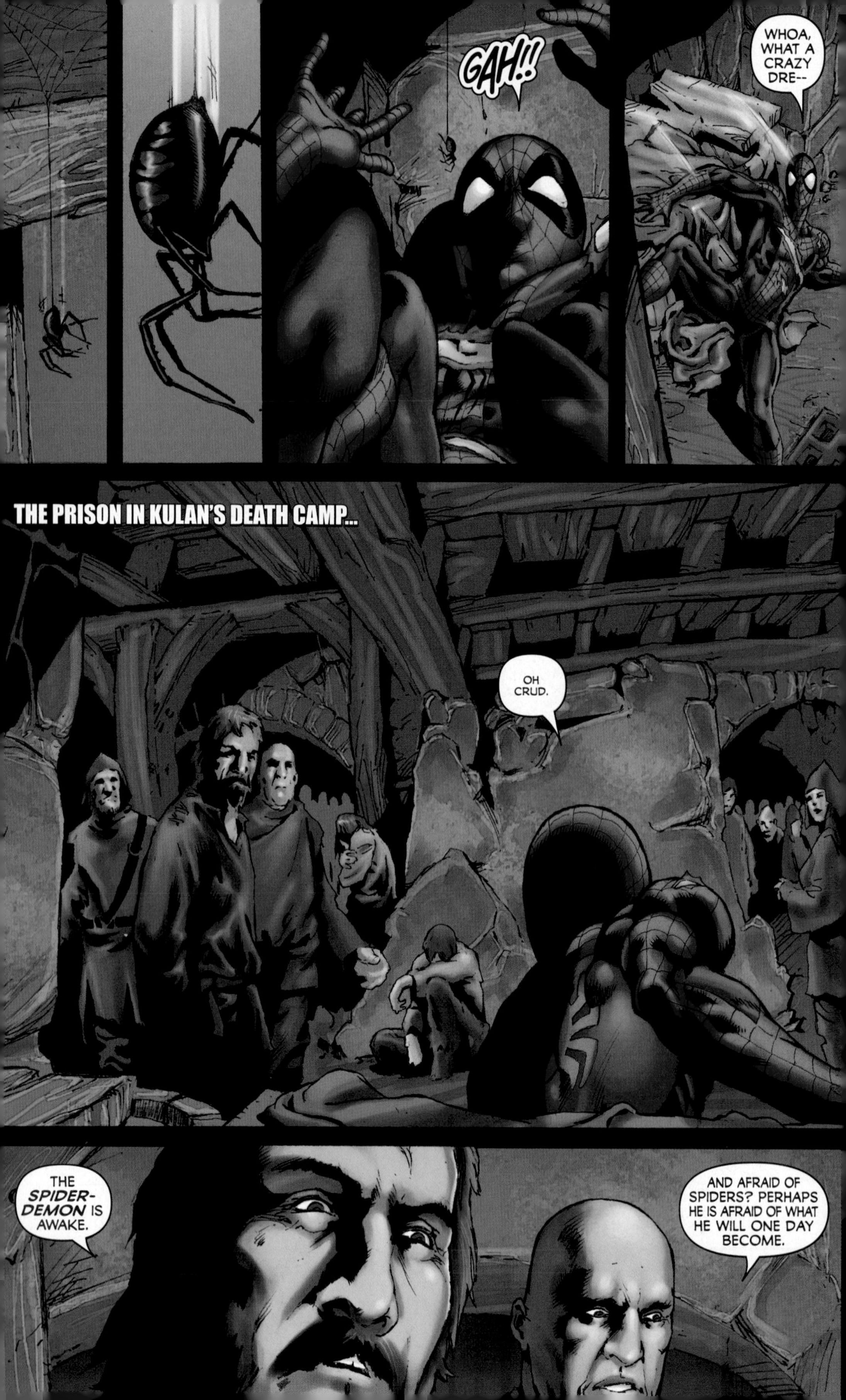
GAH!!
WHOA, WHAT A CRAZY DRE--
THE PRISON IN KULAN'S DEATH CAMP...
OH CRUD.
THE *SPIDER-DEMON* IS AWAKE.
AND AFRAID OF SPIDERS? PERHAPS HE IS AFRAID OF WHAT HE WILL ONE DAY BECOME.

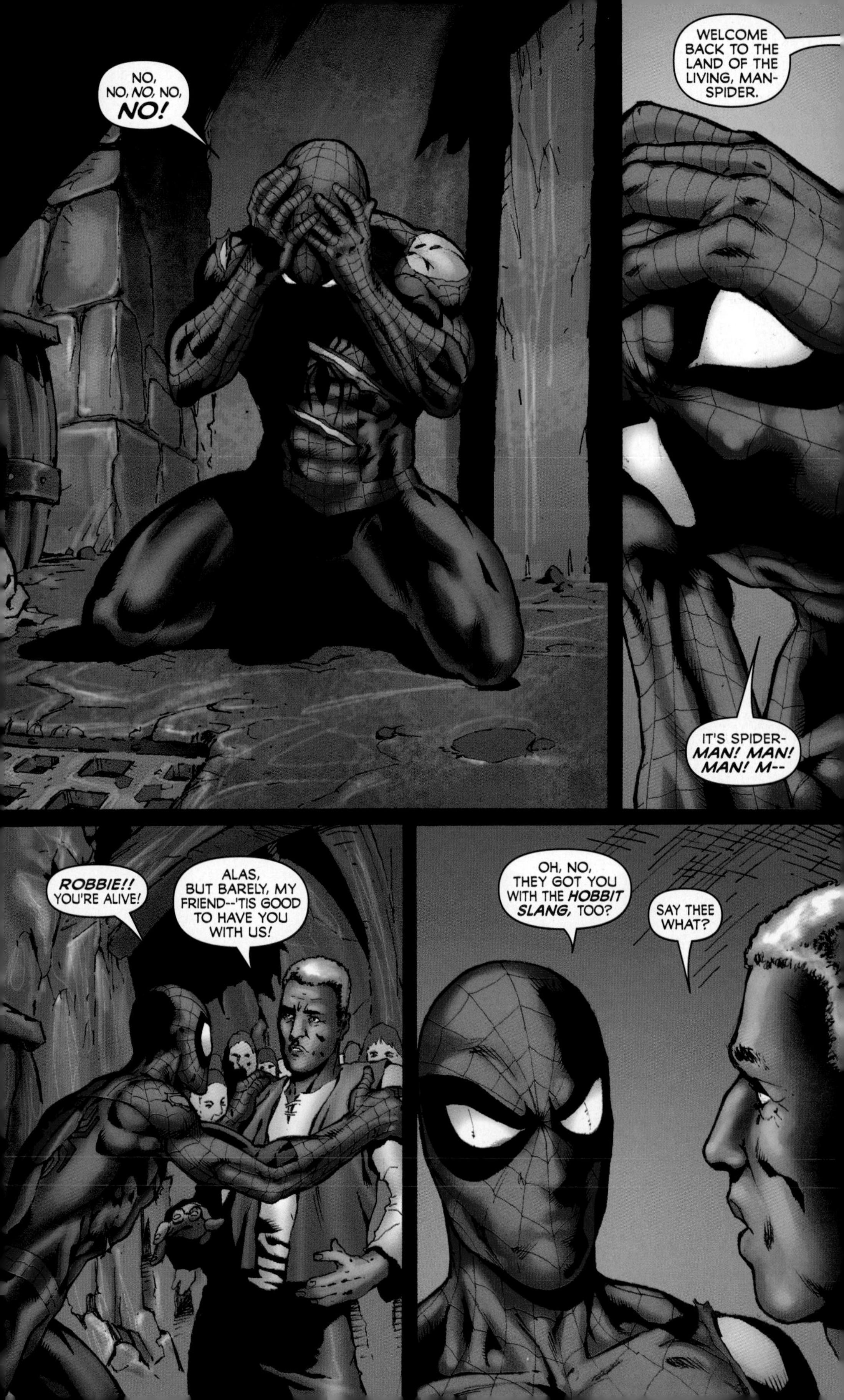
NO, NO, *NO,* NO, **NO!**
WELCOME BACK TO THE LAND OF THE LIVING, MAN-SPIDER.
IT'S SPIDER-**MAN! MAN! MAN! M--**
**ROBBIE!!** YOU'RE ALIVE!
ALAS, BUT BARELY, MY FRIEND--'TIS GOOD TO HAVE YOU WITH US!
OH, NO, THEY GOT YOU WITH THE **HOBBIT SLANG,** TOO?
SAY THEE WHAT?

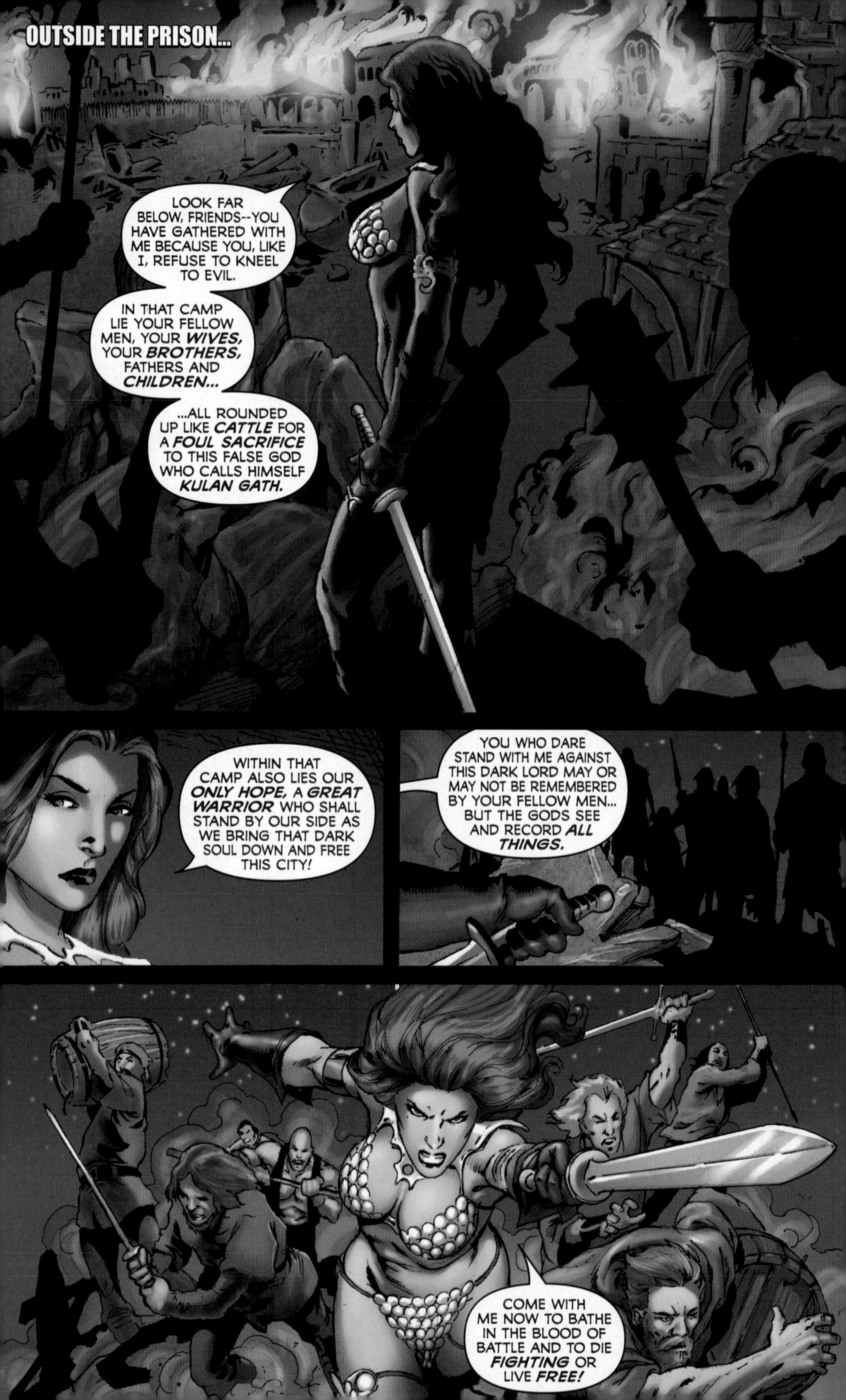
OUTSIDE THE PRISON...
LOOK FAR BELOW, FRIENDS--YOU HAVE GATHERED WITH ME BECAUSE YOU, LIKE I, REFUSE TO KNEEL TO EVIL.
IN THAT CAMP LIE YOUR FELLOW MEN, YOUR WIVES, YOUR BROTHERS, FATHERS AND CHILDREN...
...ALL ROUNDED UP LIKE CATTLE FOR A FOUL SACRIFICE TO THIS FALSE GOD WHO CALLS HIMSELF KULAN GATH.
WITHIN THAT CAMP ALSO LIES OUR ONLY HOPE, A GREAT WARRIOR WHO SHALL STAND BY OUR SIDE AS WE BRING THAT DARK SOUL DOWN AND FREE THIS CITY!
YOU WHO DARE STAND WITH ME AGAINST THIS DARK LORD MAY OR MAY NOT BE REMEMBERED BY YOUR FELLOW MEN... BUT THE GODS SEE AND RECORD ALL THINGS.
COME WITH ME NOW TO BATHE IN THE BLOOD OF BATTLE AND TO DIE FIGHTING OR LIVE FREE!

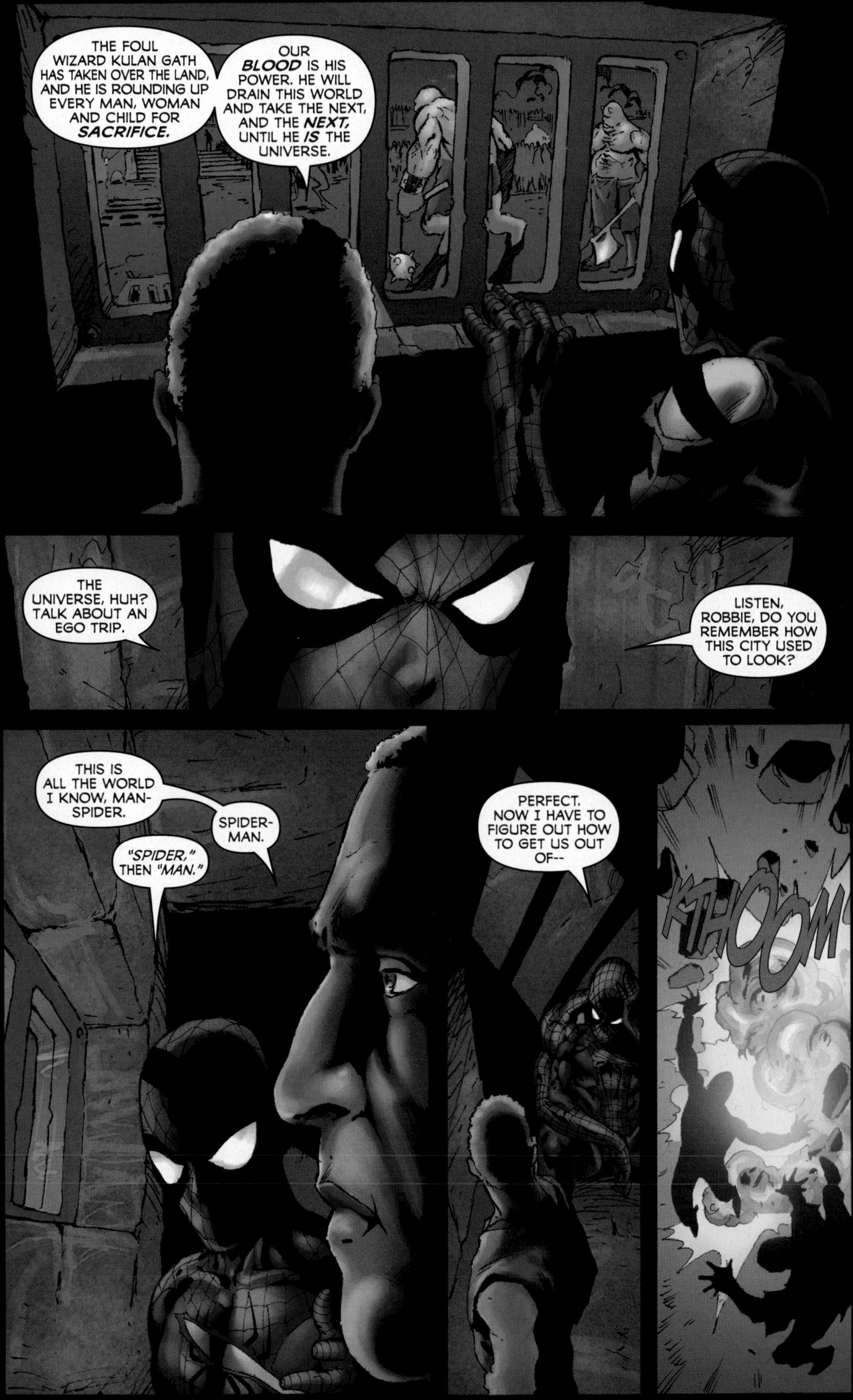
THE FOUL WIZARD KULAN GATH HAS TAKEN OVER THE LAND, AND HE IS ROUNDING UP EVERY MAN, WOMAN AND CHILD FOR *SACRIFICE.*
OUR *BLOOD* IS HIS POWER. HE WILL DRAIN THIS WORLD AND TAKE THE NEXT, AND THE *NEXT,* UNTIL HE *IS* THE UNIVERSE.
THE UNIVERSE, HUH? TALK ABOUT AN EGO TRIP.
LISTEN, ROBBIE, DO YOU REMEMBER HOW THIS CITY USED TO LOOK?
THIS IS ALL THE WORLD I KNOW, MAN-SPIDER.
SPIDER-MAN.
*"SPIDER,"* THEN *"MAN."*
PERFECT. NOW I HAVE TO FIGURE OUT HOW TO GET US OUT OF--
KTHOOM

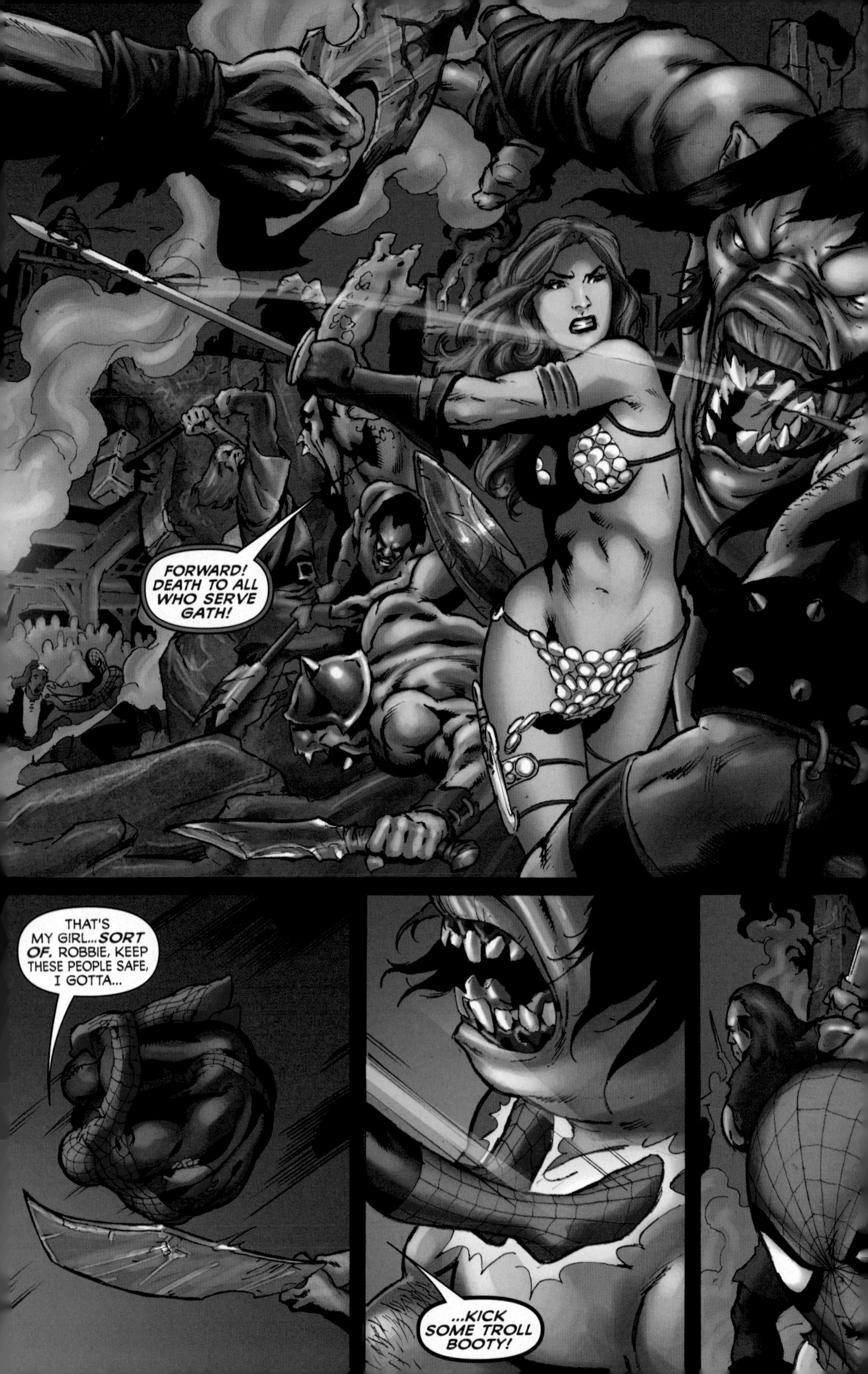
FORWARD! DEATH TO ALL WHO SERVE GATH!
THAT'S MY GIRL...SORT OF. ROBBIE, KEEP THESE PEOPLE SAFE, I GOTTA...
...KICK SOME TROLL BOOTY!

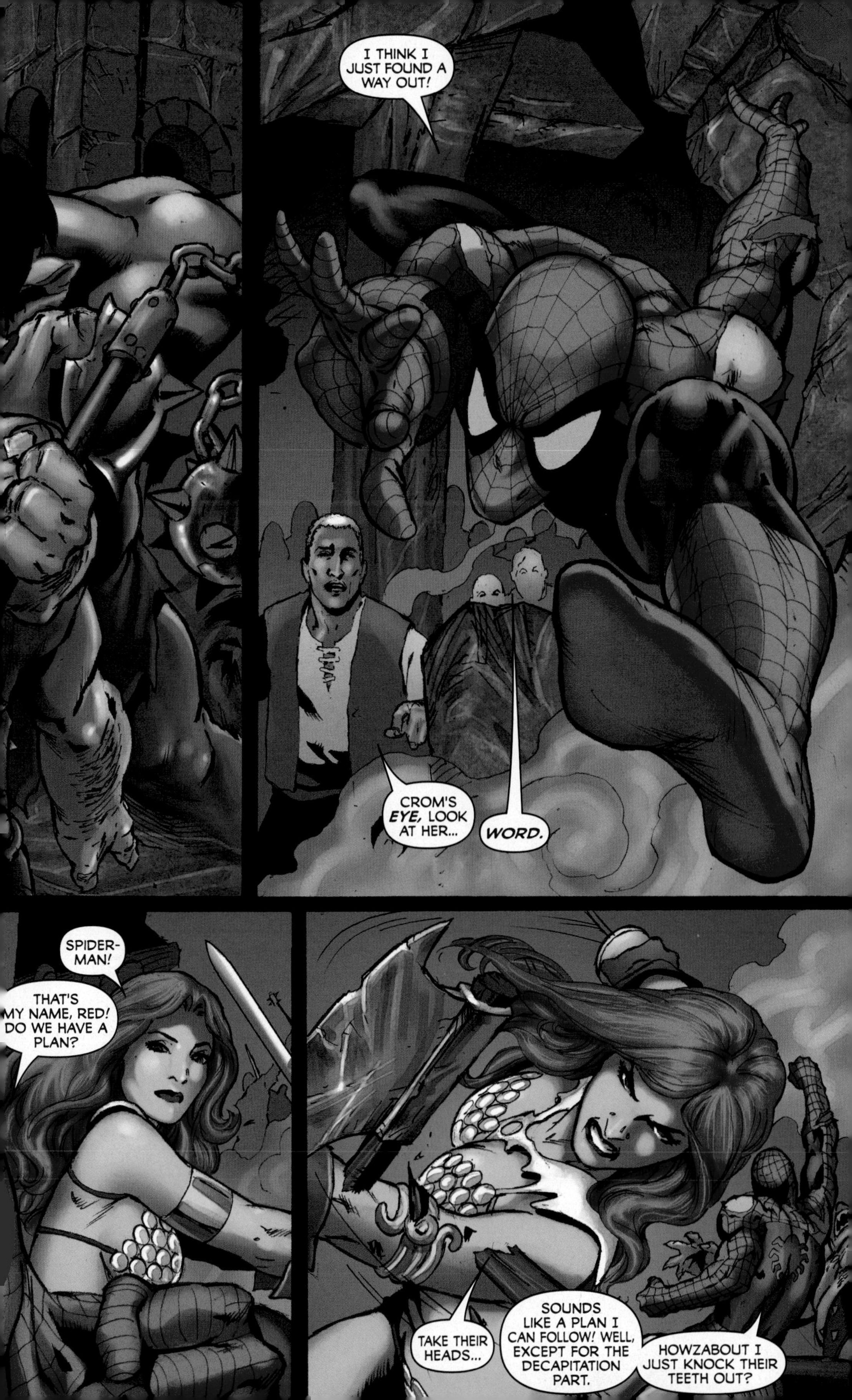
I THINK I JUST FOUND A WAY OUT!
CROM'S *EYE,* LOOK AT HER...
***WORD.***
SPIDER-MAN!
THAT'S MY NAME, RED! DO WE HAVE A PLAN?
TAKE THEIR HEADS...
SOUNDS LIKE A PLAN I CAN FOLLOW! WELL, EXCEPT FOR THE DECAPITATION PART.
HOWZABOUT I JUST KNOCK THEIR TEETH OUT?

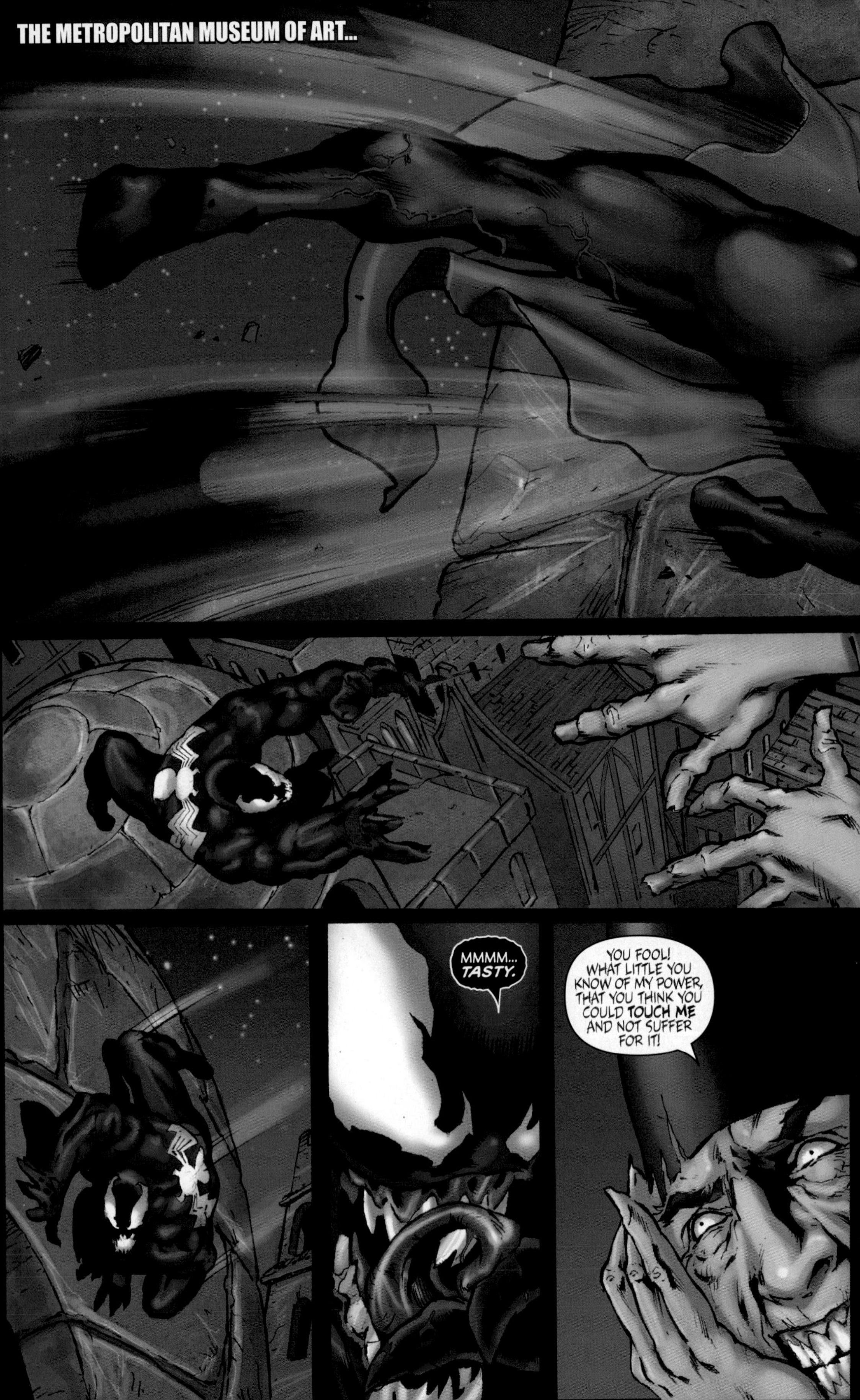
THE METROPOLITAN MUSEUM OF ART...
MMMM... TASTY.
YOU FOOL! WHAT LITTLE YOU KNOW OF MY POWER, THAT YOU THINK YOU COULD TOUCH ME AND NOT SUFFER FOR IT!

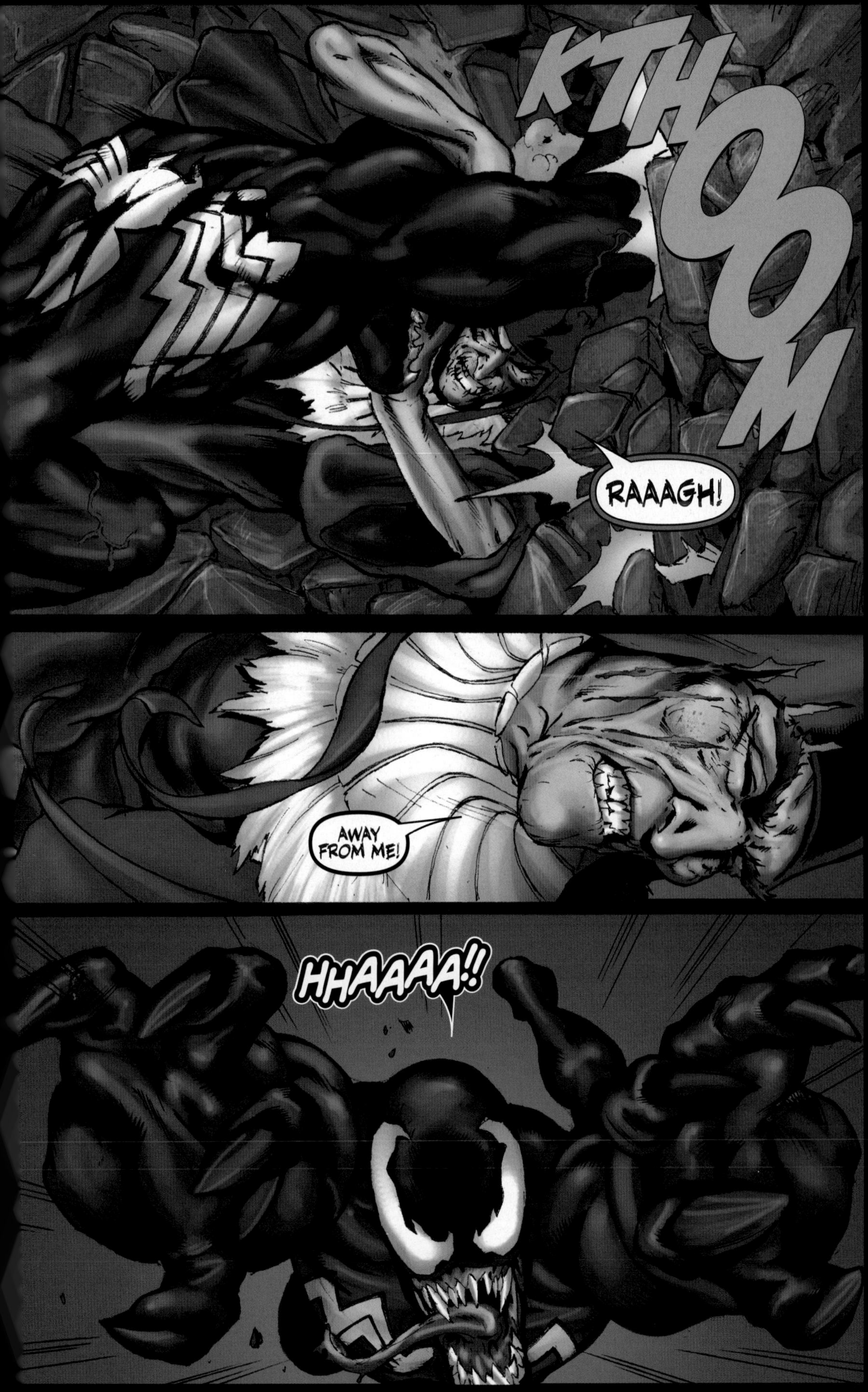
KTHOOOM
RAAAGH!
AWAY FROM ME!
HHAAAAA!!

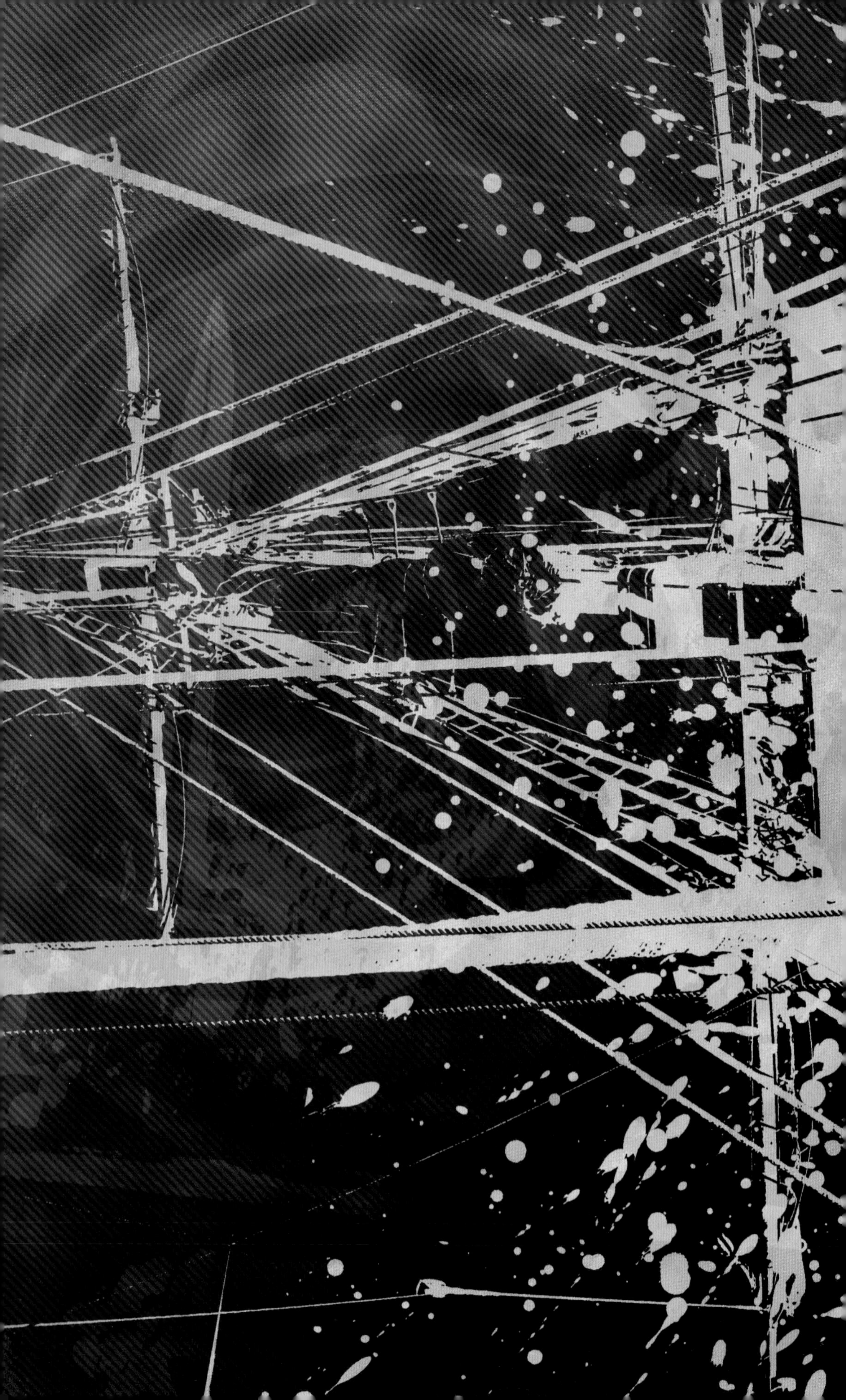

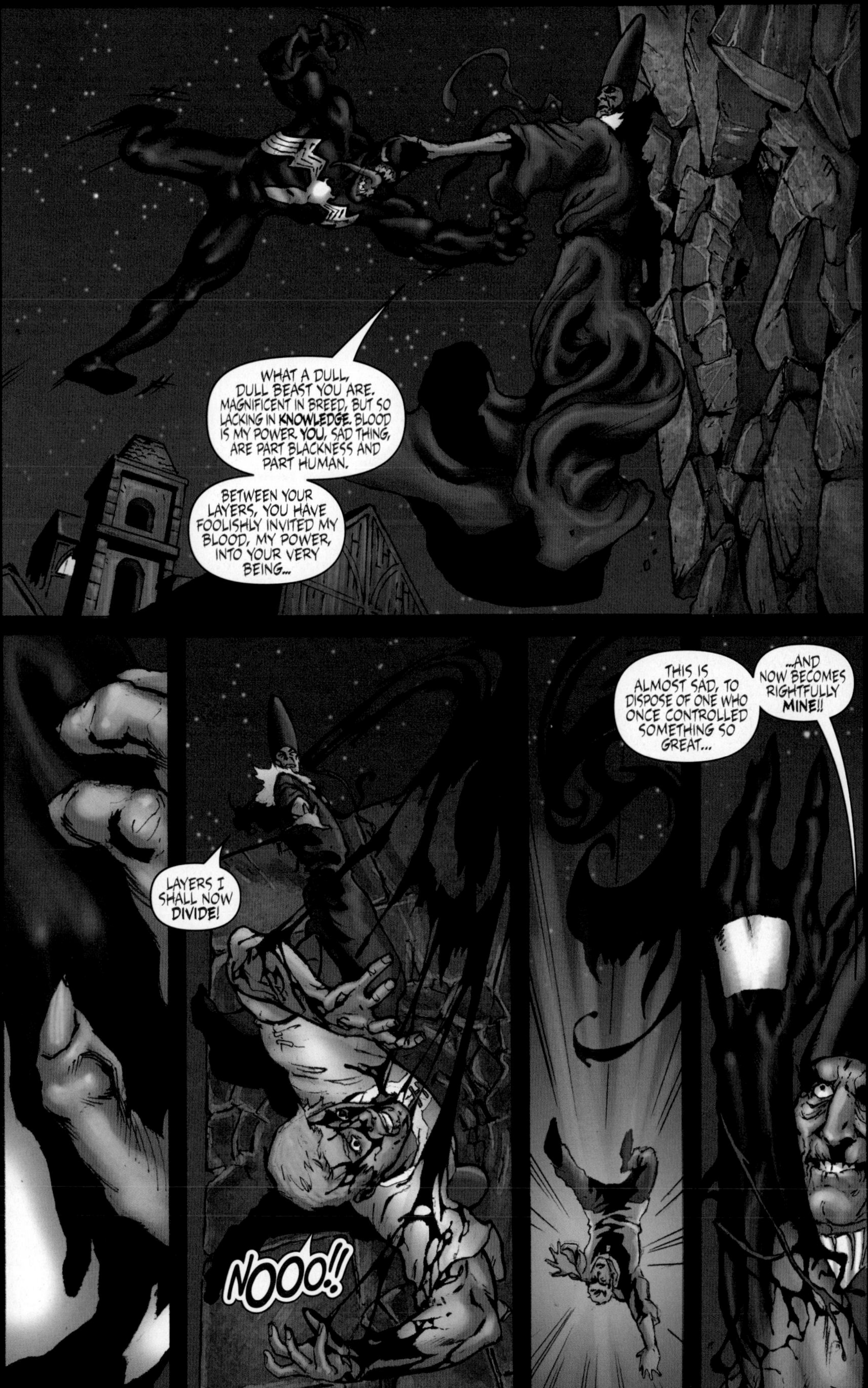
WHAT A DULL, DULL BEAST YOU ARE. MAGNIFICENT IN BREED, BUT SO LACKING IN KNOWLEDGE. BLOOD IS MY POWER. YOU, SAD THING, ARE PART BLACKNESS AND PART HUMAN.
BETWEEN YOUR LAYERS, YOU HAVE FOOLISHLY INVITED MY BLOOD, MY POWER, INTO YOUR VERY BEING...
LAYERS I SHALL NOW DIVIDE!
NOOO!!
THIS IS ALMOST SAD, TO DISPOSE OF ONE WHO ONCE CONTROLLED SOMETHING SO GREAT...
...AND NOW BECOMES RIGHTFULLY MINE!!

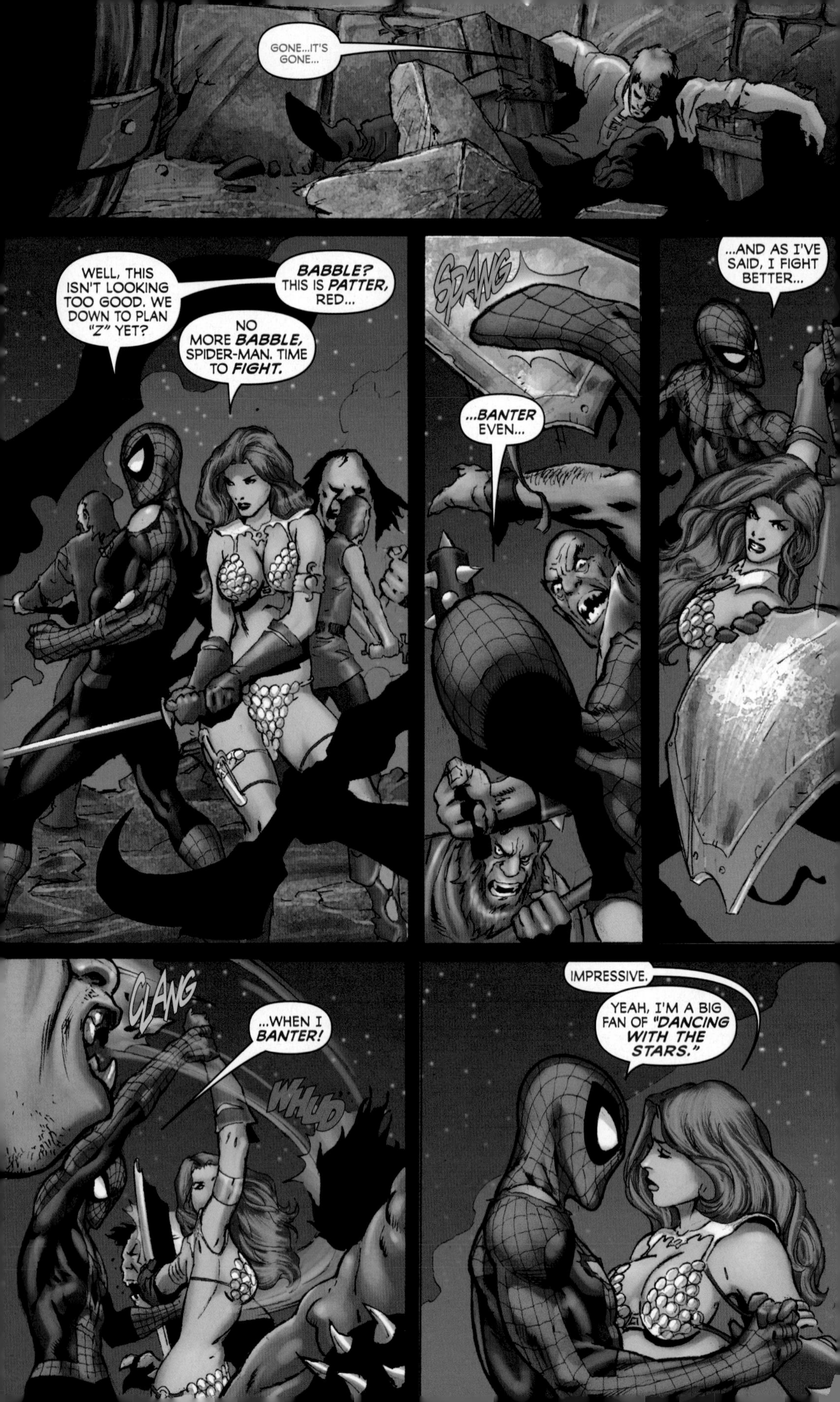
GONE...IT'S GONE...
WELL, THIS ISN'T LOOKING TOO GOOD. WE DOWN TO PLAN "Z" YET?
NO MORE BABBLE, SPIDER-MAN. TIME TO FIGHT.
BABBLE? THIS IS PATTER, RED...
SPANG
...BANTER EVEN...
...AND AS I'VE SAID, I FIGHT BETTER...
CLANG
...WHEN I BANTER!
WHUD
IMPRESSIVE.
YEAH, I'M A BIG FAN OF "DANCING WITH THE STARS."

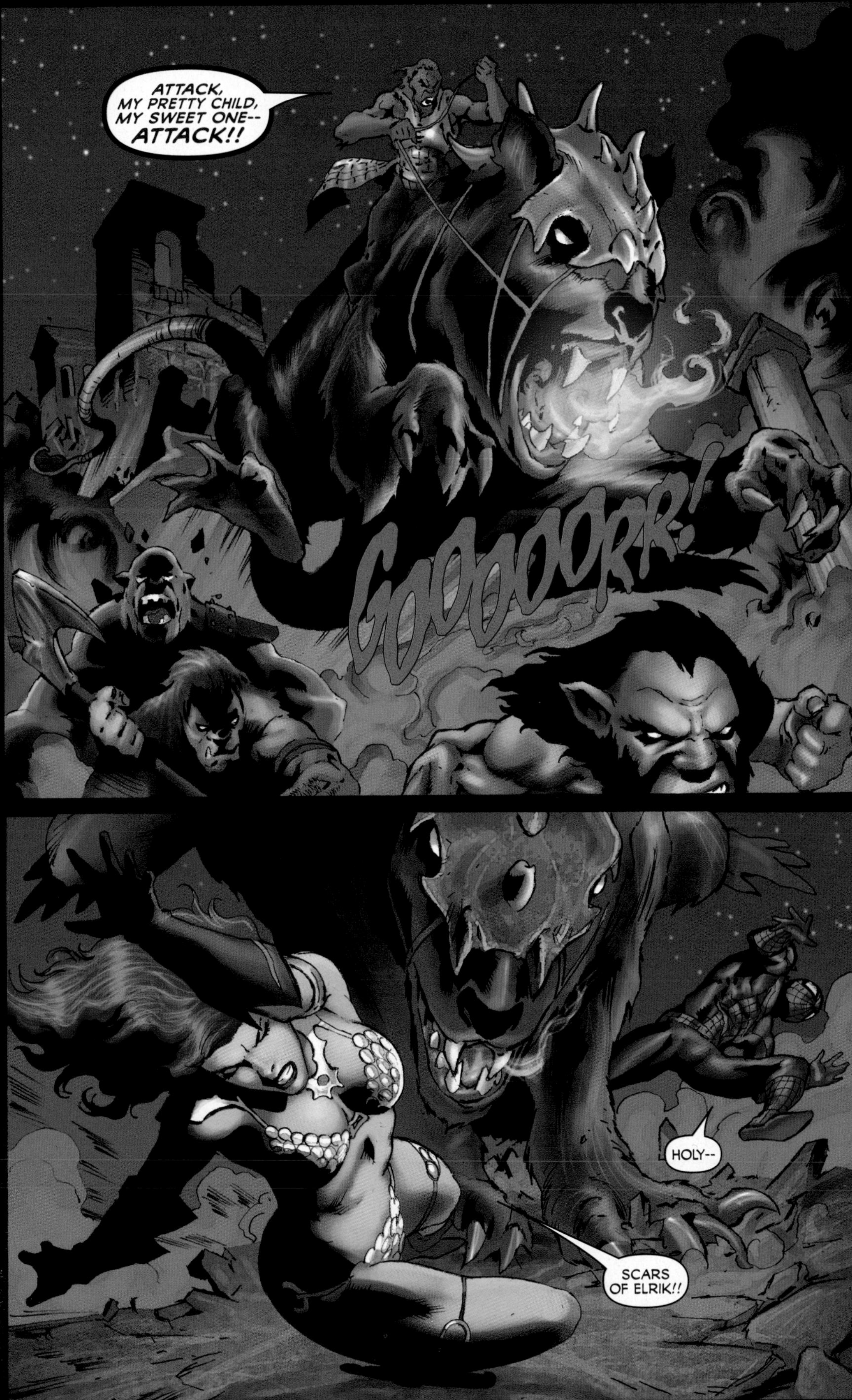
ATTACK, MY PRETTY CHILD, MY SWEET ONE-- ATTACK!!
GOOOOORR!
HOLY--
SCARS OF ELRIK!!

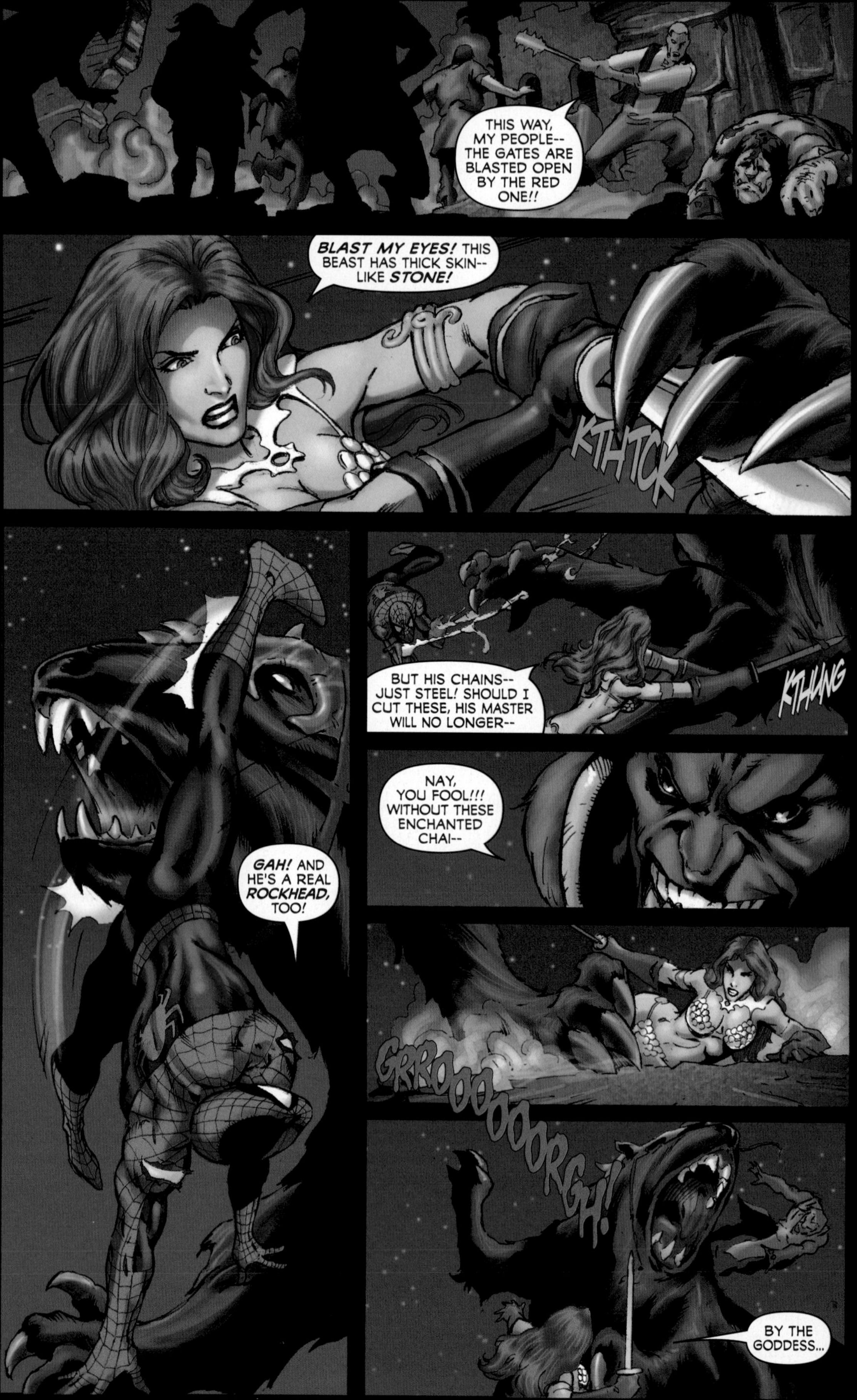
THIS WAY, MY PEOPLE-- THE GATES ARE BLASTED OPEN BY THE RED ONE!!
BLAST MY EYES! THIS BEAST HAS THICK SKIN-- LIKE STONE!
KTHTCK
GAH! AND HE'S A REAL ROCKHEAD, TOO!
BUT HIS CHAINS-- JUST STEEL! SHOULD I CUT THESE, HIS MASTER WILL NO LONGER--
KTHUNG
NAY, YOU FOOL!!! WITHOUT THESE ENCHANTED CHAI--
GRROOOOOOORGH!!
BY THE GODDESS...

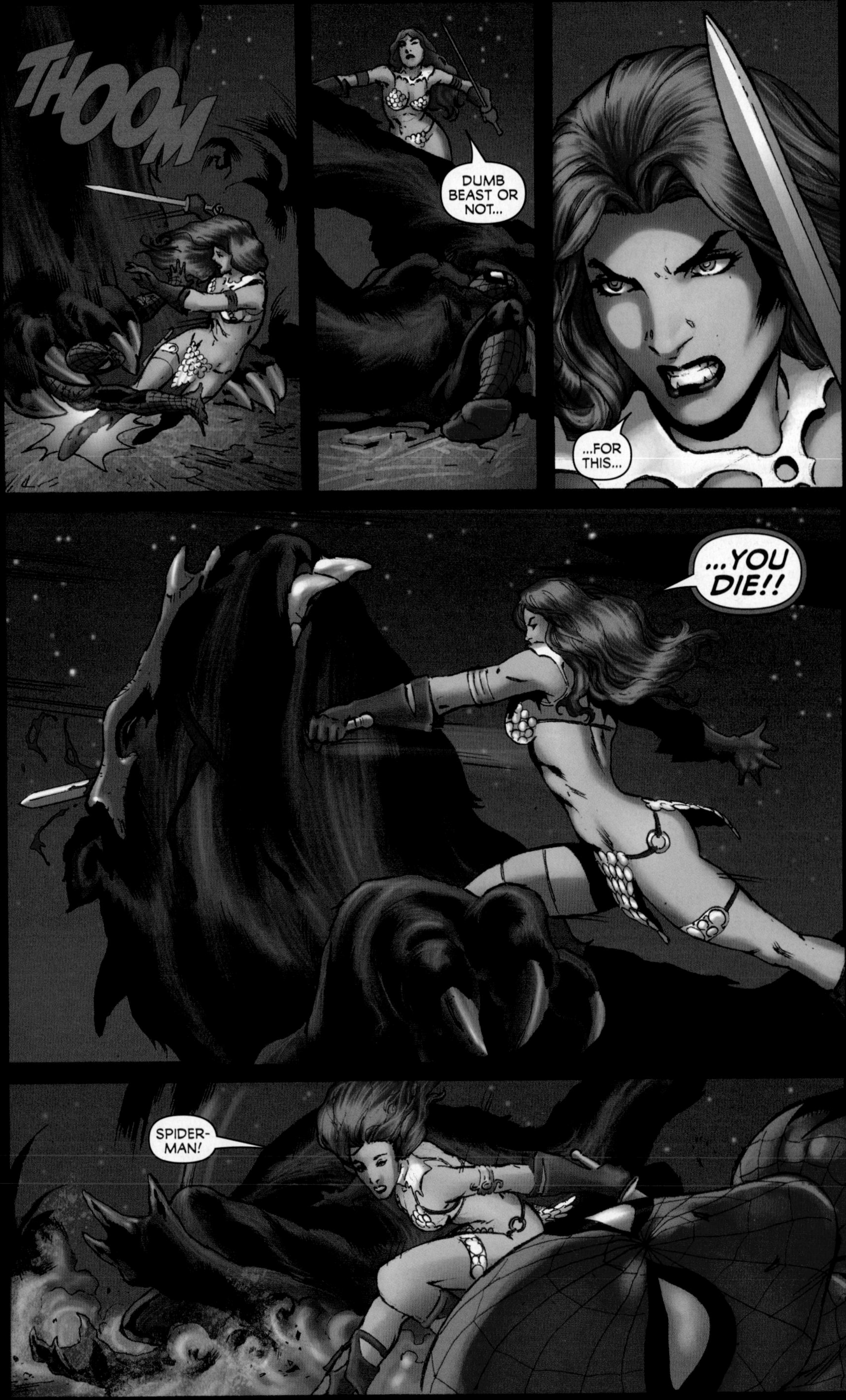
THOOM
DUMB BEAST OR NOT...
...FOR THIS...
...YOU DIE!!
SPIDER-MAN!

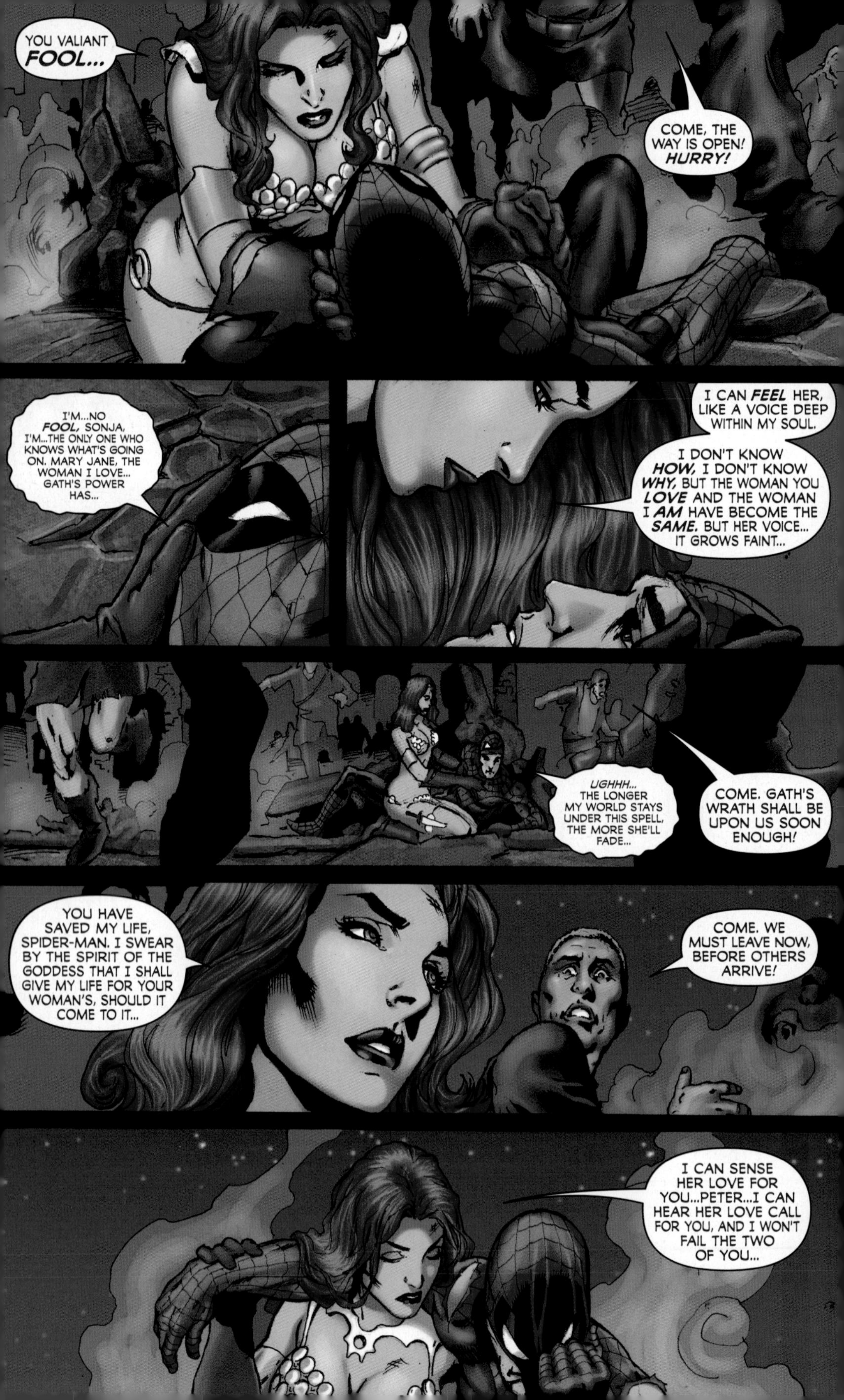
YOU VALIANT FOOL...
COME, THE WAY IS OPEN! HURRY!
I'M...NO FOOL, SONJA, I'M...THE ONLY ONE WHO KNOWS WHAT'S GOING ON. MARY JANE, THE WOMAN I LOVE... GATH'S POWER HAS...
I CAN FEEL HER, LIKE A VOICE DEEP WITHIN MY SOUL.
I DON'T KNOW HOW, I DON'T KNOW WHY, BUT THE WOMAN YOU LOVE AND THE WOMAN I AM HAVE BECOME THE SAME. BUT HER VOICE... IT GROWS FAINT...
UGHHH... THE LONGER MY WORLD STAYS UNDER THIS SPELL, THE MORE SHE'LL FADE...
COME. GATH'S WRATH SHALL BE UPON US SOON ENOUGH!
YOU HAVE SAVED MY LIFE, SPIDER-MAN. I SWEAR BY THE SPIRIT OF THE GODDESS THAT I SHALL GIVE MY LIFE FOR YOUR WOMAN'S, SHOULD IT COME TO IT...
COME. WE MUST LEAVE NOW, BEFORE OTHERS ARRIVE!
I CAN SENSE HER LOVE FOR YOU...PETER...I CAN HEAR HER LOVE CALL FOR YOU, AND I WON'T FAIL THE TWO OF YOU...

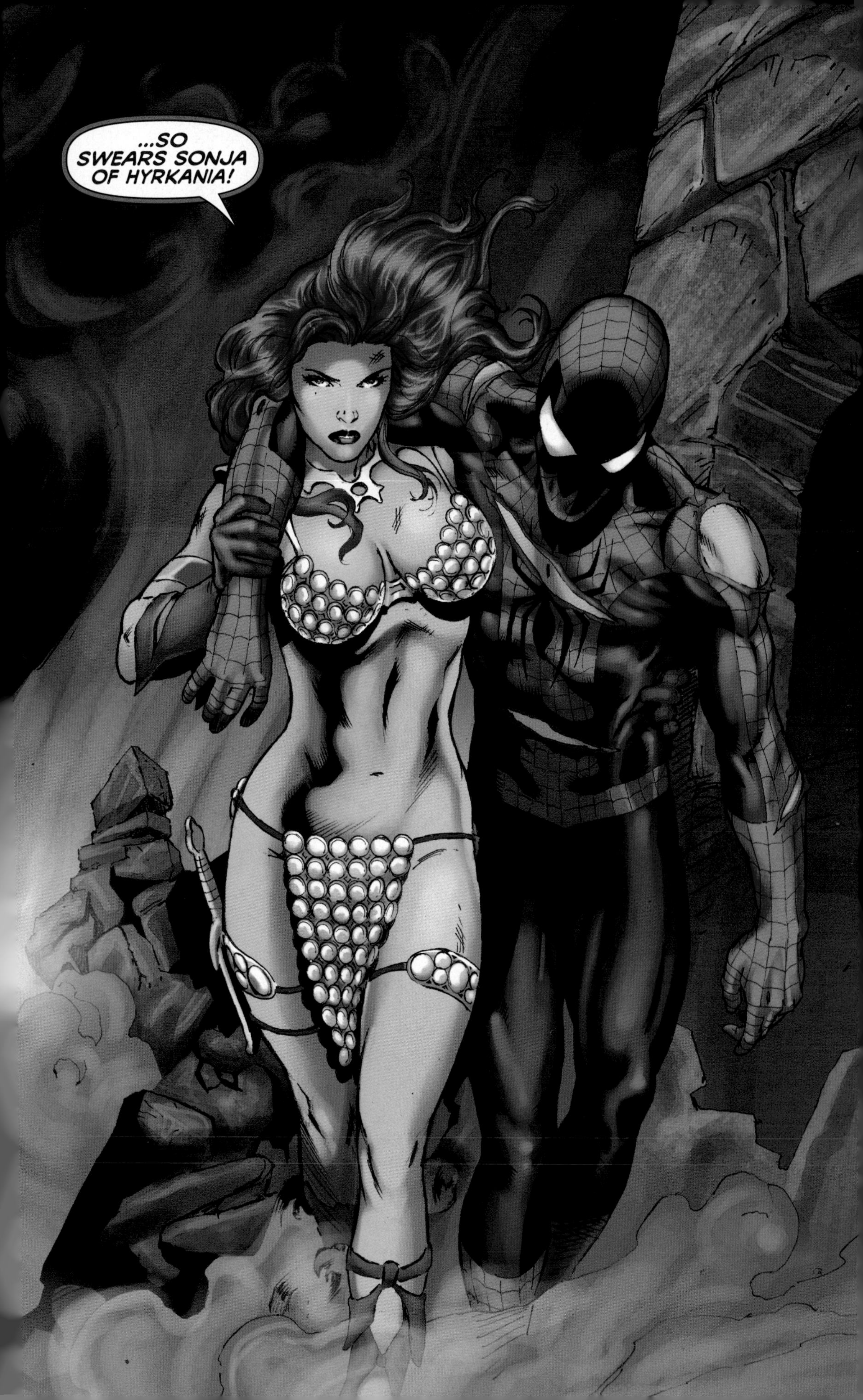
...SO SWEARS SONJA OF HYRKANIA!

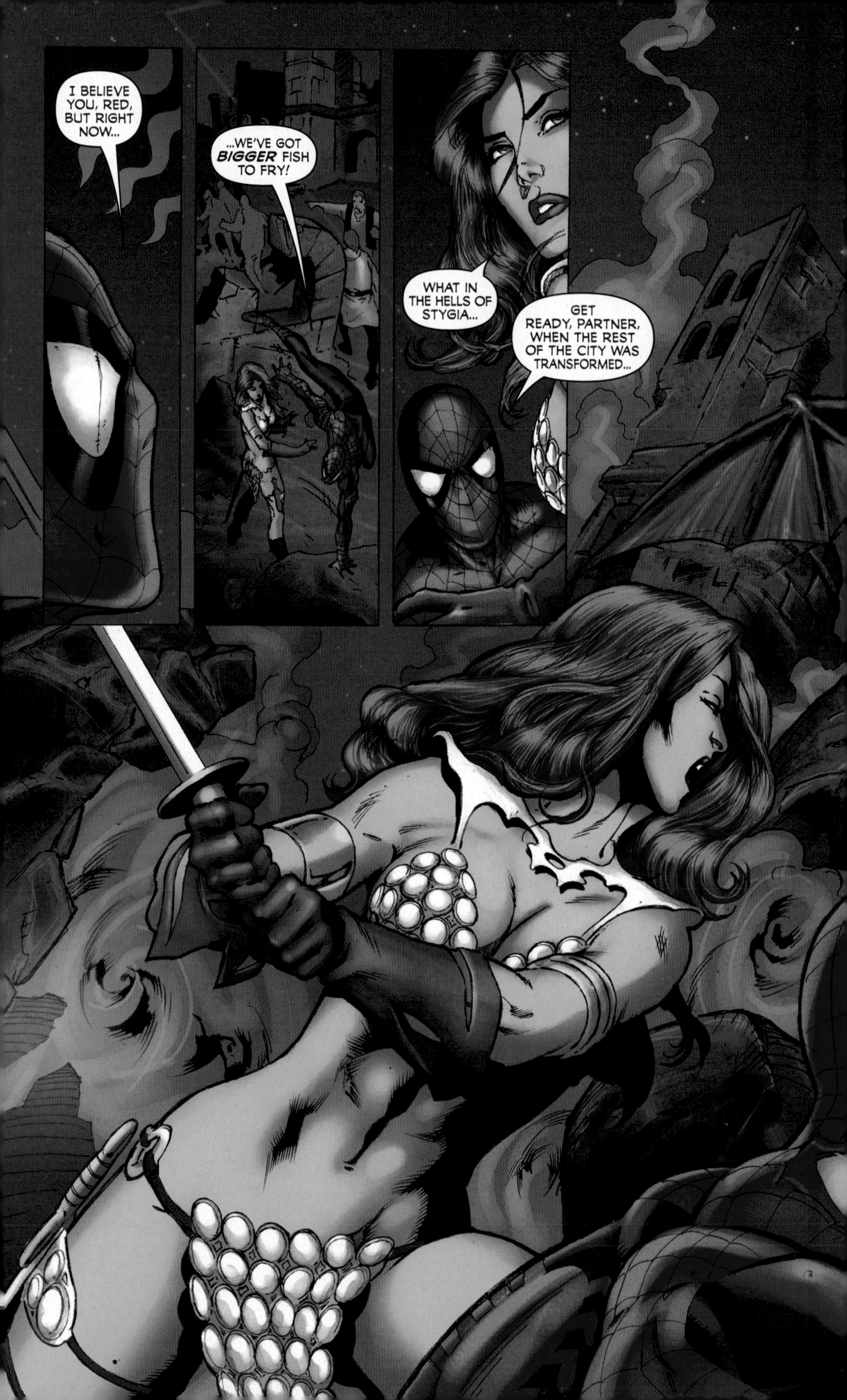
I BELIEVE YOU, RED, BUT RIGHT NOW...
...WE'VE GOT *BIGGER* FISH TO FRY!
WHAT IN THE HELLS OF STYGIA...
GET READY, PARTNER, WHEN THE REST OF THE CITY WAS TRANSFORMED...

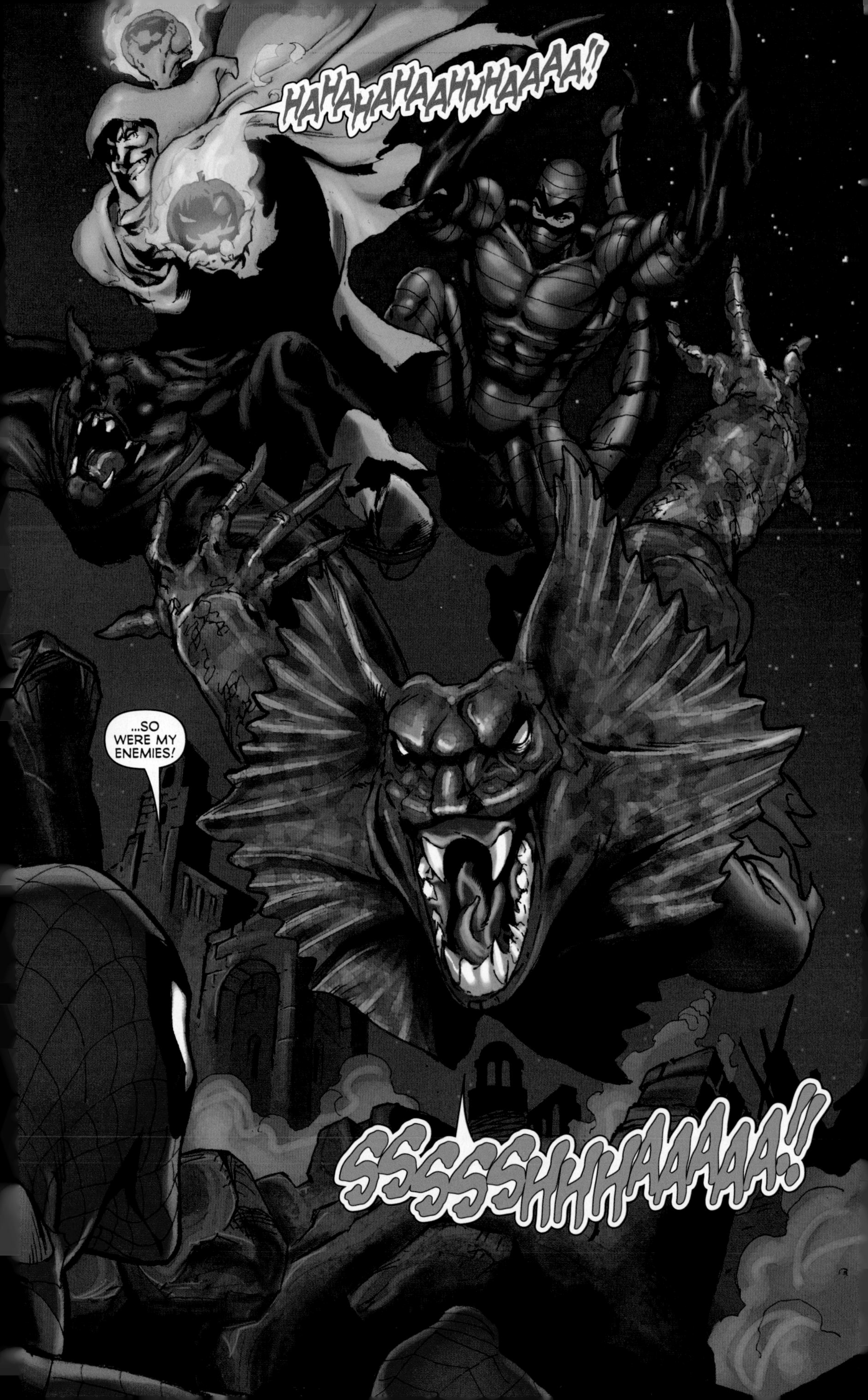
HAHAHAHAAHHAAAA!!
...SO WERE MY ENEMIES!
SSSSSHHHAAAAAA!!

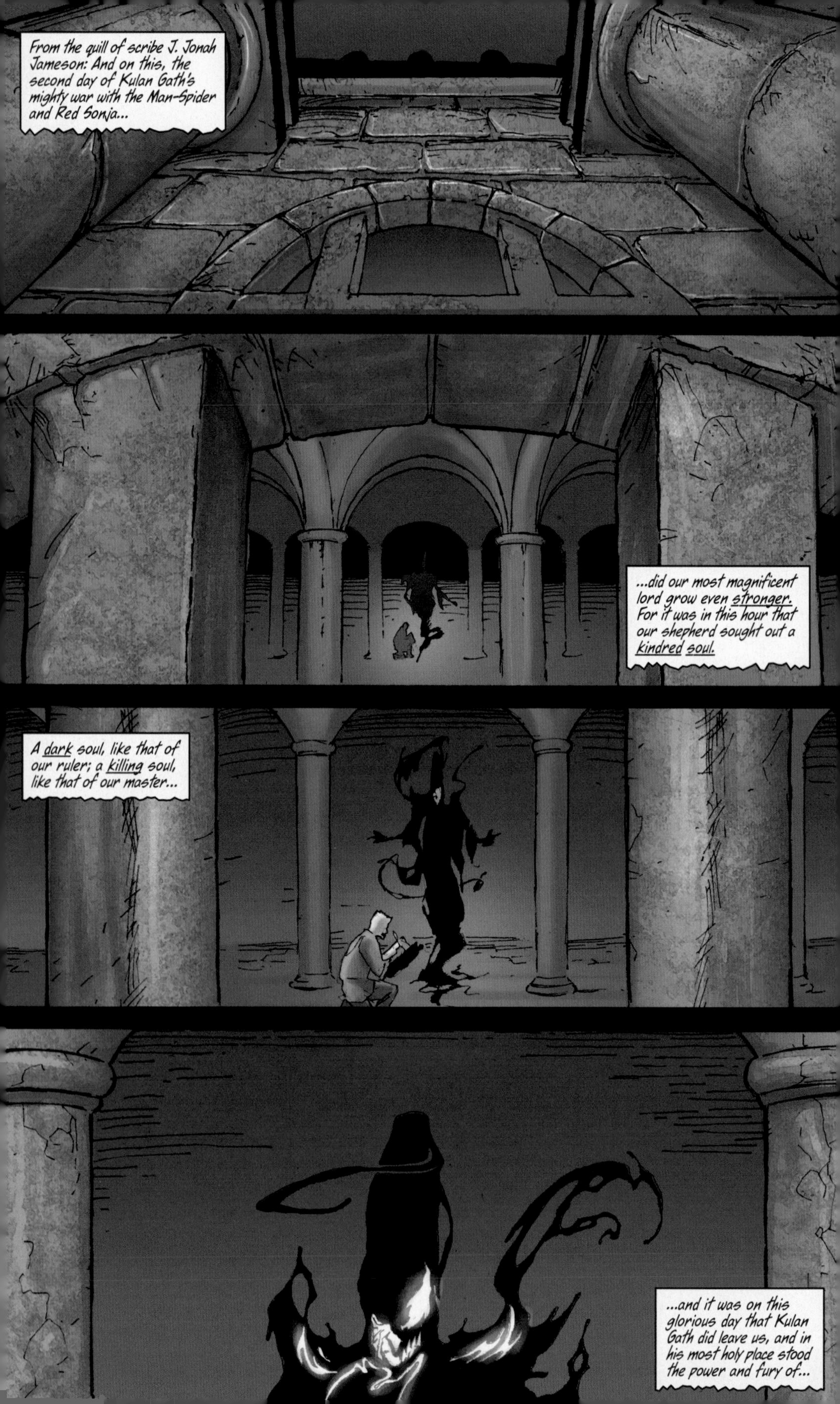
From the quill of scribe J. Jonah Jameson: And on this, the second day of Kulan Gath's mighty war with the Man-Spider and Red Sonja...
...did our most magnificent lord grow even stronger. For it was in this hour that our shepherd sought out a kindred soul.
A dark soul, like that of our ruler; a killing soul, like that of our master...
...and it was on this glorious day that Kulan Gath did leave us, and in his most holy place stood the power and fury of...

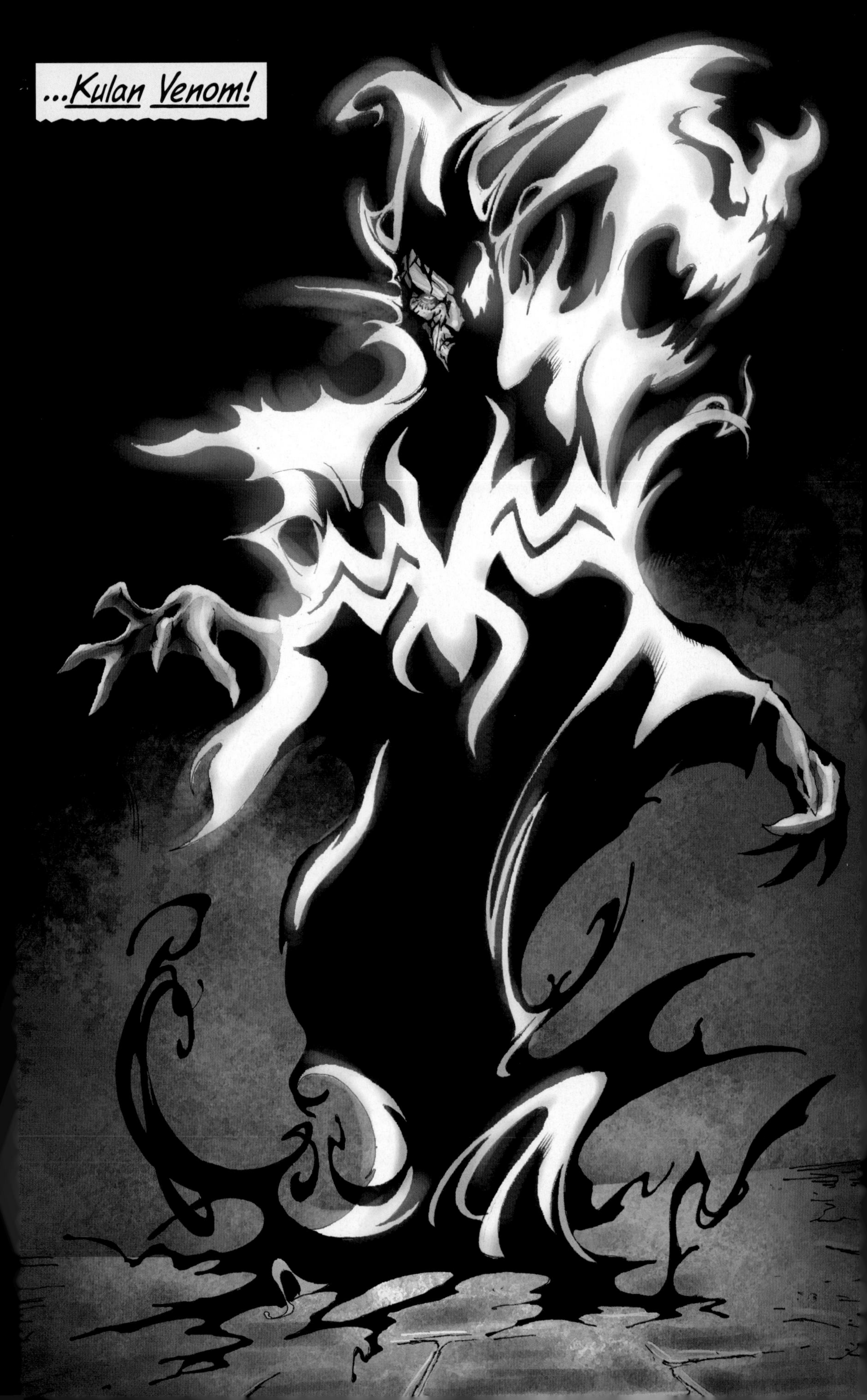
...Kulan Venom!

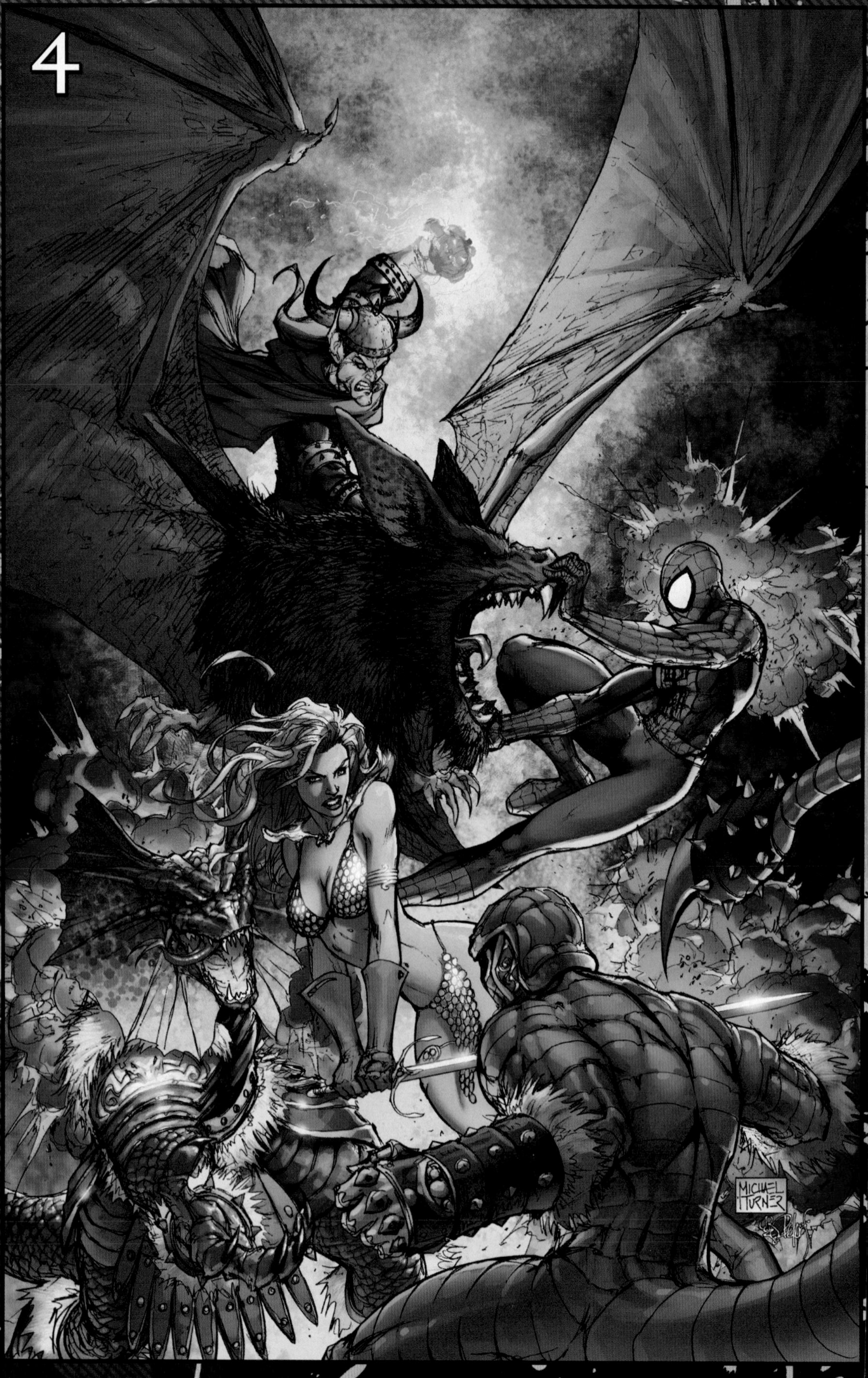
4
MICHAEL TURNER

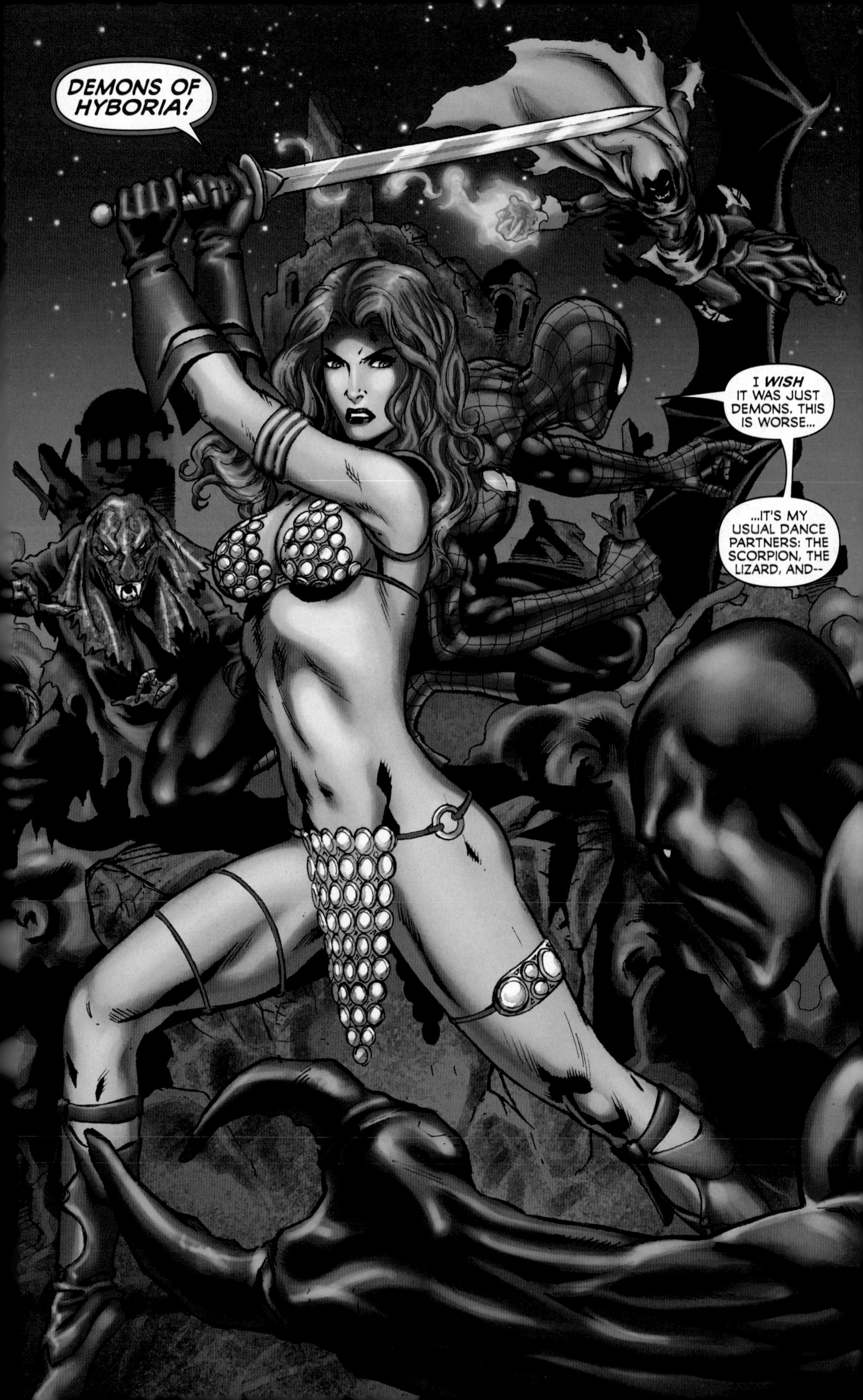
DEMONS OF HYBORIA!
I WISH IT WAS JUST DEMONS. THIS IS WORSE...
...IT'S MY USUAL DANCE PARTNERS: THE SCORPION, THE LIZARD, AND--

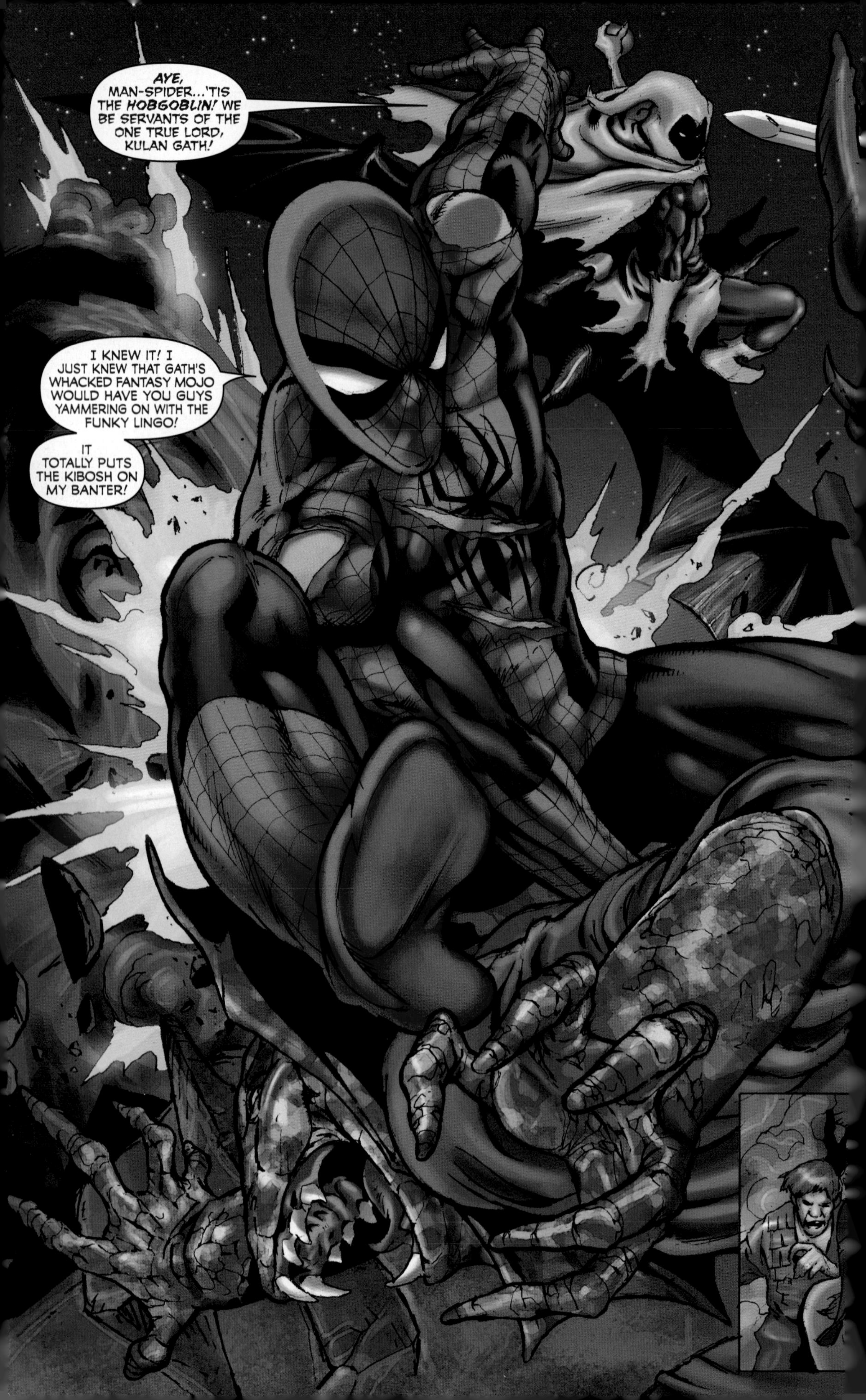
AYE, MAN-SPIDER...'TIS THE HOBGOBLIN! WE BE SERVANTS OF THE ONE TRUE LORD, KULAN GATH!
I KNEW IT! I JUST KNEW THAT GATH'S WHACKED FANTASY MOJO WOULD HAVE YOU GUYS YAMMERING ON WITH THE FUNKY LINGO!
IT TOTALLY PUTS THE KIBOSH ON MY BANTER!

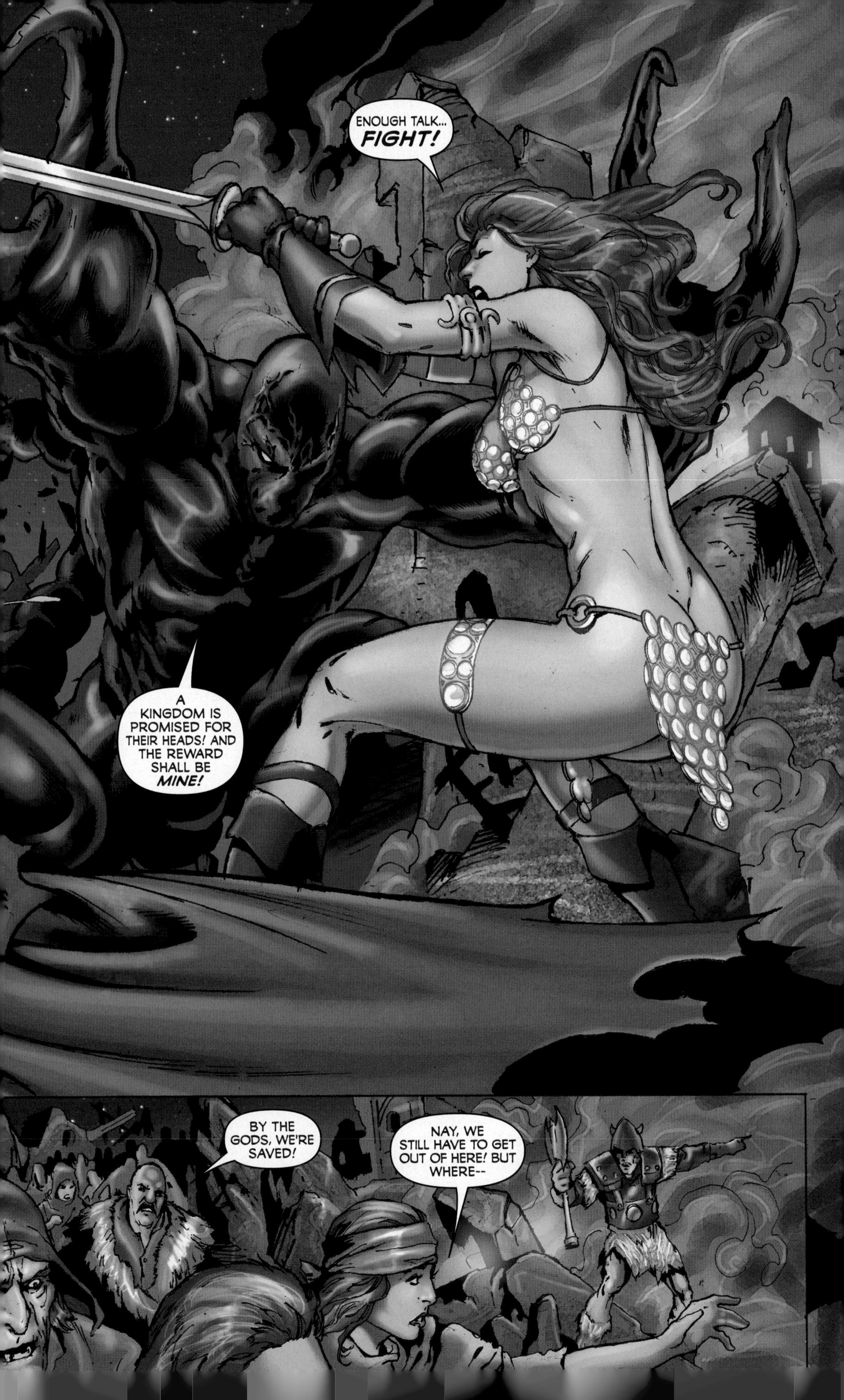

ENOUGH TALK... FIGHT!
A KINGDOM IS PROMISED FOR THEIR HEADS! AND THE REWARD SHALL BE MINE!
BY THE GODS, WE'RE SAVED!
NAY, WE STILL HAVE TO GET OUT OF HERE! BUT WHERE--

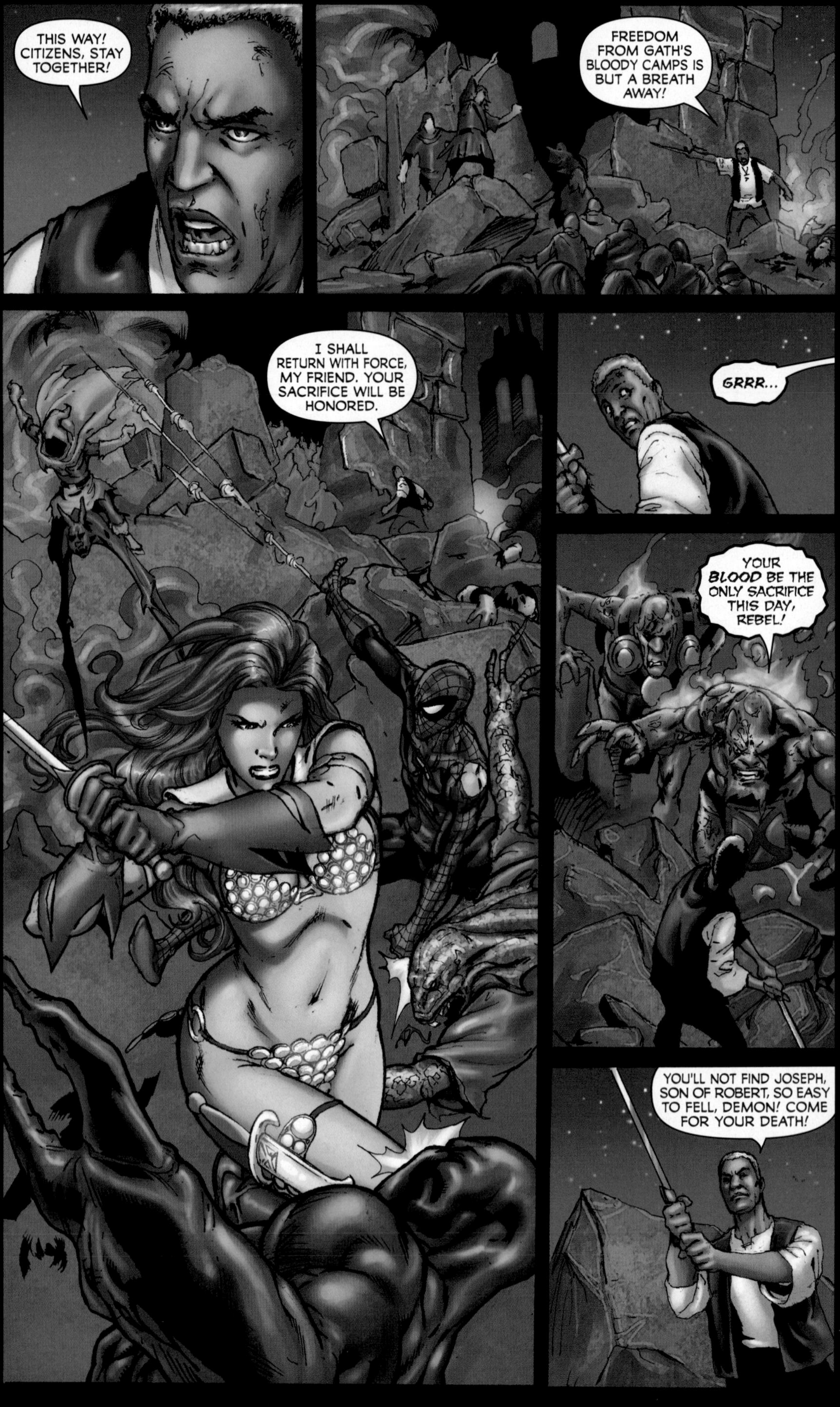
THIS WAY! CITIZENS, STAY TOGETHER!
FREEDOM FROM GATH'S BLOODY CAMPS IS BUT A BREATH AWAY!
I SHALL RETURN WITH FORCE, MY FRIEND. YOUR SACRIFICE WILL BE HONORED.
GRRR...
YOUR BLOOD BE THE ONLY SACRIFICE THIS DAY, REBEL!
YOU'LL NOT FIND JOSEPH, SON OF ROBERT, SO EASY TO FELL, DEMON! COME FOR YOUR DEATH!

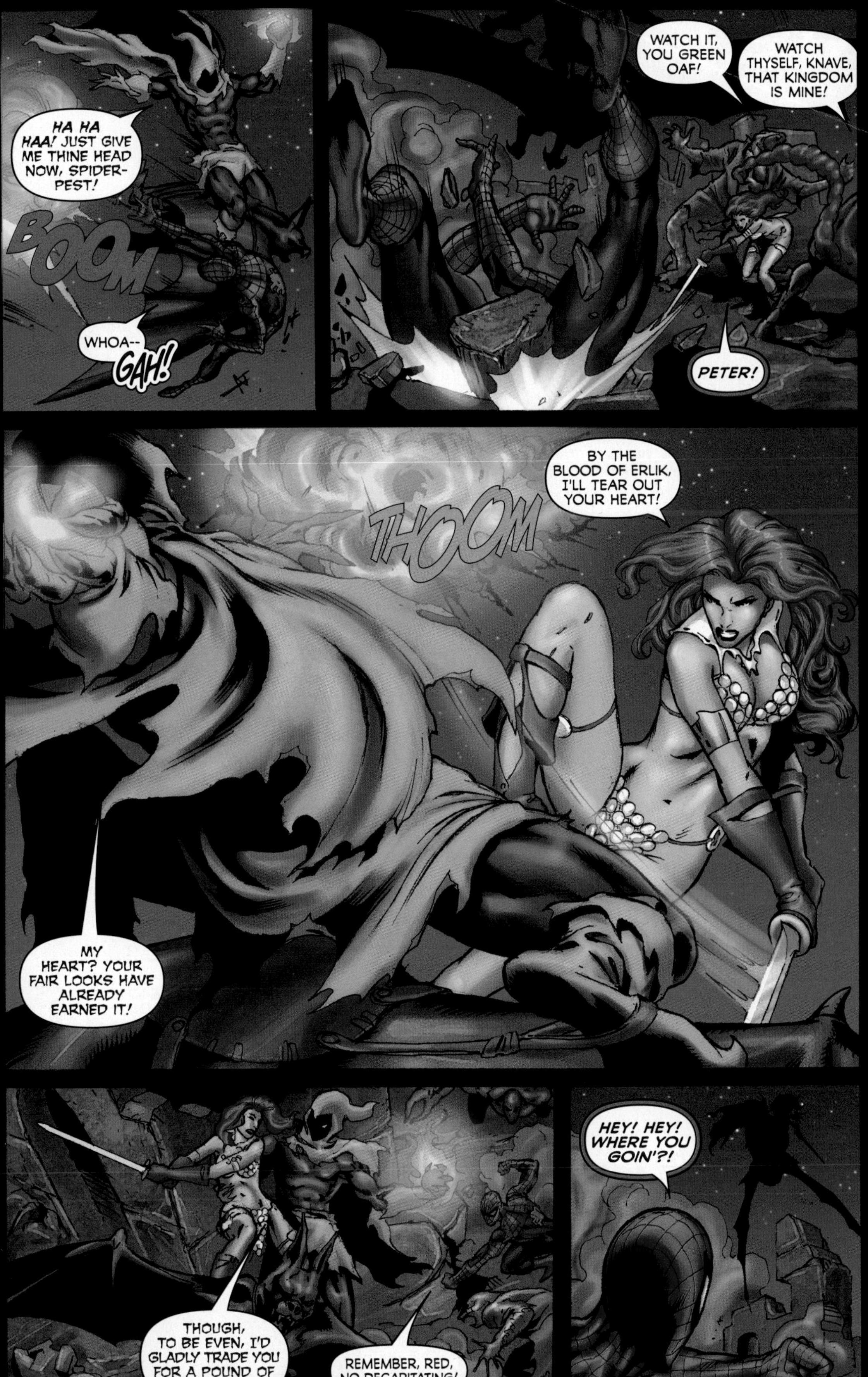
HA HA HAA! JUST GIVE ME THINE HEAD NOW, SPIDER-PEST!
BOOM
WHOA--GAH!
WATCH IT, YOU GREEN OAF!
WATCH THYSELF, KNAVE, THAT KINGDOM IS MINE!
PETER!
BY THE BLOOD OF ERLIK, I'LL TEAR OUT YOUR HEART!
THOOM
MY HEART? YOUR FAIR LOOKS HAVE ALREADY EARNED IT!
THOUGH, TO BE EVEN, I'D GLADLY TRADE YOU FOR A POUND OF YOUR FLESH!
REMEMBER, RED, NO DECAPITATING!
HEY! HEY! WHERE YOU GOIN'?!

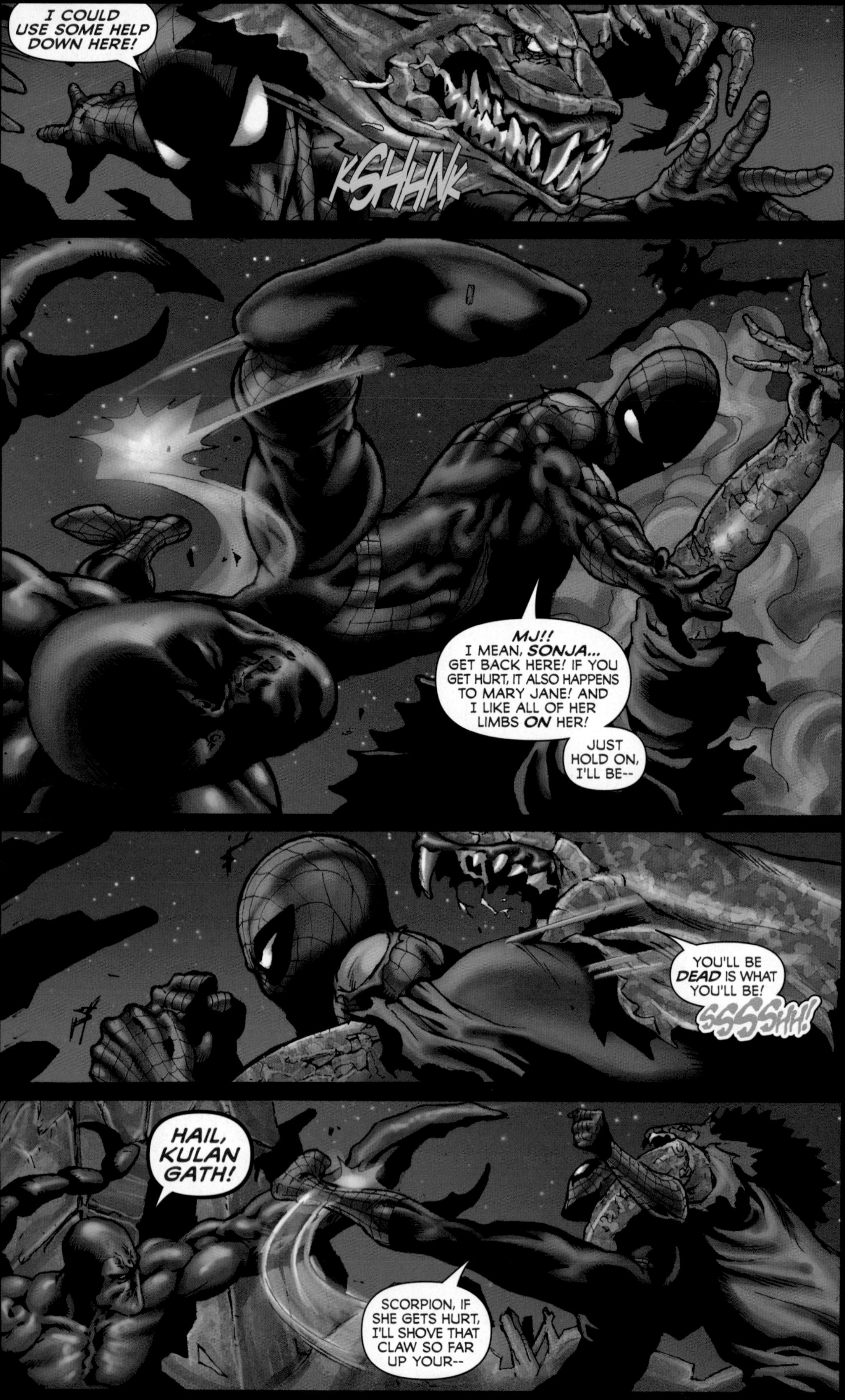
I COULD USE SOME HELP DOWN HERE!
KSHUNK
MJ!! I MEAN, SONJA... GET BACK HERE! IF YOU GET HURT, IT ALSO HAPPENS TO MARY JANE! AND I LIKE ALL OF HER LIMBS ON HER!
JUST HOLD ON, I'LL BE--
YOU'LL BE DEAD IS WHAT YOU'LL BE!
SSSSHH!
HAIL, KULAN GATH!
SCORPION, IF SHE GETS HURT, I'LL SHOVE THAT CLAW SO FAR UP YOUR--

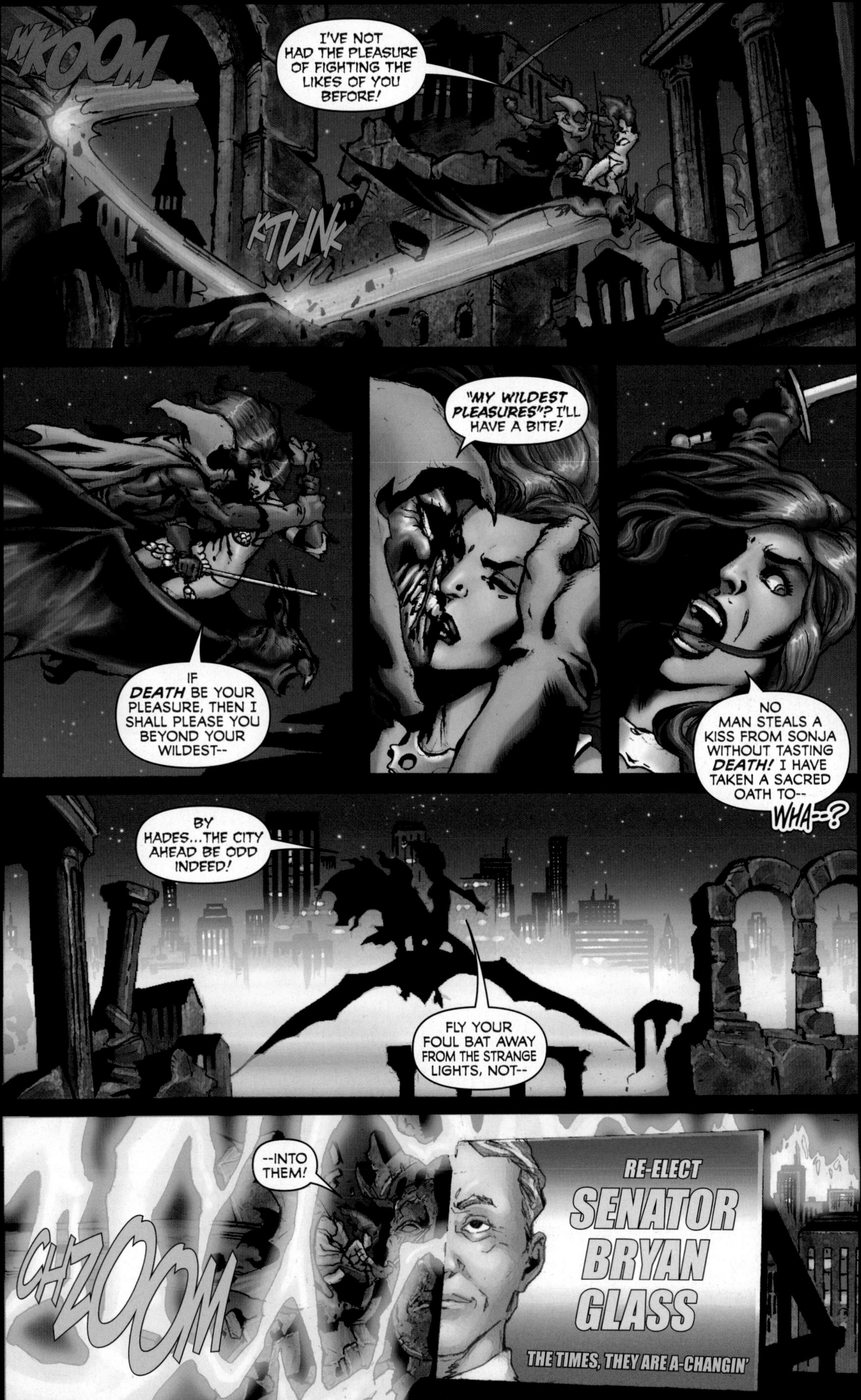
WKOOM
I'VE NOT HAD THE PLEASURE OF FIGHTING THE LIKES OF YOU BEFORE!
KTUNK
IF DEATH BE YOUR PLEASURE, THEN I SHALL PLEASE YOU BEYOND YOUR WILDEST--
"MY WILDEST PLEASURES"? I'LL HAVE A BITE!
NO MAN STEALS A KISS FROM SONJA WITHOUT TASTING DEATH! I HAVE TAKEN A SACRED OATH TO--
WHA--?
BY HADES...THE CITY AHEAD BE ODD INDEED!
FLY YOUR FOUL BAT AWAY FROM THE STRANGE LIGHTS, NOT--
--INTO THEM!
CHZOOM
RE-ELECT
SENATOR BRYAN GLASS
THE TIMES, THEY ARE A-CHANGIN'

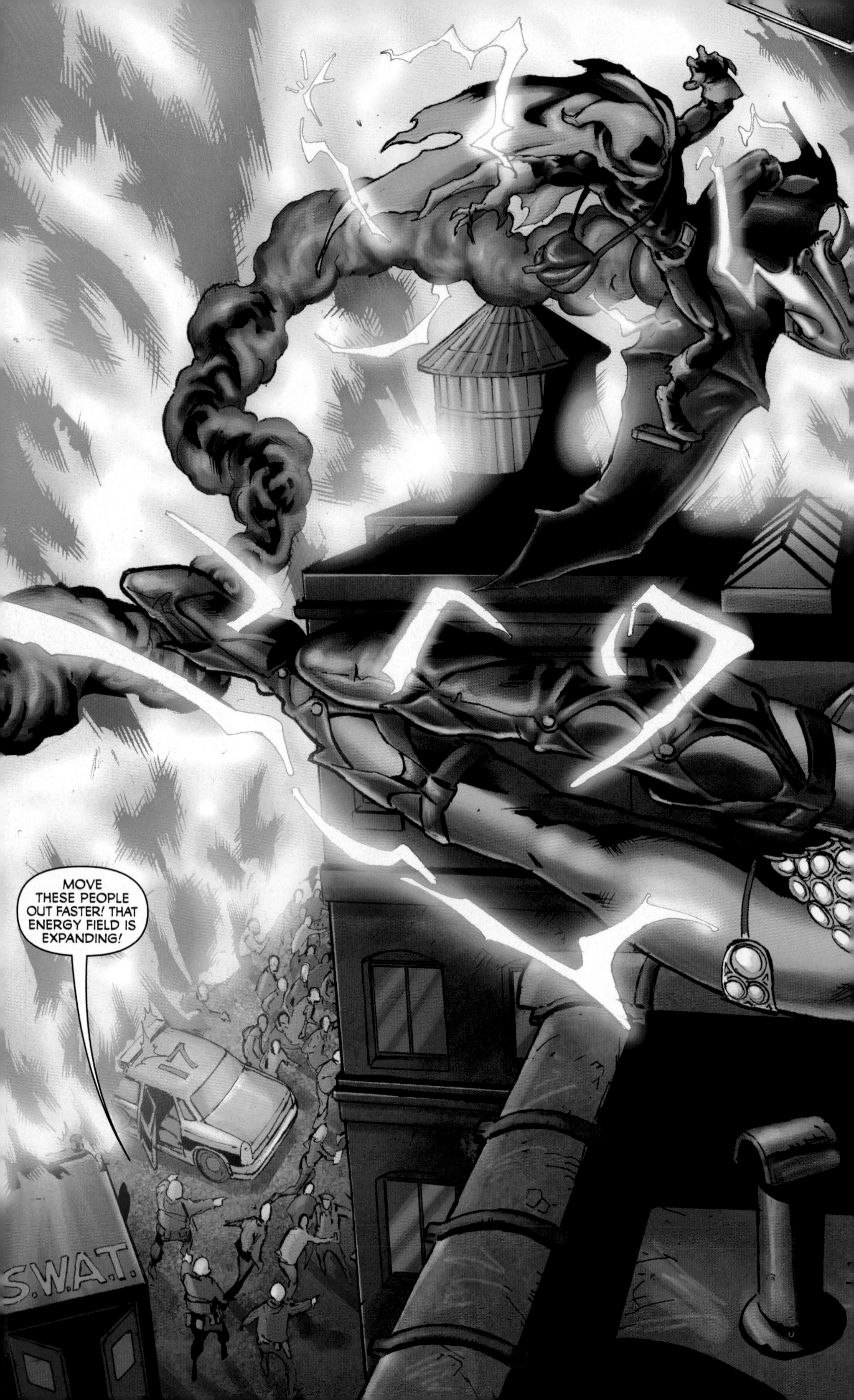
MOVE THESE PEOPLE OUT FASTER! THAT ENERGY FIELD IS EXPANDING!
S.W.A.T.

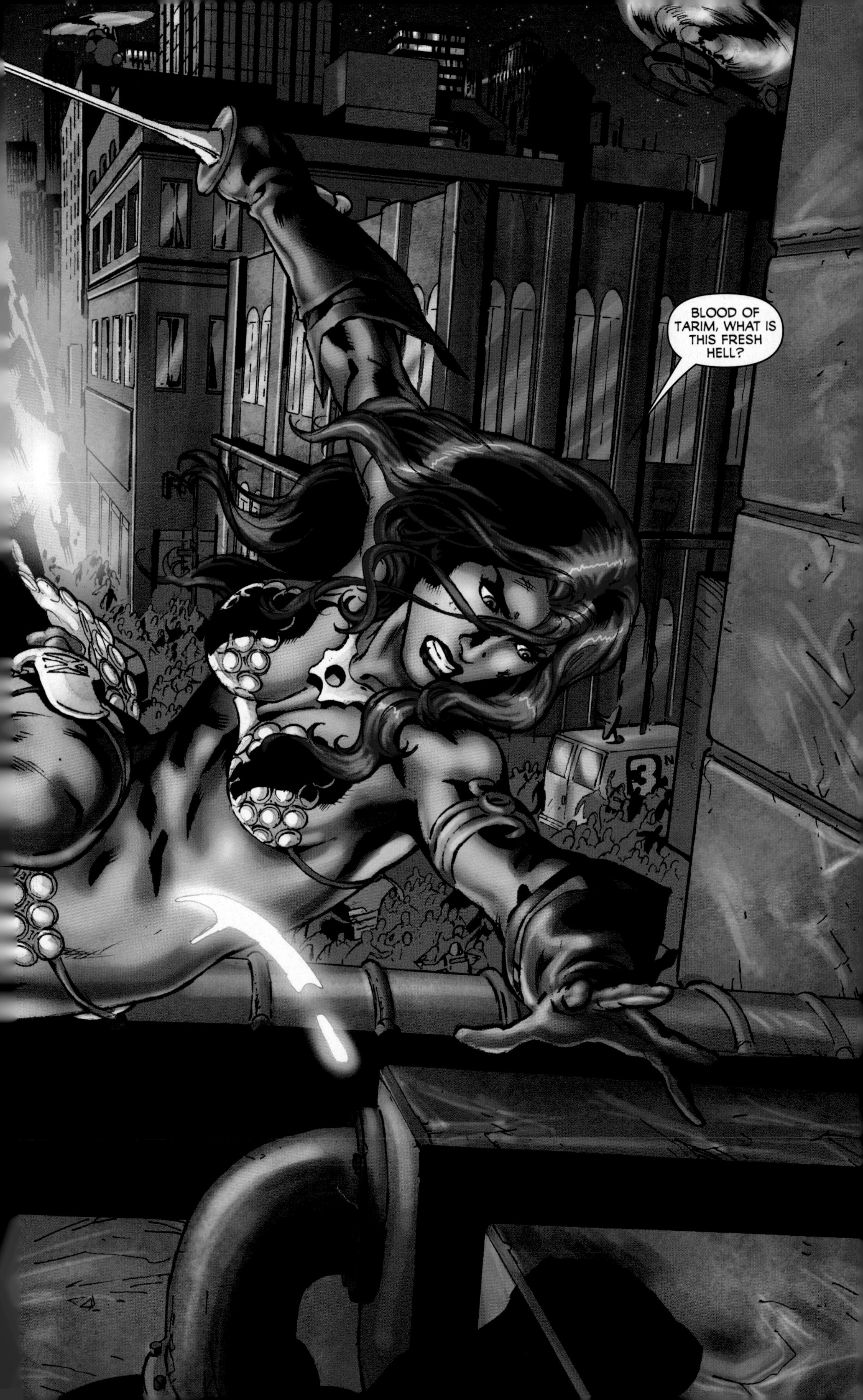
BLOOD OF TARIM, WHAT IS THIS FRESH HELL?

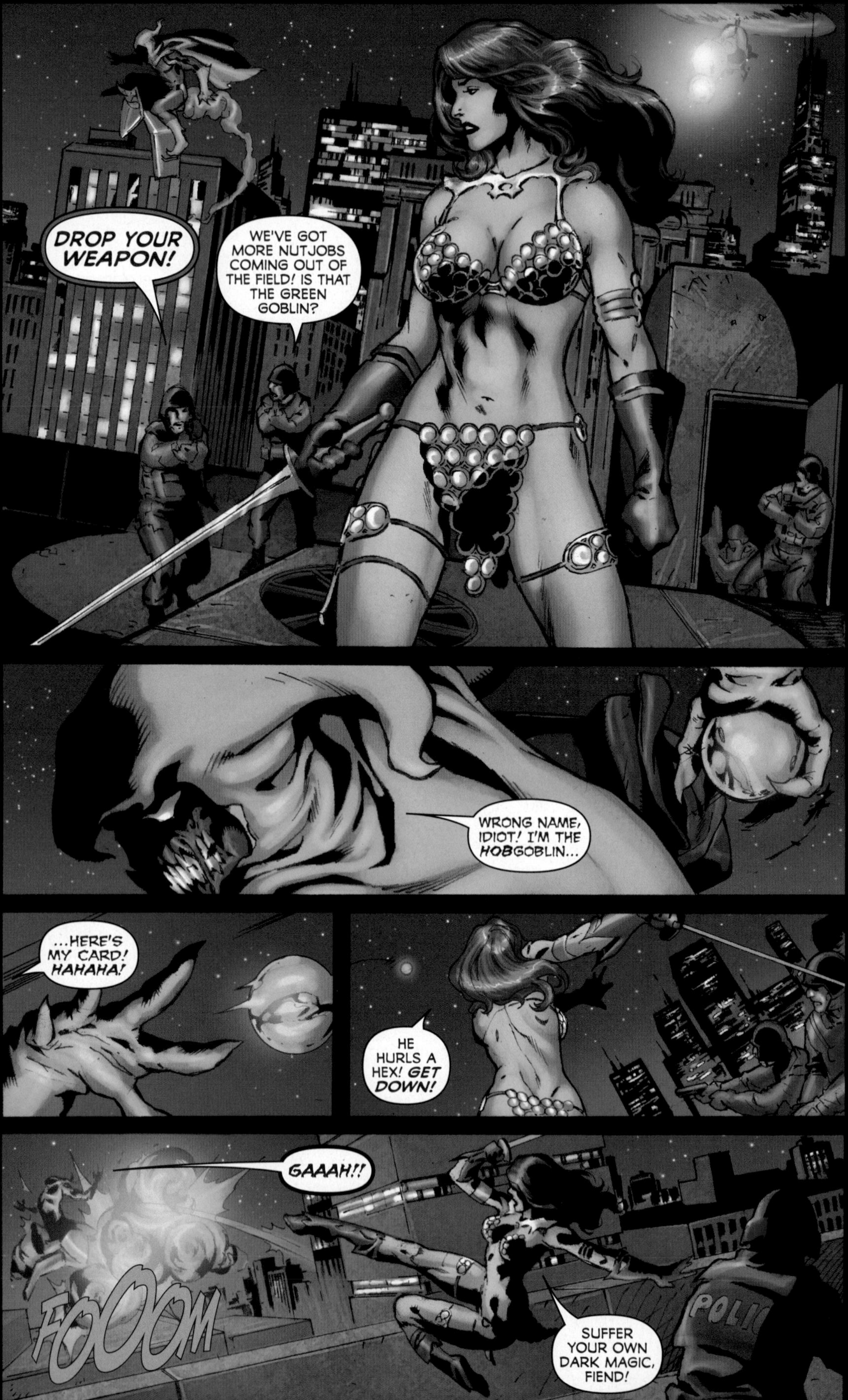
DROP YOUR WEAPON!
WE'VE GOT MORE NUTJOBS COMING OUT OF THE FIELD! IS THAT THE GREEN GOBLIN?
WRONG NAME, IDIOT! I'M THE HOBGOBLIN...
...HERE'S MY CARD! HAHAHA!
HE HURLS A HEX! GET DOWN!
GAAAH!!
FOOOM
SUFFER YOUR OWN DARK MAGIC, FIEND!
POLI

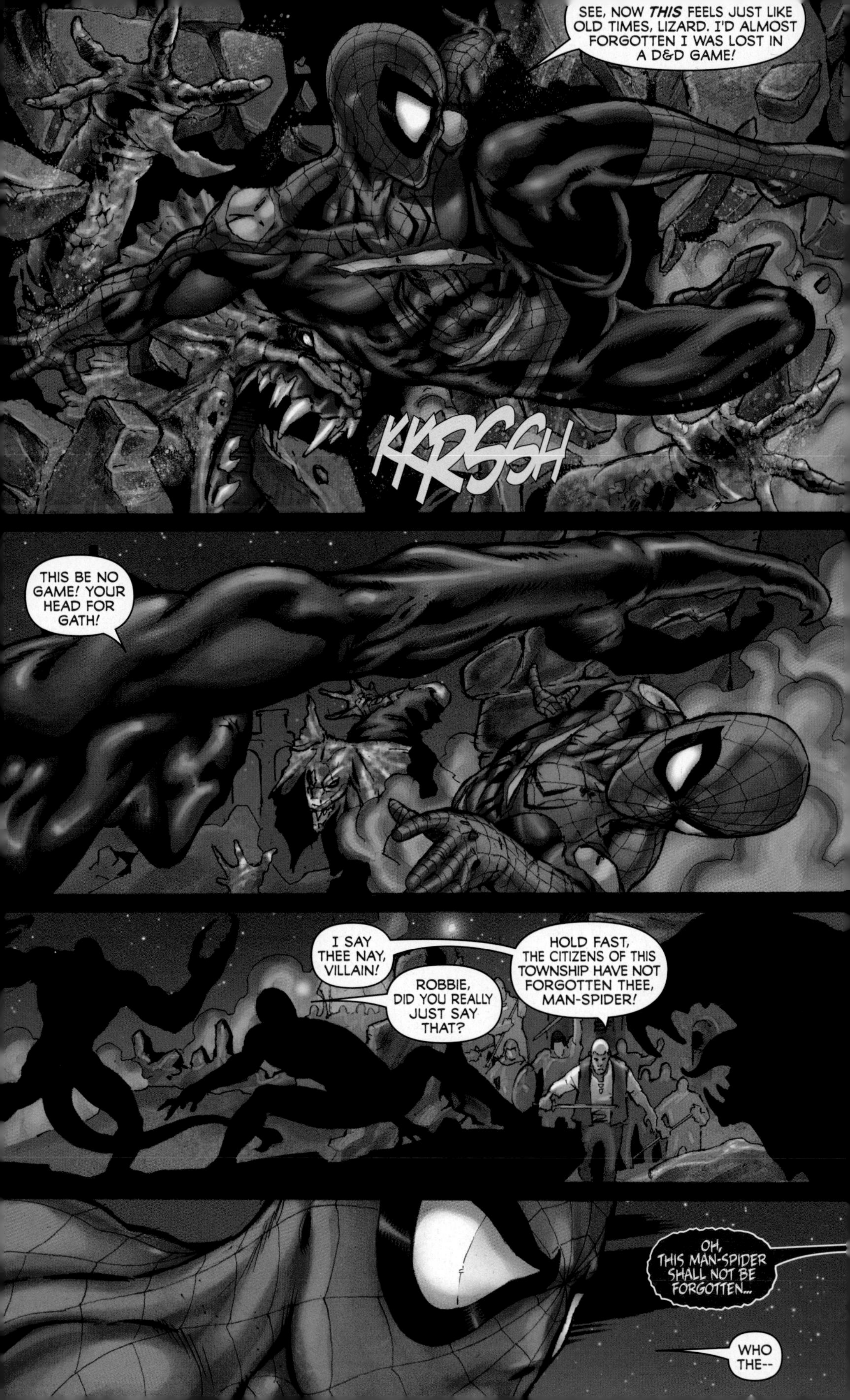
SEE, NOW THIS FEELS JUST LIKE OLD TIMES, LIZARD. I'D ALMOST FORGOTTEN I WAS LOST IN A D&D GAME!
KKRSSH
THIS BE NO GAME! YOUR HEAD FOR GATH!
I SAY THEE NAY, VILLAIN!
HOLD FAST, THE CITIZENS OF THIS TOWNSHIP HAVE NOT FORGOTTEN THEE, MAN-SPIDER!
ROBBIE, DID YOU REALLY JUST SAY THAT?
OH, THIS MAN-SPIDER SHALL NOT BE FORGOTTEN...
WHO THE--

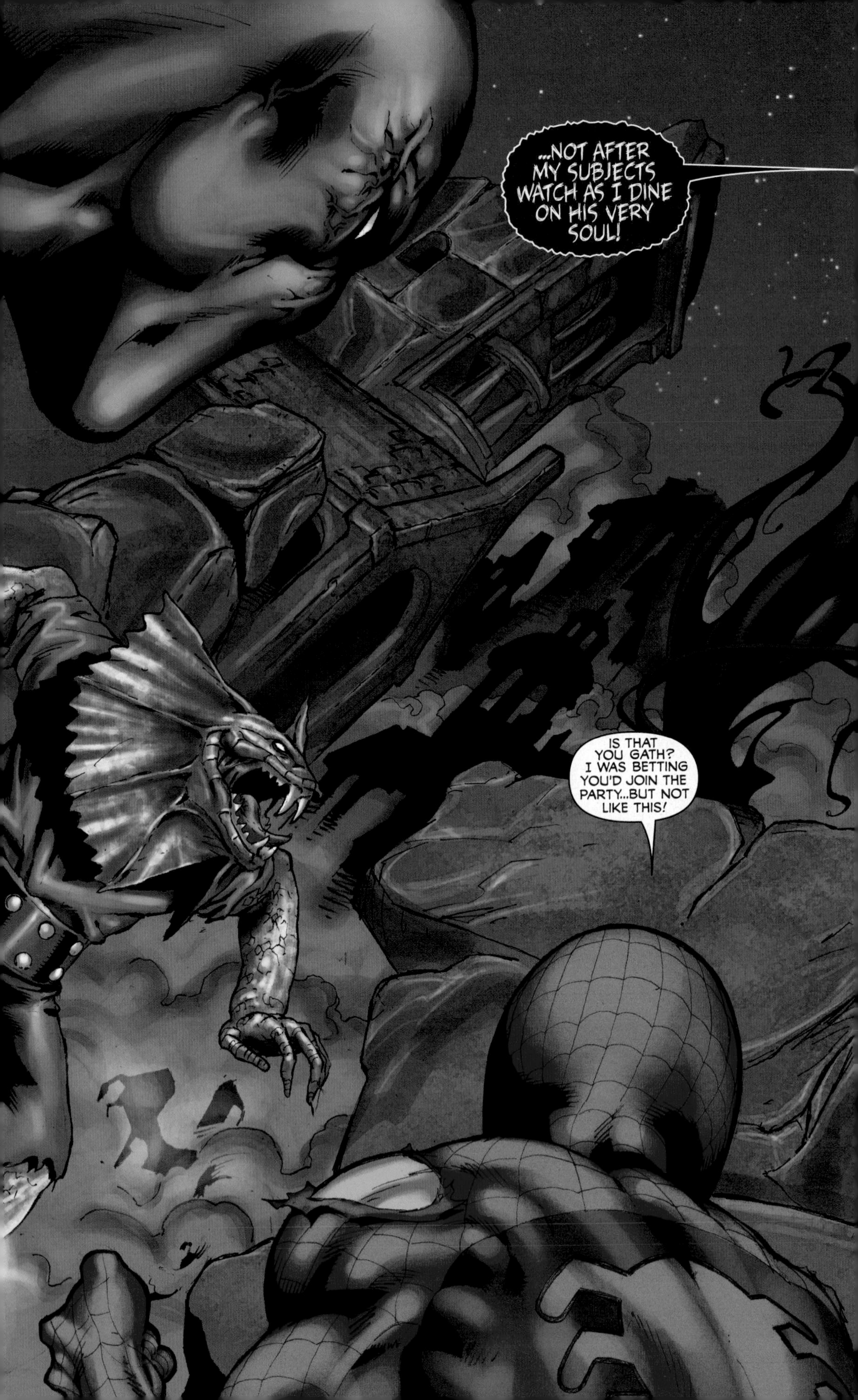
...NOT AFTER MY SUBJECTS WATCH AS I DINE ON HIS VERY SOUL!
IS THAT YOU GATH? I WAS BETTING YOU'D JOIN THE PARTY...BUT NOT LIKE THIS!

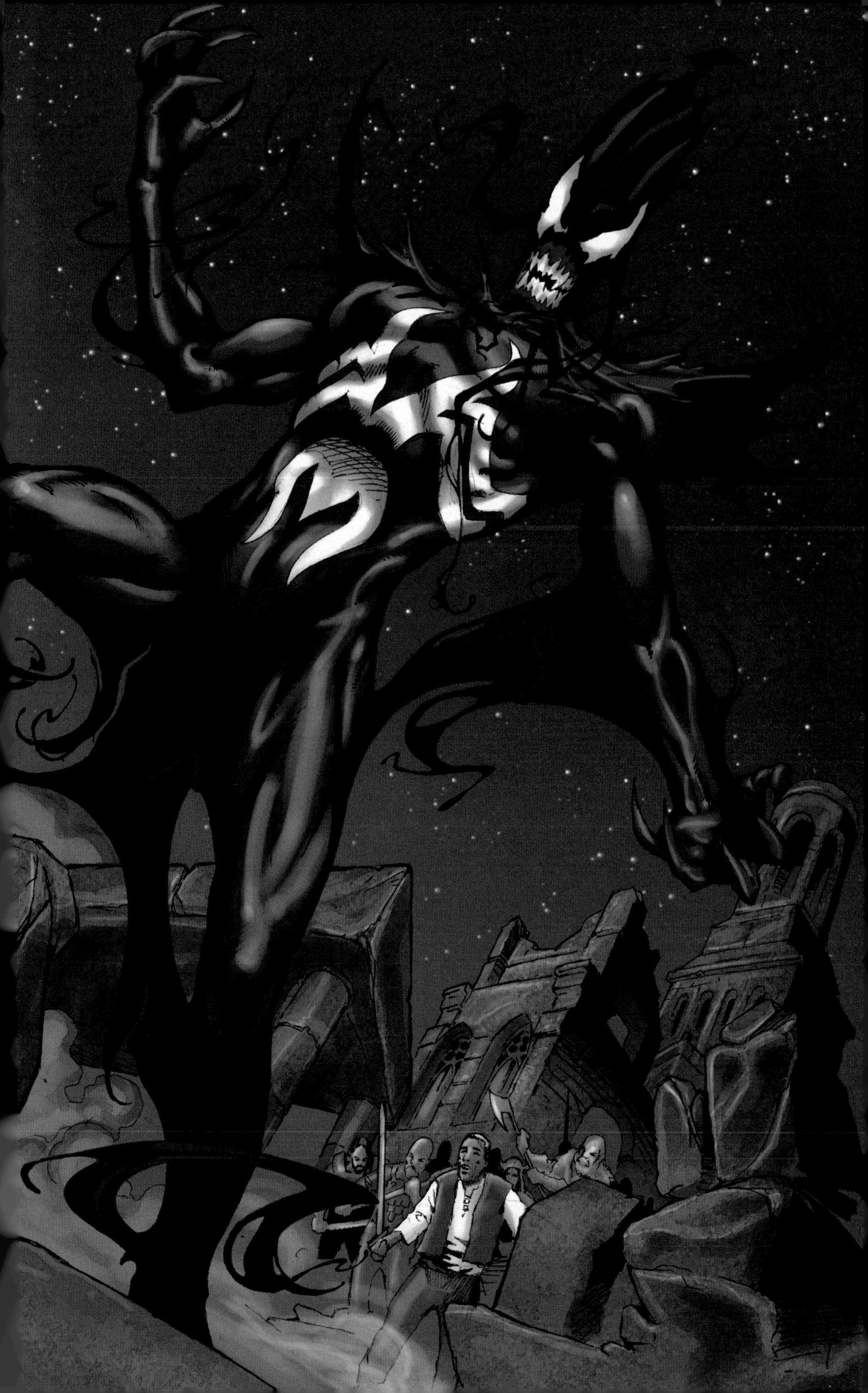

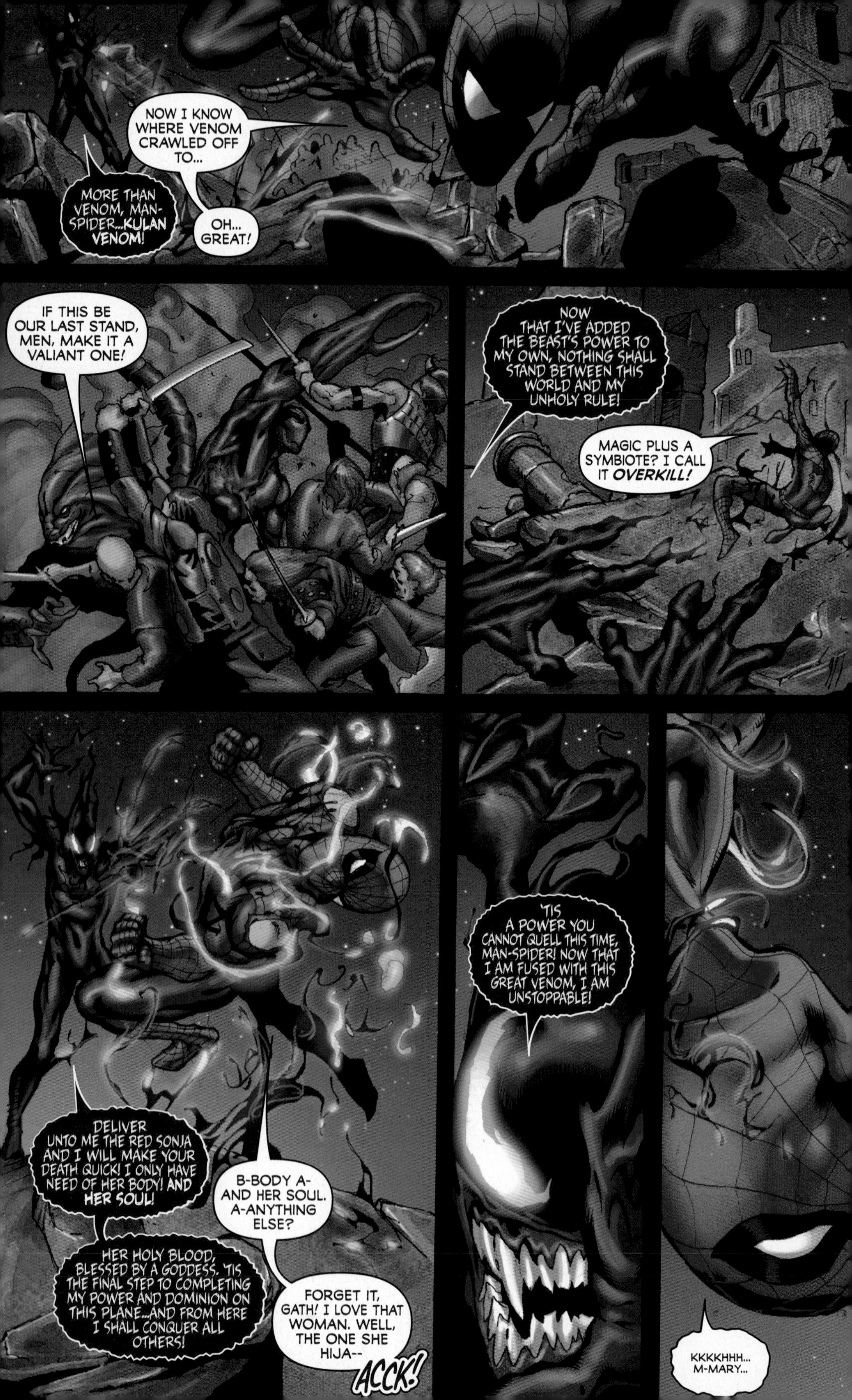
NOW I KNOW WHERE VENOM CRAWLED OFF TO...
MORE THAN VENOM, MAN-SPIDER...KULAN VENOM!
OH... GREAT!
IF THIS BE OUR LAST STAND, MEN, MAKE IT A VALIANT ONE!
NOW THAT I'VE ADDED THE BEAST'S POWER TO MY OWN, NOTHING SHALL STAND BETWEEN THIS WORLD AND MY UNHOLY RULE!
MAGIC PLUS A SYMBIOTE? I CALL IT OVERKILL!
DELIVER UNTO ME THE RED SONJA AND I WILL MAKE YOUR DEATH QUICK! I ONLY HAVE NEED OF HER BODY! AND HER SOUL!
B-BODY A-AND HER SOUL. A-ANYTHING ELSE?
HER HOLY BLOOD, BLESSED BY A GODDESS. 'TIS THE FINAL STEP TO COMPLETING MY POWER AND DOMINION ON THIS PLANE...AND FROM HERE I SHALL CONQUER ALL OTHERS!
FORGET IT, GATH! I LOVE THAT WOMAN. WELL, THE ONE SHE HIJA--
ACCK!
'TIS A POWER YOU CANNOT QUELL THIS TIME, MAN-SPIDER! NOW THAT I AM FUSED WITH THIS GREAT VENOM, I AM UNSTOPPABLE!
KKKKHHH... M-MARY...

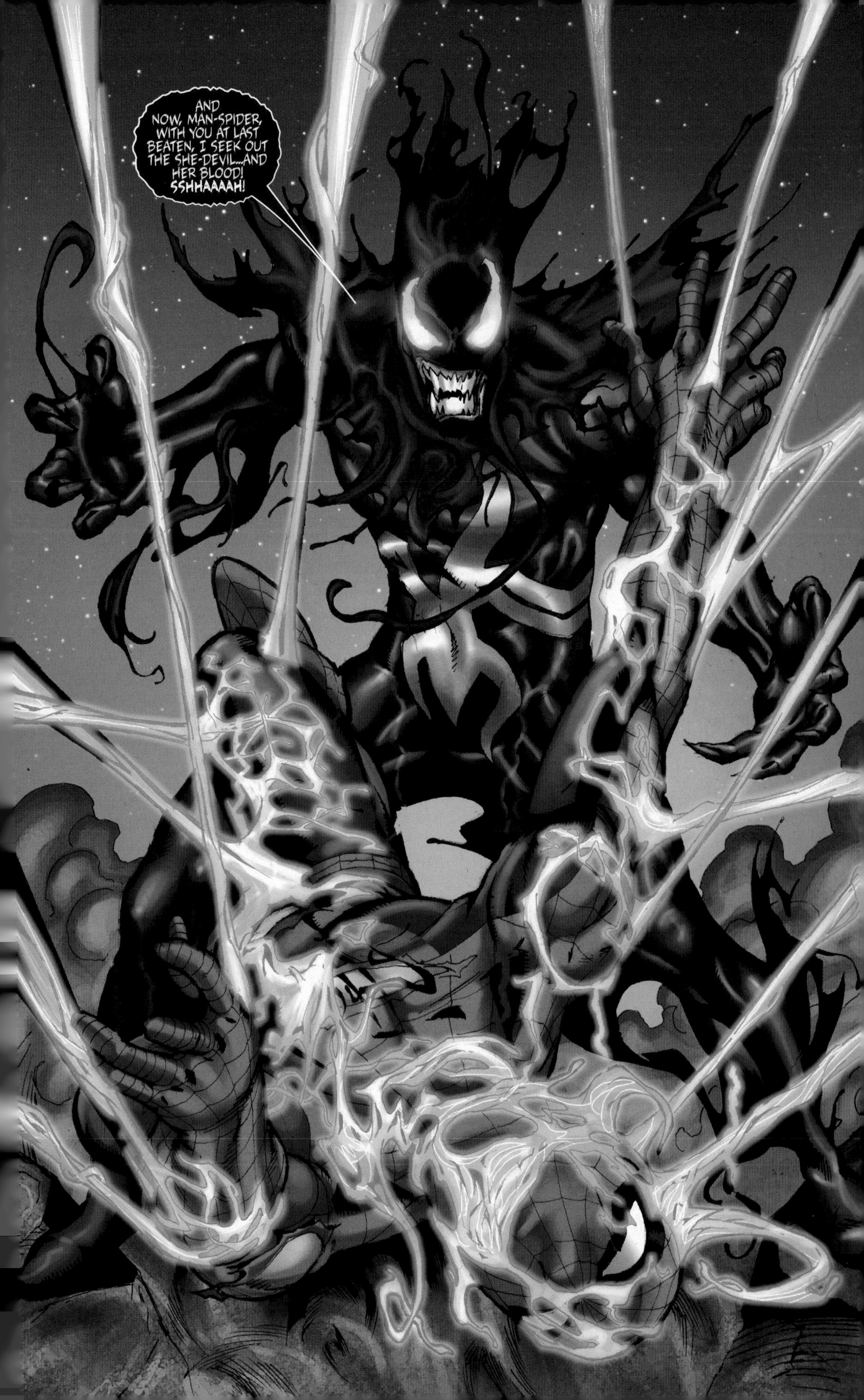
AND NOW, MAN-SPIDER, WITH YOU AT LAST BEATEN, I SEEK OUT THE SHE-DEVIL...AND HER BLOOD! SSHHAAAAH!

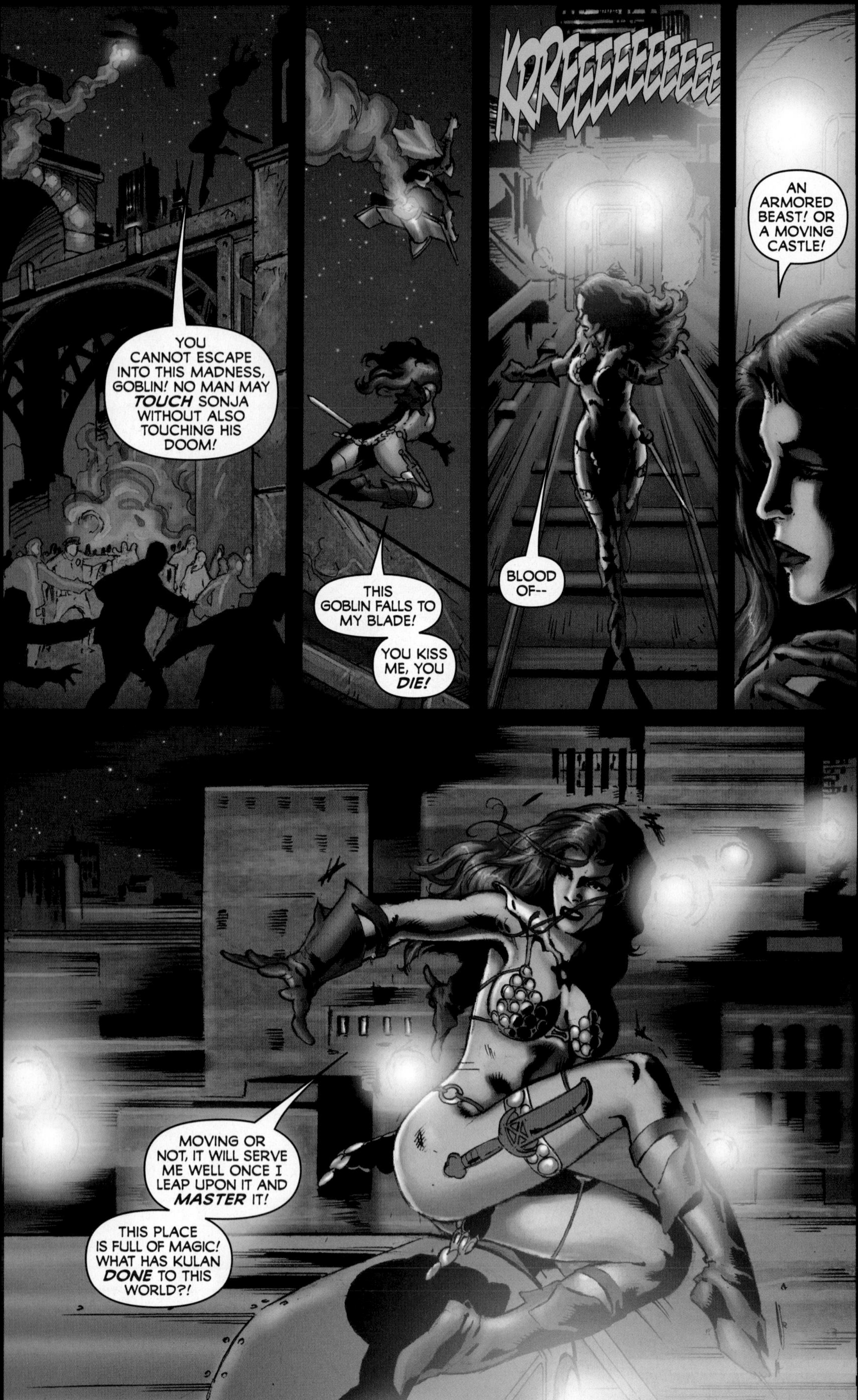

YOU CANNOT ESCAPE INTO THIS MADNESS, GOBLIN! NO MAN MAY TOUCH SONJA WITHOUT ALSO TOUCHING HIS DOOM!
THIS GOBLIN FALLS TO MY BLADE!
YOU KISS ME, YOU DIE!
KRREEEEEEEEEEE
BLOOD OF--
AN ARMORED BEAST! OR A MOVING CASTLE!
MOVING OR NOT, IT WILL SERVE ME WELL ONCE I LEAP UPON IT AND MASTER IT!
THIS PLACE IS FULL OF MAGIC! WHAT HAS KULAN DONE TO THIS WORLD?!

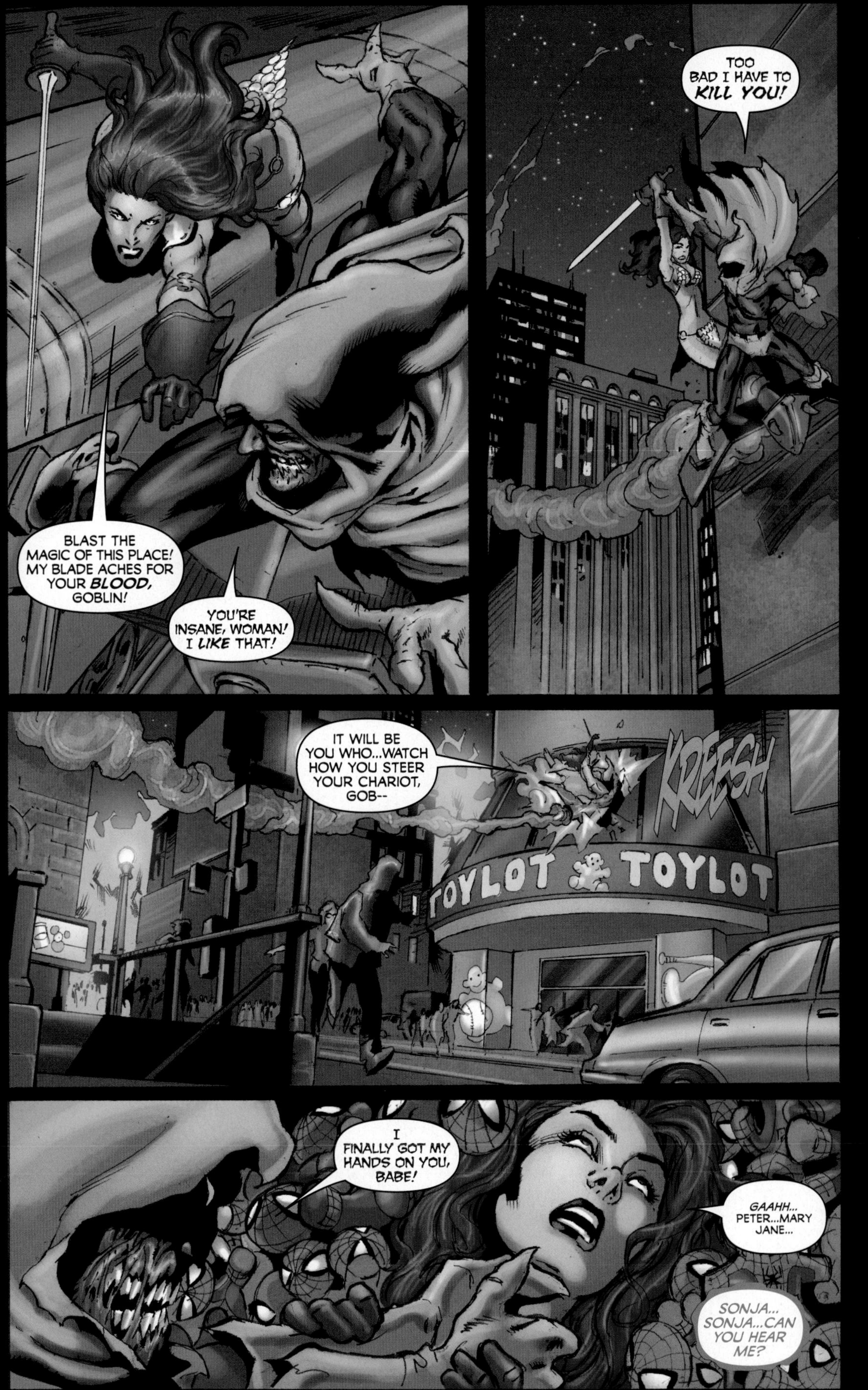

BLAST THE MAGIC OF THIS PLACE! MY BLADE ACHES FOR YOUR **BLOOD,** GOBLIN!
YOU'RE INSANE, WOMAN! I **LIKE** THAT!
TOO BAD I HAVE TO **KILL YOU!**
IT WILL BE YOU WHO...WATCH HOW YOU STEER YOUR CHARIOT, GOB--
KREESH
TOYLOT TOYLOT
I FINALLY GOT MY HANDS ON YOU, BABE!
*GAAHH... PETER...MARY JANE...*
*SONJA... SONJA...CAN YOU HEAR ME?*

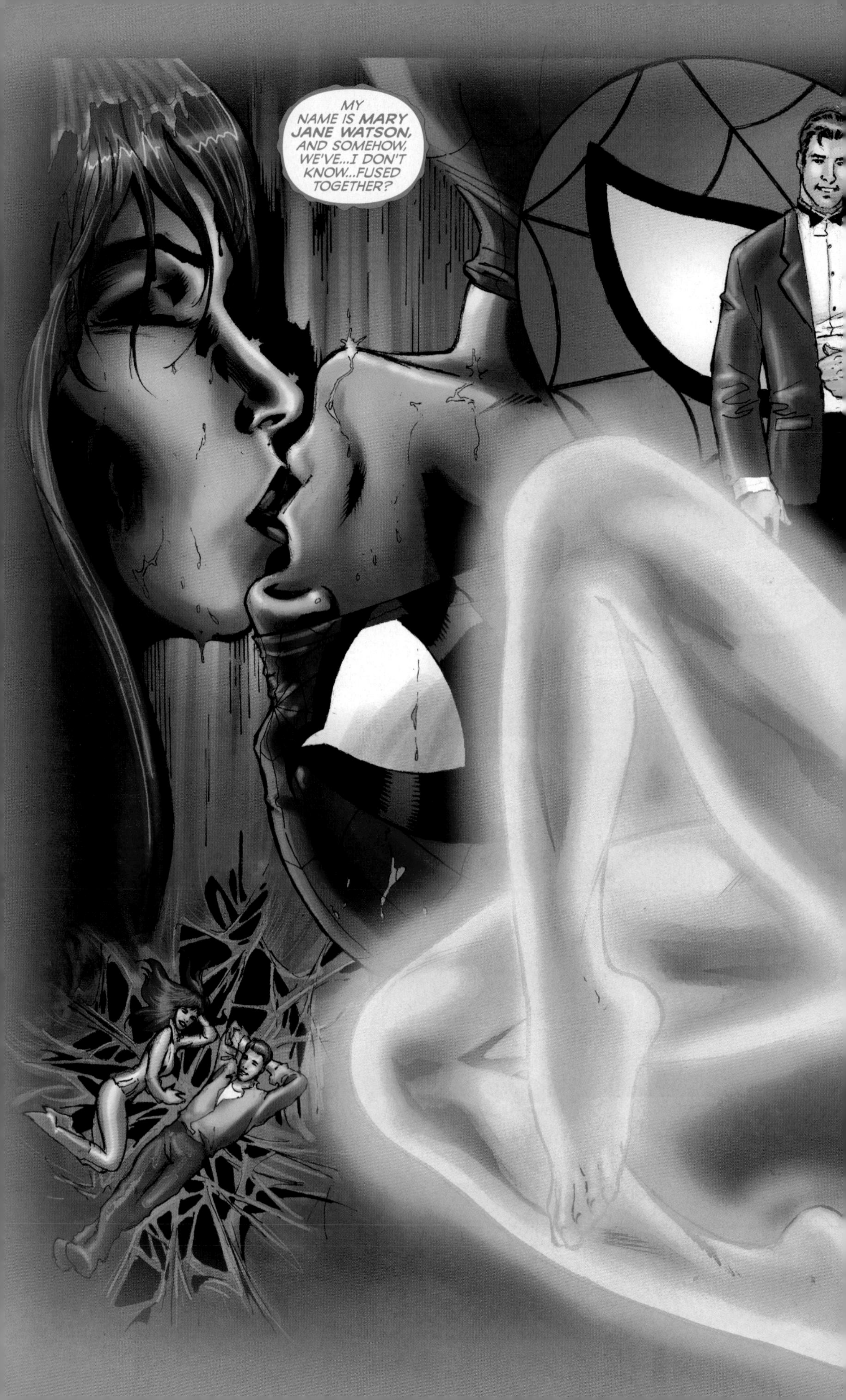
MY NAME IS **MARY JANE WATSON,** AND SOMEHOW, WE'VE...I DON'T KNOW...FUSED TOGETHER?

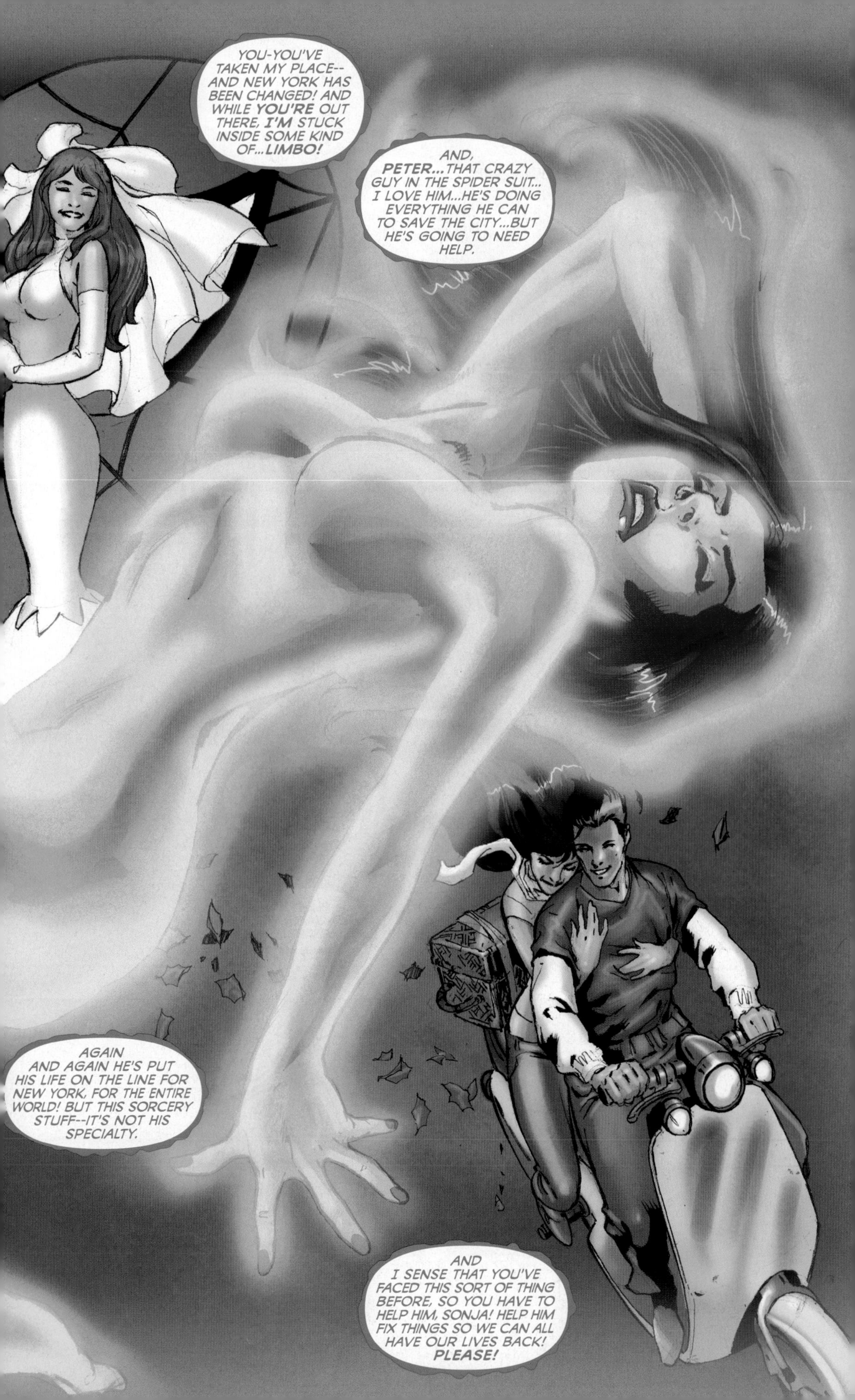
YOU-YOU'VE TAKEN MY PLACE-- AND NEW YORK HAS BEEN CHANGED! AND WHILE YOU'RE OUT THERE, I'M STUCK INSIDE SOME KIND OF...LIMBO!
AND, PETER...THAT CRAZY GUY IN THE SPIDER SUIT... I LOVE HIM...HE'S DOING EVERYTHING HE CAN TO SAVE THE CITY...BUT HE'S GOING TO NEED HELP.
AGAIN AND AGAIN HE'S PUT HIS LIFE ON THE LINE FOR NEW YORK, FOR THE ENTIRE WORLD! BUT THIS SORCERY STUFF--IT'S NOT HIS SPECIALTY.
AND I SENSE THAT YOU'VE FACED THIS SORT OF THING BEFORE, SO YOU HAVE TO HELP HIM, SONJA! HELP HIM FIX THINGS SO WE CAN ALL HAVE OUR LIVES BACK! PLEASE!

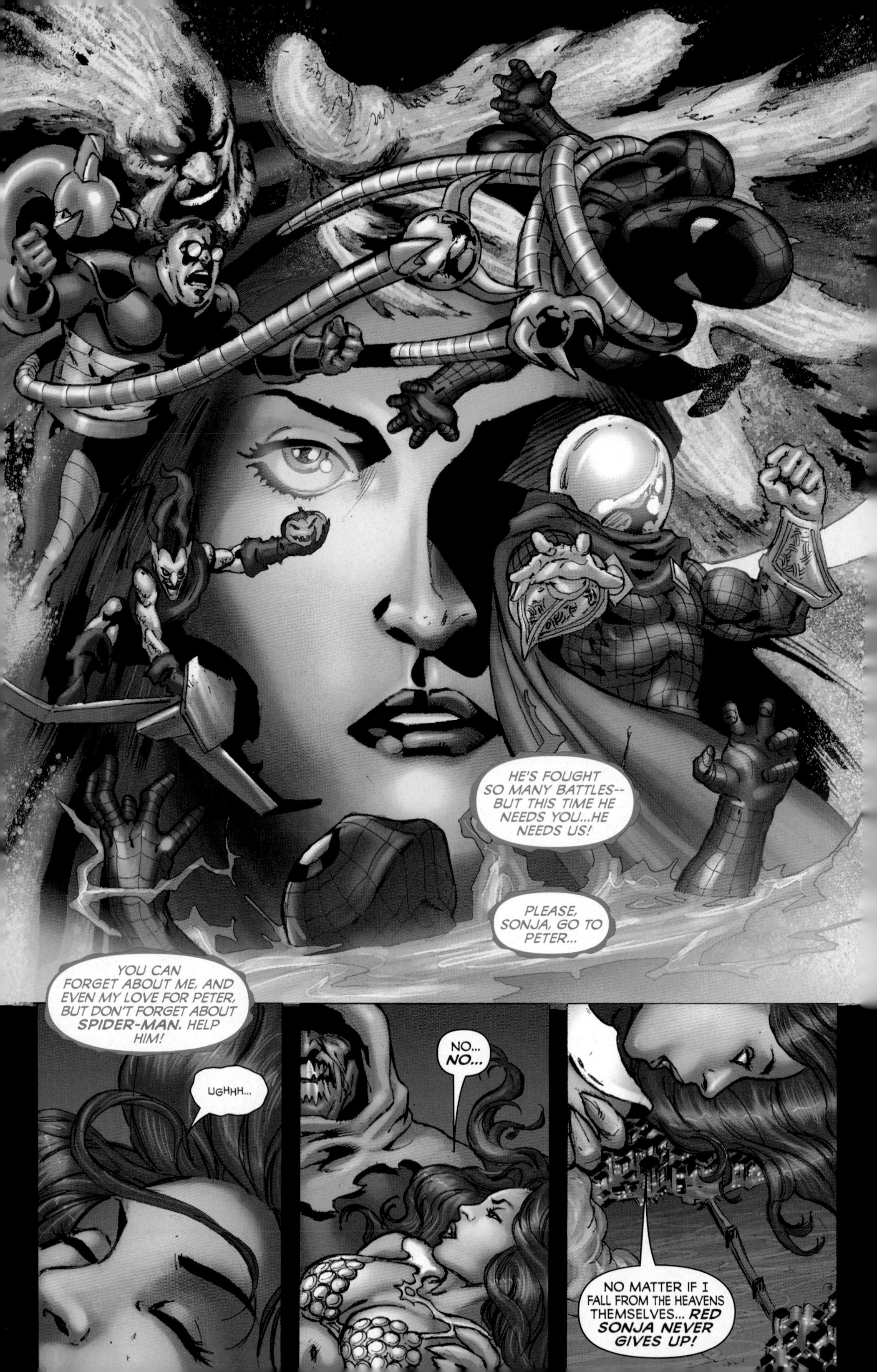
HE'S FOUGHT SO MANY BATTLES-- BUT THIS TIME HE NEEDS YOU...HE NEEDS US!
PLEASE, SONJA, GO TO PETER...
YOU CAN FORGET ABOUT ME, AND EVEN MY LOVE FOR PETER, BUT DON'T FORGET ABOUT SPIDER-MAN. HELP HIM!
UGHHH...
NO... NO...
NO MATTER IF I FALL FROM THE HEAVENS THEMSELVES... RED SONJA NEVER GIVES UP!

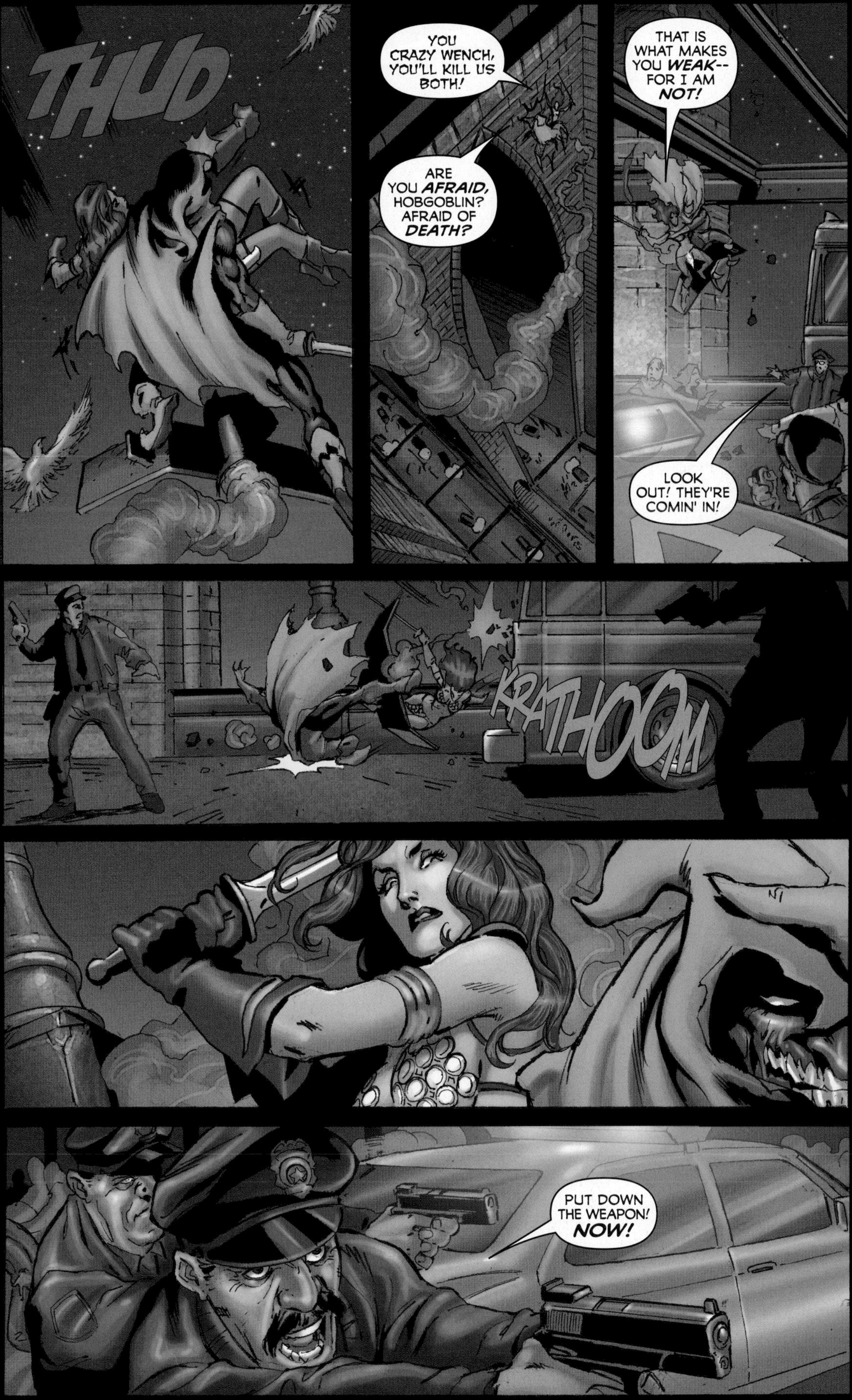
THUD
YOU CRAZY WENCH, YOU'LL KILL US BOTH!
ARE YOU AFRAID, HOBGOBLIN? AFRAID OF DEATH?
THAT IS WHAT MAKES YOU WEAK-- FOR I AM NOT!
LOOK OUT! THEY'RE COMIN' IN!
KRATHOOM
PUT DOWN THE WEAPON! NOW!

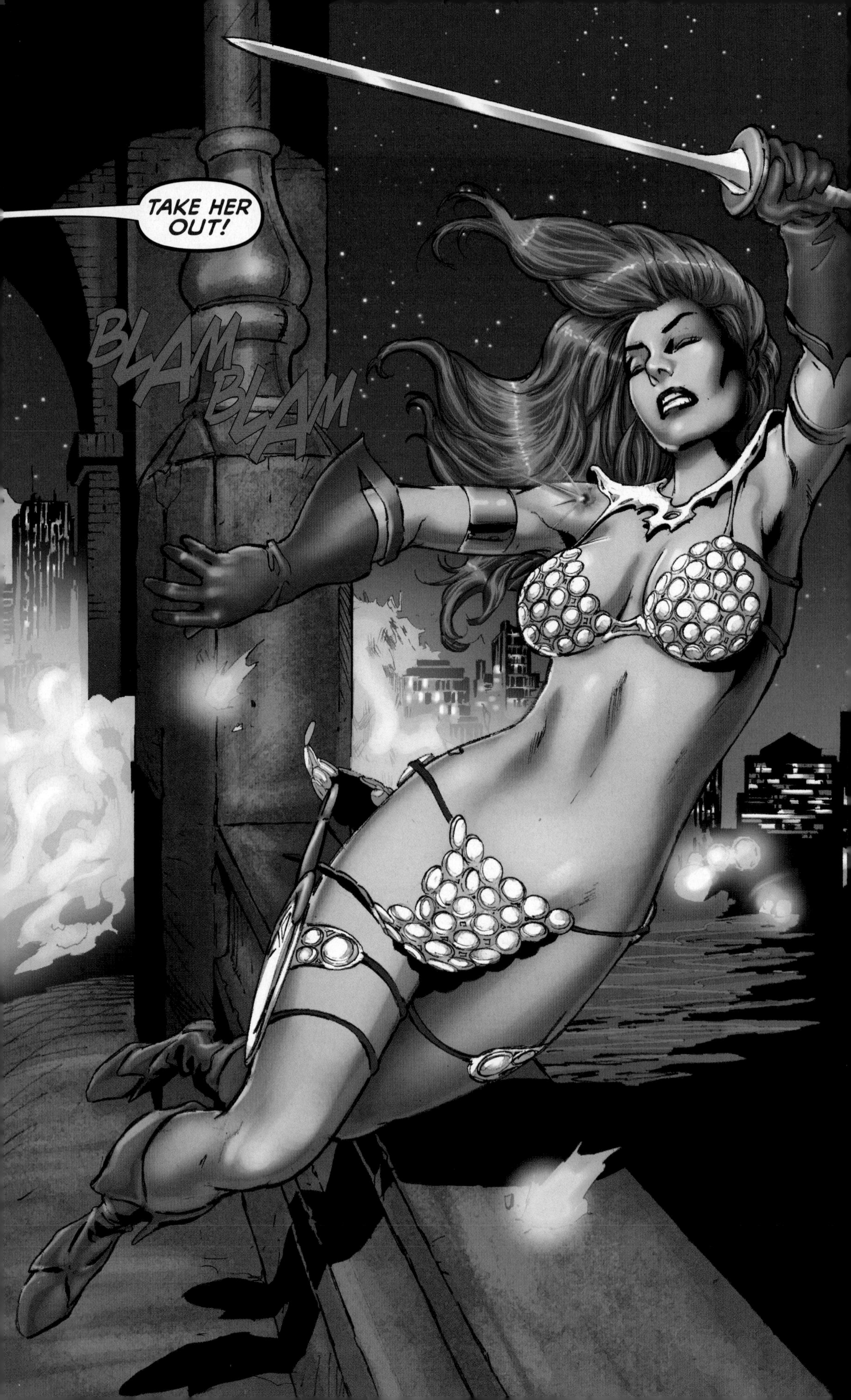
TAKE HER OUT!
BLAM
BLAM

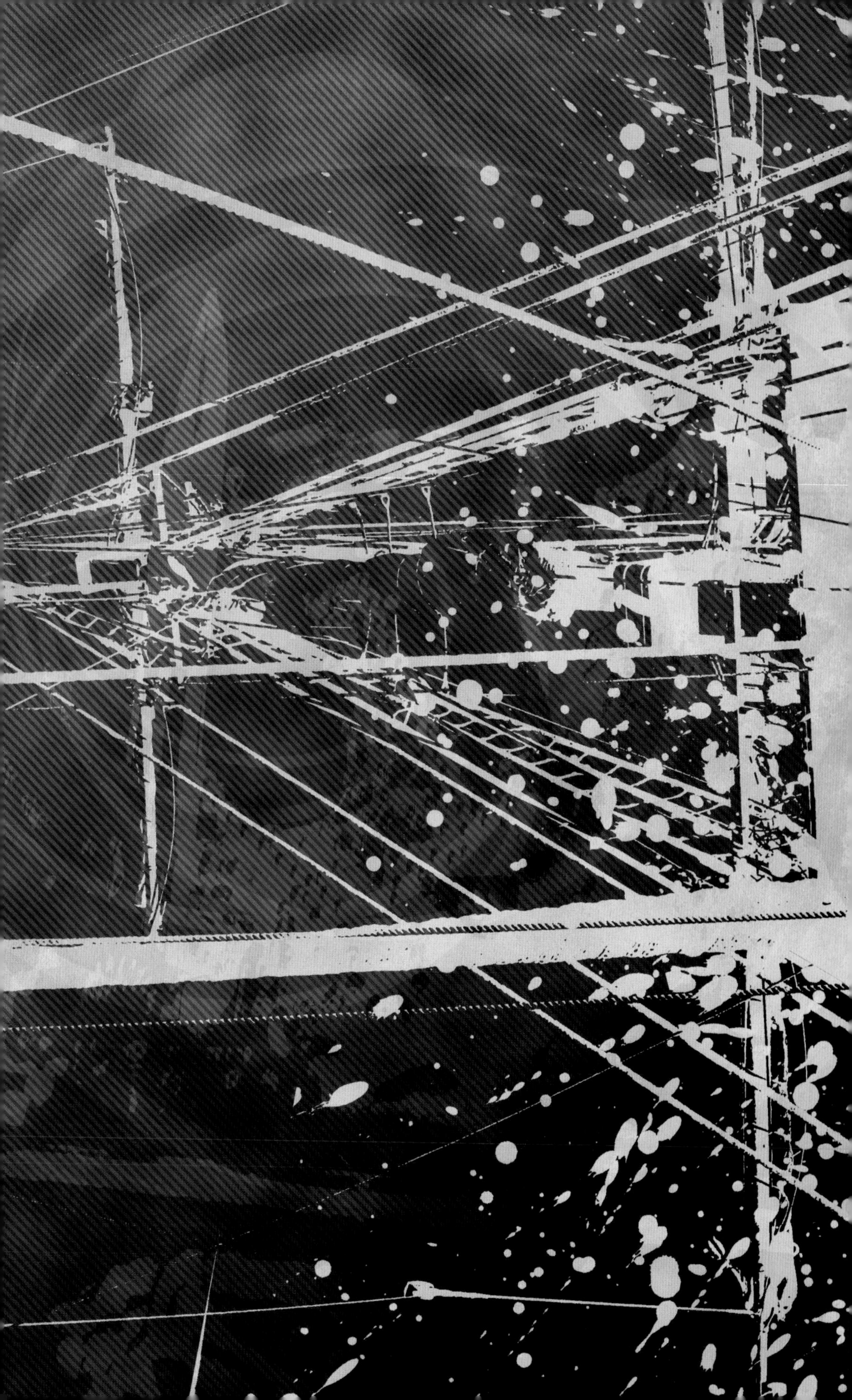

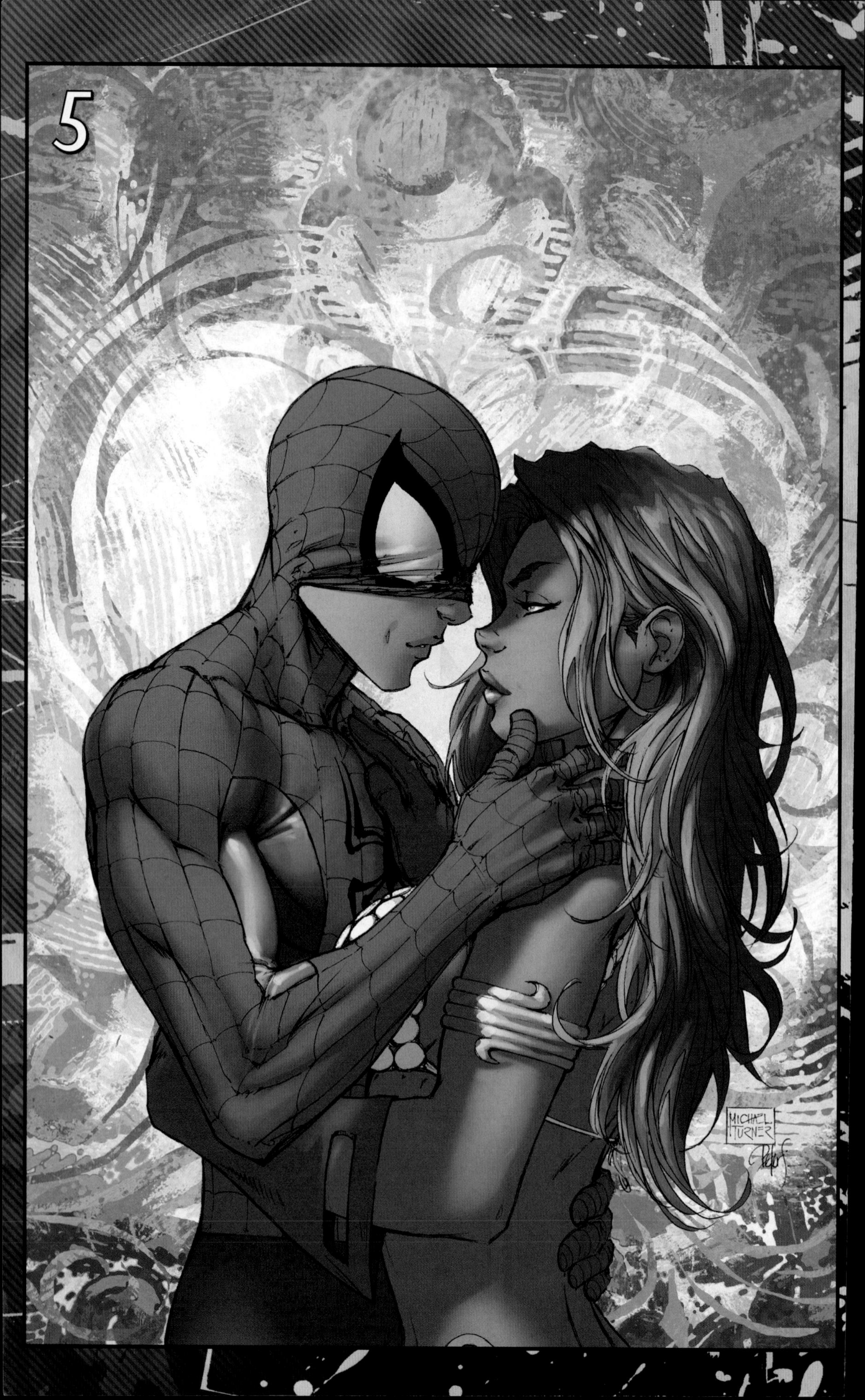
5
MICHAEL TURNER

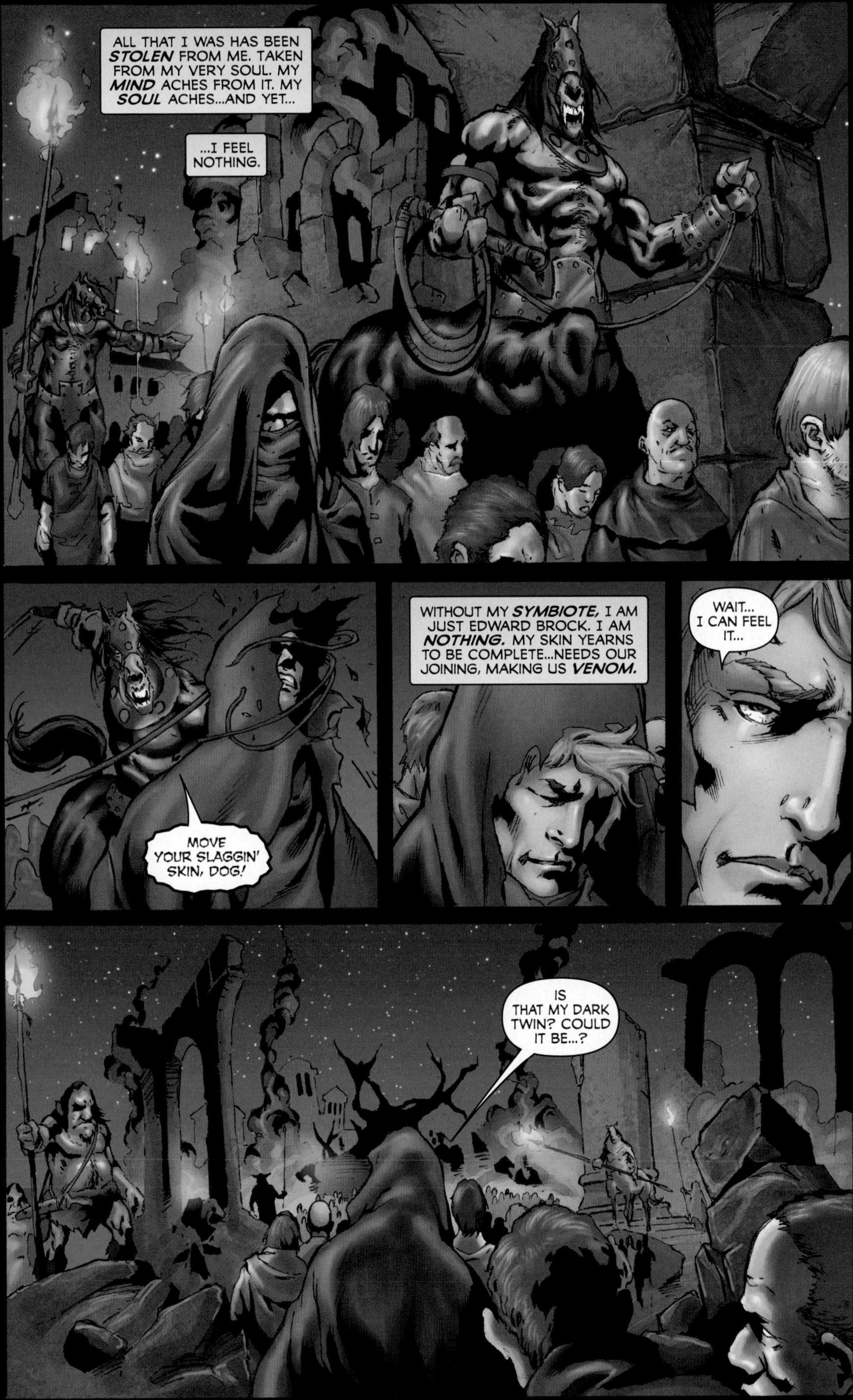
ALL THAT I WAS HAS BEEN *STOLEN* FROM ME. TAKEN FROM MY VERY SOUL. MY *MIND* ACHES FROM IT. MY *SOUL* ACHES...AND YET...
...I FEEL NOTHING.
MOVE YOUR SLAGGIN' SKIN, DOG!
WITHOUT MY *SYMBIOTE,* I AM JUST EDWARD BROCK. I AM *NOTHING.* MY SKIN YEARNS TO BE COMPLETE...NEEDS OUR JOINING, MAKING US *VENOM.*
WAIT... I CAN FEEL IT...
IS THAT MY DARK TWIN? COULD IT BE...?

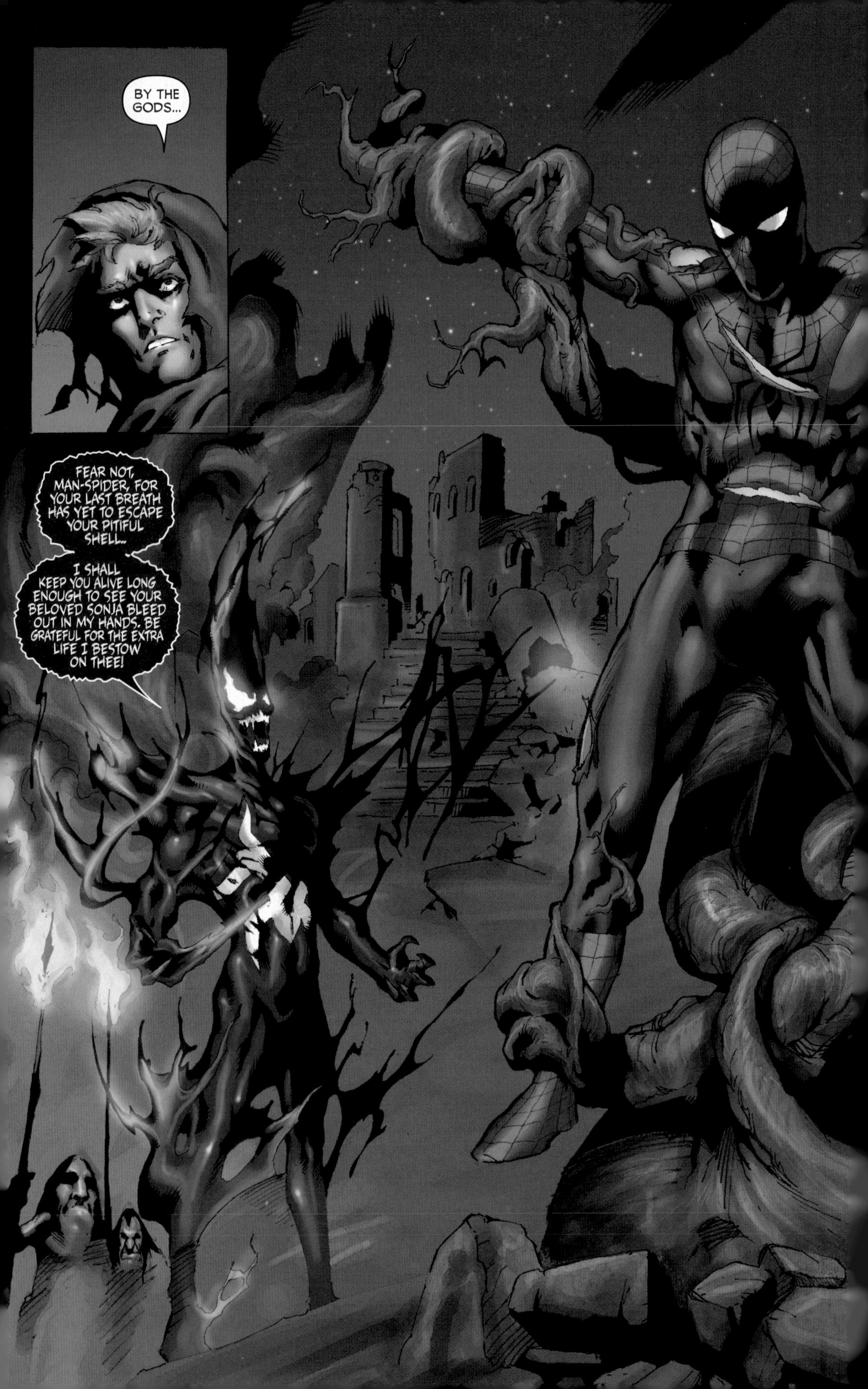
BY THE GODS...
FEAR NOT, MAN-SPIDER, FOR YOUR LAST BREATH HAS YET TO ESCAPE YOUR PITIFUL SHELL..
I SHALL KEEP YOU ALIVE LONG ENOUGH TO SEE YOUR BELOVED SONJA BLEED OUT IN MY HANDS. BE GRATEFUL FOR THE EXTRA LIFE I BESTOW ON THEE!

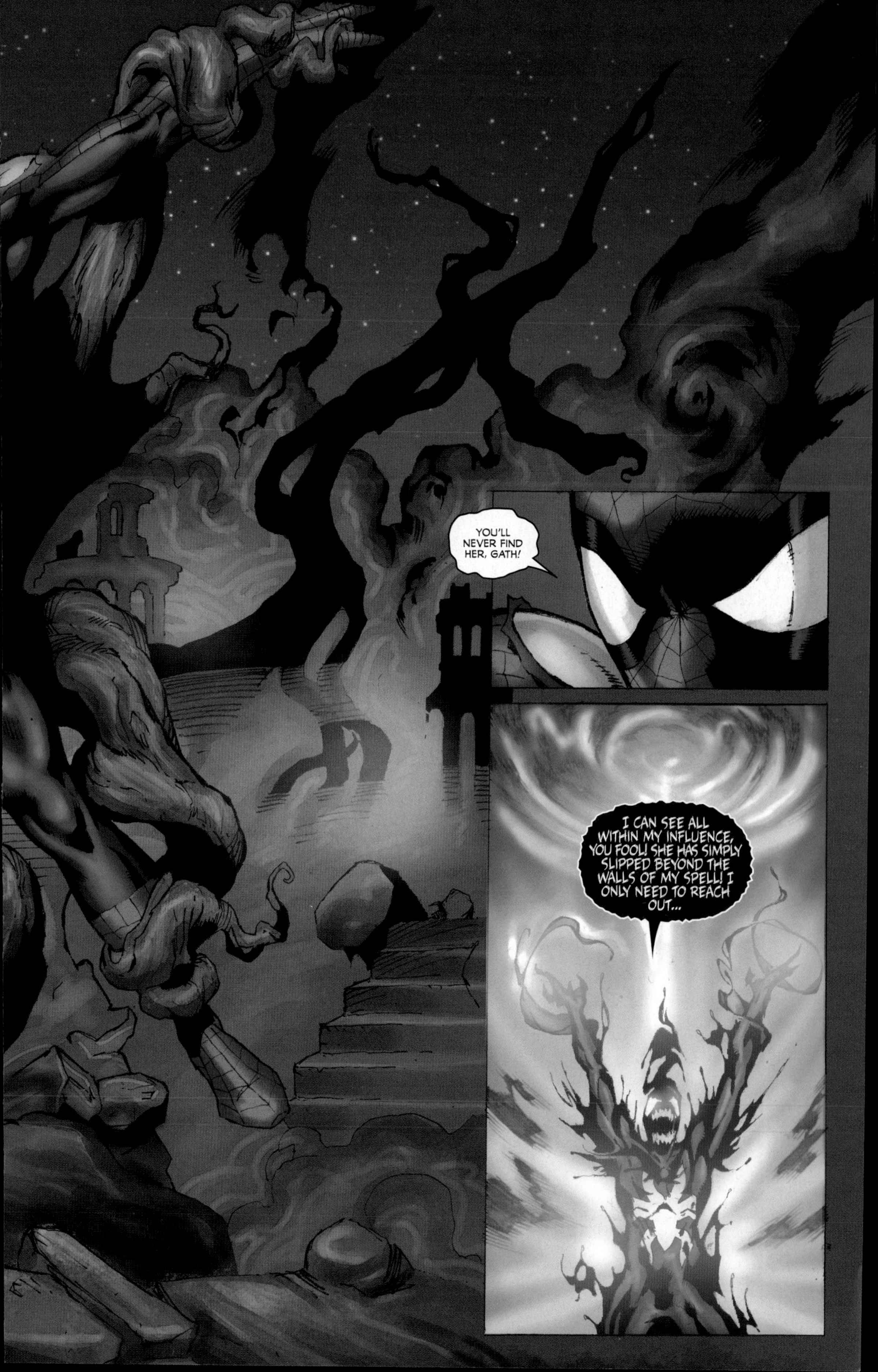
YOU'LL NEVER FIND HER, GATH!
I CAN SEE ALL WITHIN MY INFLUENCE, YOU FOOL! SHE HAS SIMPLY SLIPPED BEYOND THE WALLS OF MY SPELL! I ONLY NEED TO REACH OUT...

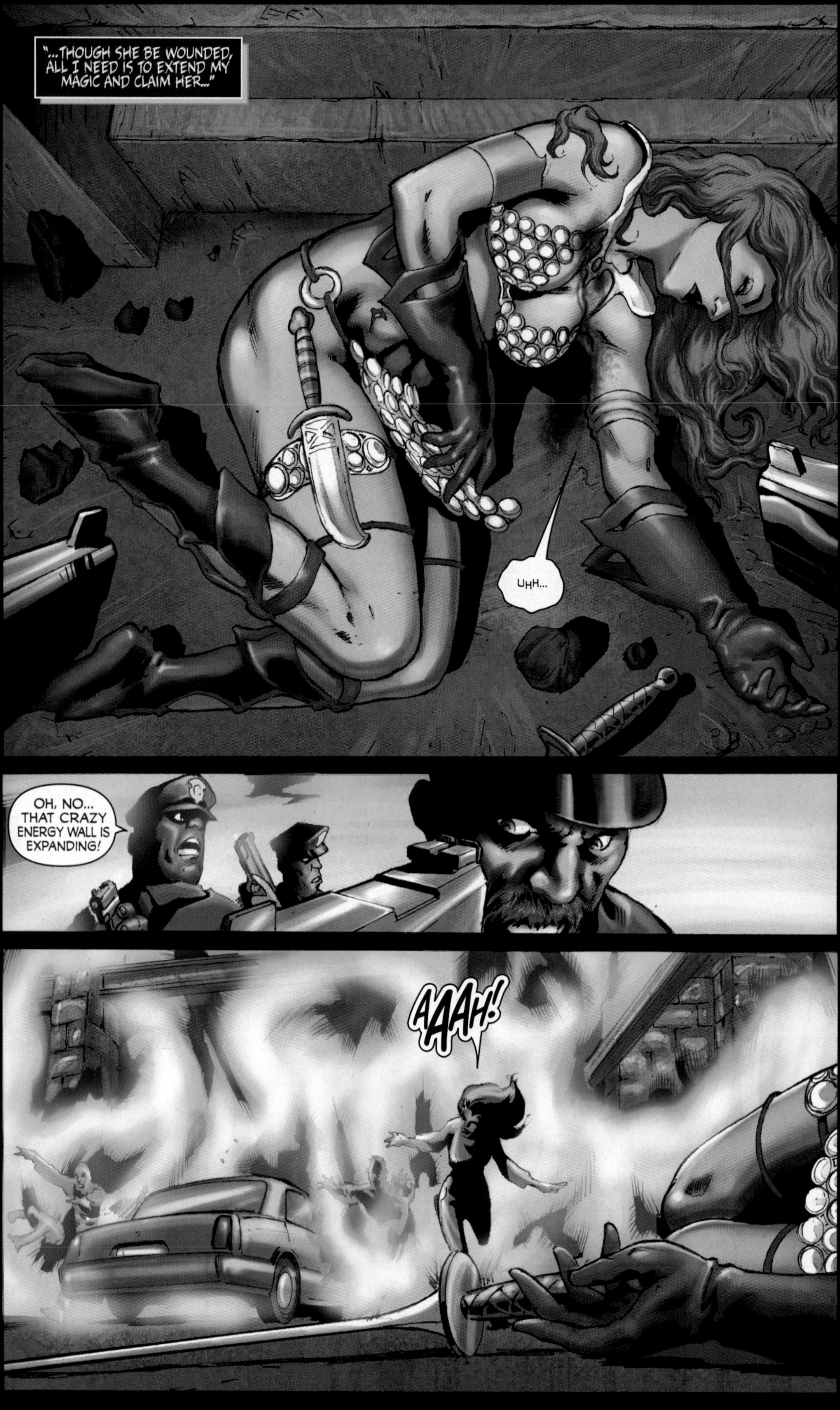
"...THOUGH SHE BE WOUNDED, ALL I NEED IS TO EXTEND MY MAGIC AND CLAIM HER..."
UHH...
OH, NO... THAT CRAZY ENERGY WALL IS EXPANDING!
AAAH!

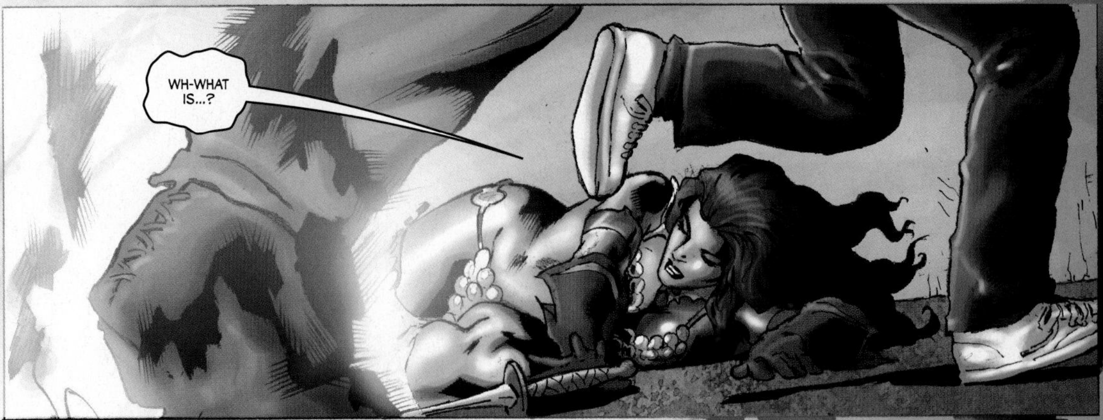
WH-WHAT IS...?

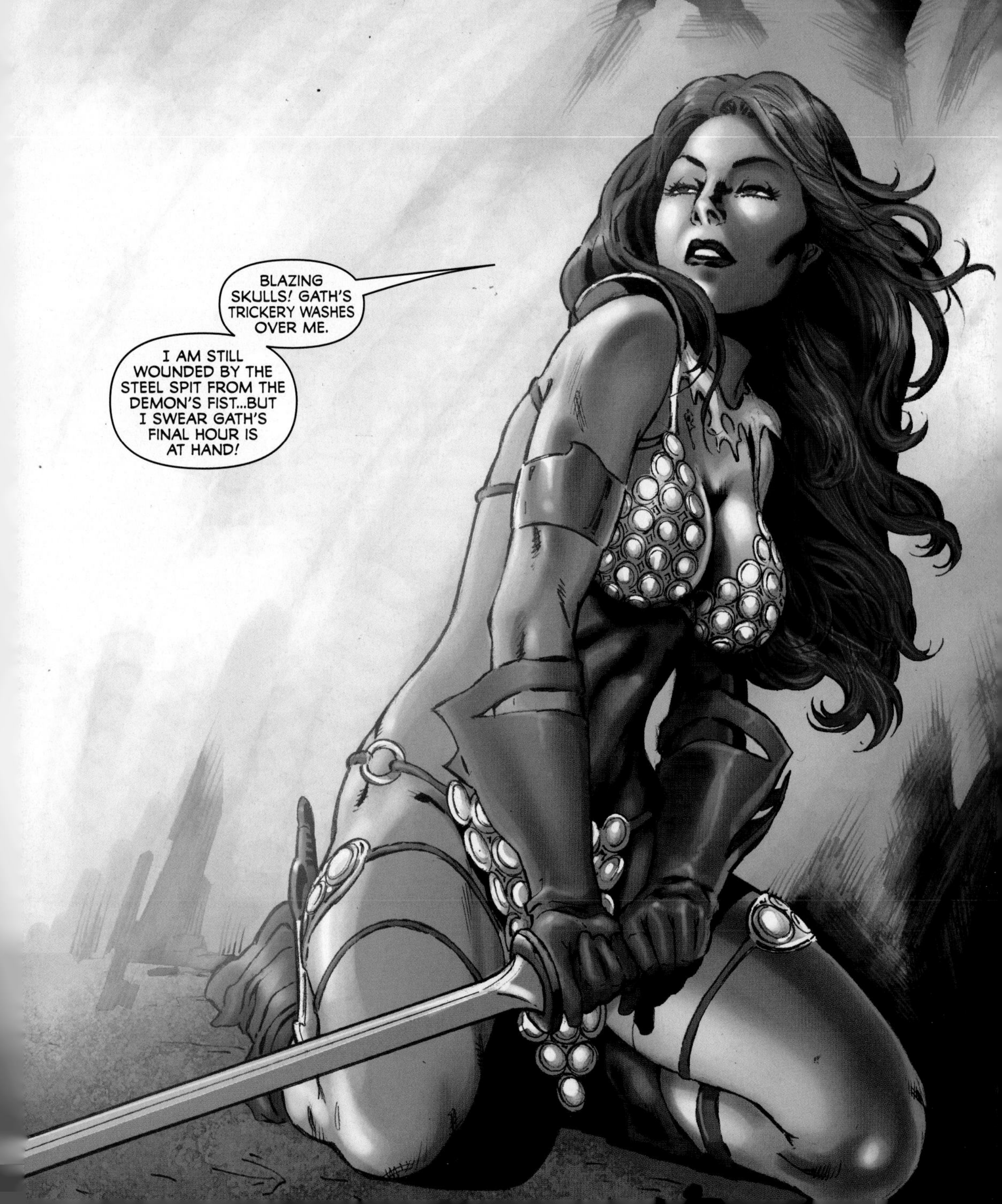
BLAZING SKULLS! GATH'S TRICKERY WASHES OVER ME.
I AM STILL WOUNDED BY THE STEEL SPIT FROM THE DEMON'S FIST...BUT I SWEAR GATH'S FINAL HOUR IS AT HAND!

"WITHIN MY SPHERE OF POWER, NOTHING ESCAPES MY SIGHT NOR MY INFLUENCE. **ALL** IS KULAN VENOM'S, AS IT **SHOULD** BE..."

"BRING THE SACRIFICE TO ME, BEFORE SHE SPILLS MORE OF THAT MOST HOLY BLOOD. ALREADY I CAN FEEL A LESSENING OF HER GIFT."

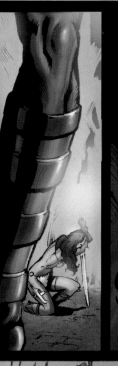

WE SHALL BRING HER TO OUR LORD, KULAN VENOM, ALIVE.

YOU'LL BRING ME IN DEAD OR NOT AT ALL! *RAAAA!*

YOU SHOULD BE HONORED, RED ONE.

*WHUD*

IF ONLY *I* WERE WORTHY ENOUGH TO GIVE MY LIFE...

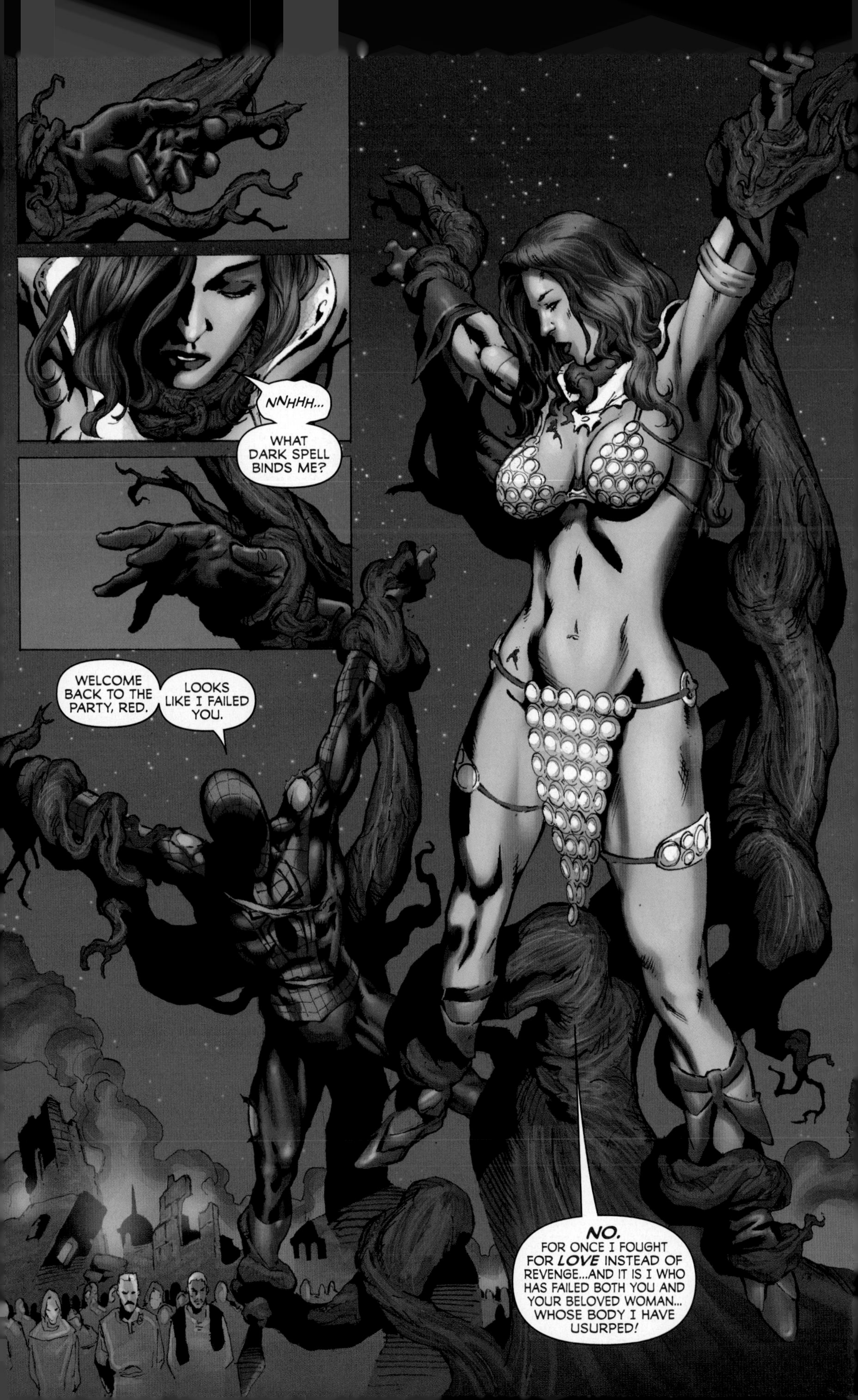
NNHHH...
WHAT DARK SPELL BINDS ME?
WELCOME BACK TO THE PARTY, RED.
LOOKS LIKE I FAILED YOU.
NO. FOR ONCE I FOUGHT FOR LOVE INSTEAD OF REVENGE...AND IT IS I WHO HAS FAILED BOTH YOU AND YOUR BELOVED WOMAN... WHOSE BODY I HAVE USURPED!

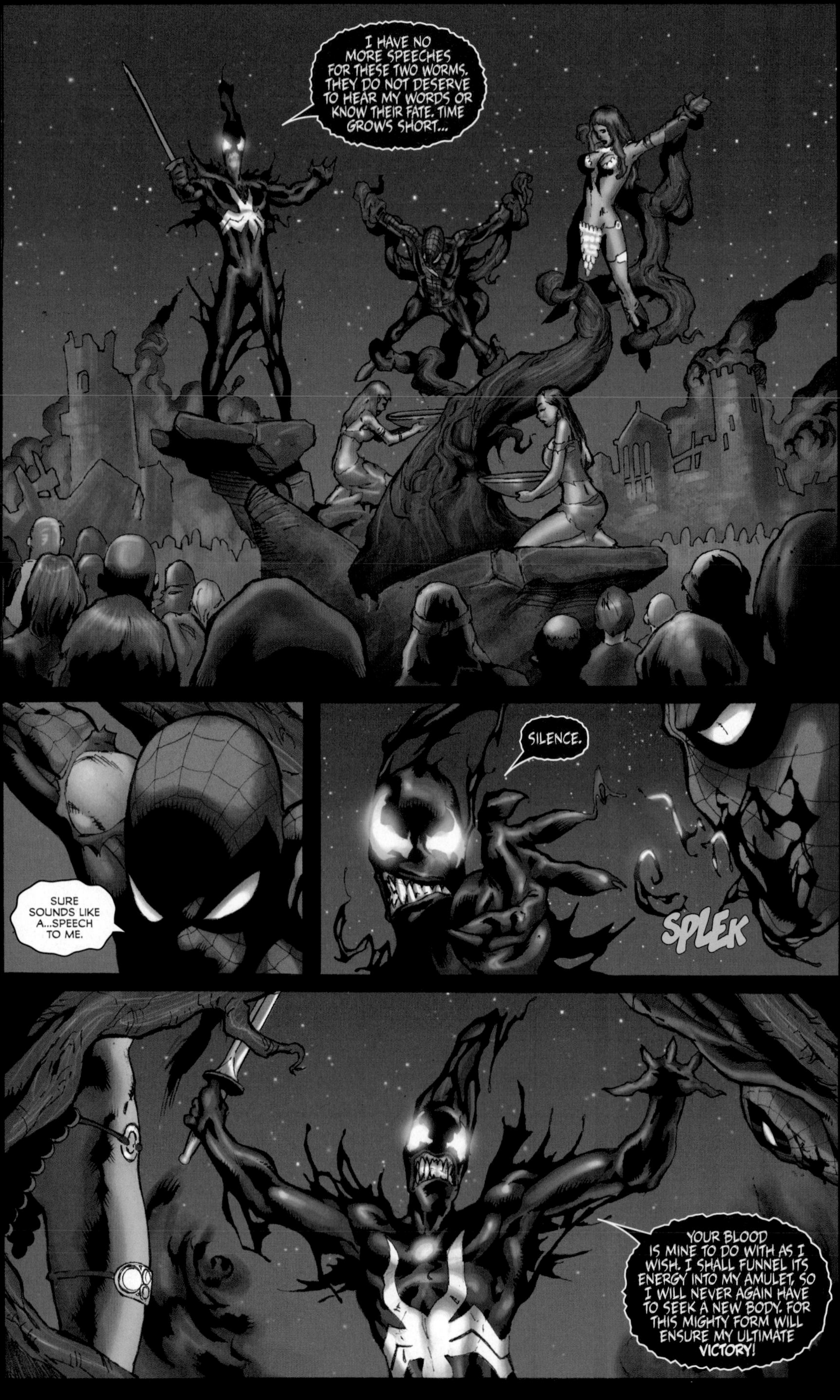

I HAVE NO MORE SPEECHES FOR THESE TWO WORMS. THEY DO NOT DESERVE TO HEAR MY WORDS OR KNOW THEIR FATE. TIME GROWS SHORT...
SURE SOUNDS LIKE A...SPEECH TO ME.
SILENCE.
SPLEK
YOUR BLOOD IS MINE TO DO WITH AS I WISH. I SHALL FUNNEL ITS ENERGY INTO MY AMULET, SO I WILL NEVER AGAIN HAVE TO SEEK A NEW BODY. FOR THIS MIGHTY FORM WILL ENSURE MY ULTIMATE VICTORY!

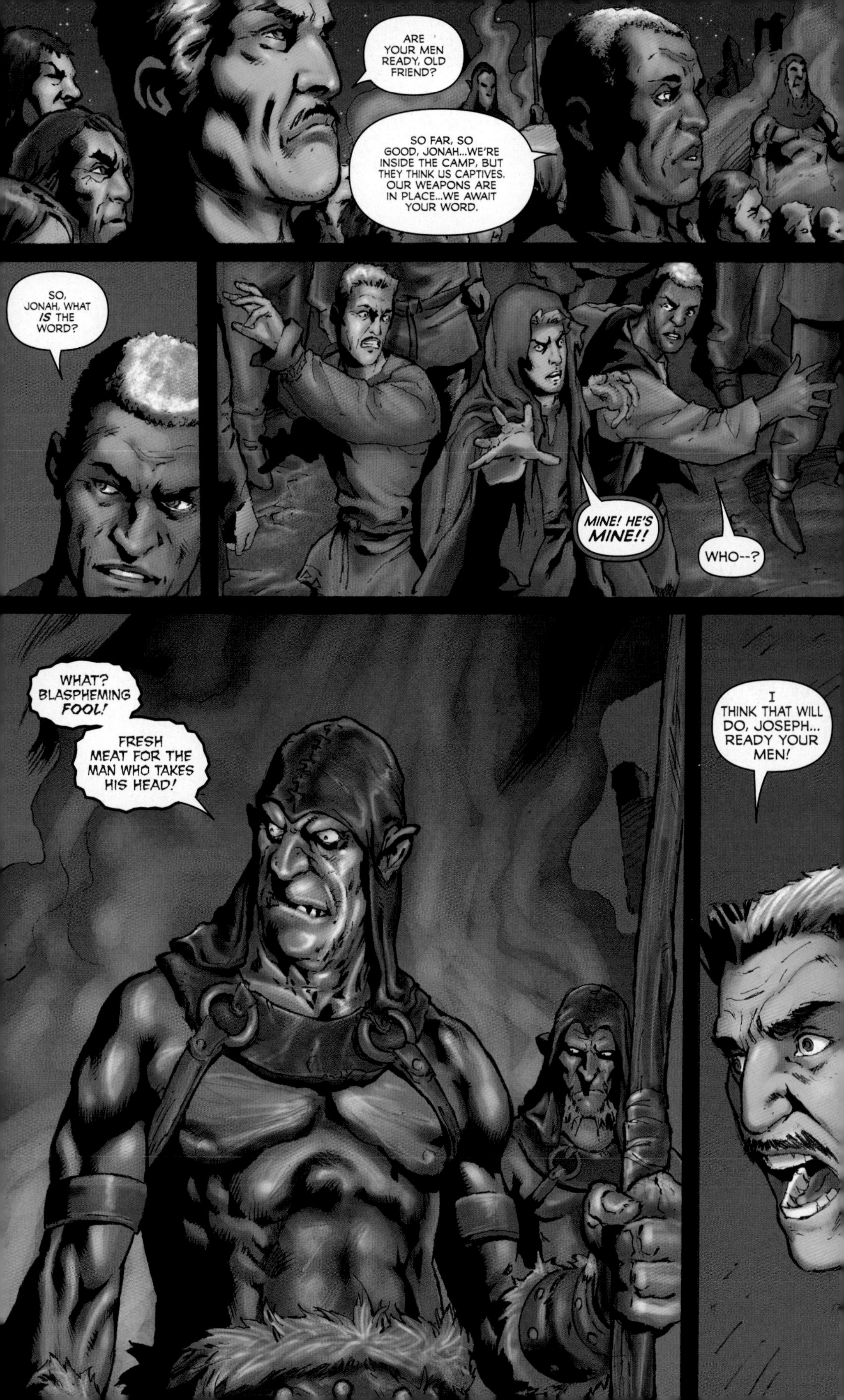
ARE YOUR MEN READY, OLD FRIEND?
SO FAR, SO GOOD, JONAH...WE'RE INSIDE THE CAMP, BUT THEY THINK US CAPTIVES. OUR WEAPONS ARE IN PLACE...WE AWAIT YOUR WORD.
SO, JONAH, WHAT *IS* THE WORD?
*MINE! HE'S* ***MINE!!***
WHO--?
WHAT? BLASPHEMING ***FOOL!***
FRESH MEAT FOR THE MAN WHO TAKES HIS HEAD!
I THINK THAT WILL DO, JOSEPH... READY YOUR MEN!

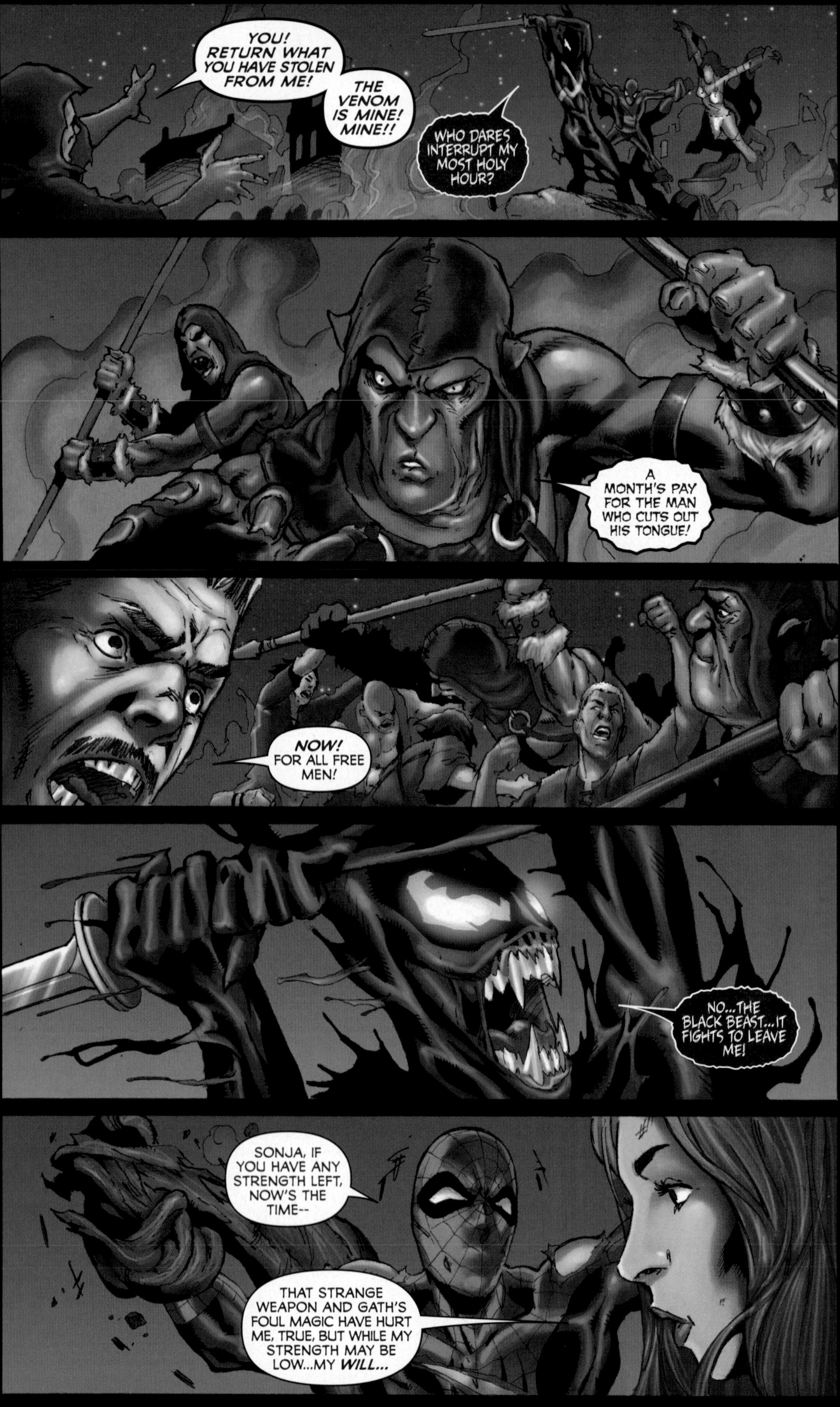
YOU! RETURN WHAT YOU HAVE STOLEN FROM ME!
THE VENOM IS MINE! MINE!!
WHO DARES INTERRUPT MY MOST HOLY HOUR?
A MONTH'S PAY FOR THE MAN WHO CUTS OUT HIS TONGUE!
NOW! FOR ALL FREE MEN!
NO...THE BLACK BEAST...IT FIGHTS TO LEAVE ME!
SONJA, IF YOU HAVE ANY STRENGTH LEFT, NOW'S THE TIME--
THAT STRANGE WEAPON AND GATH'S FOUL MAGIC HAVE HURT ME, TRUE, BUT WHILE MY STRENGTH MAY BE LOW...MY WILL...

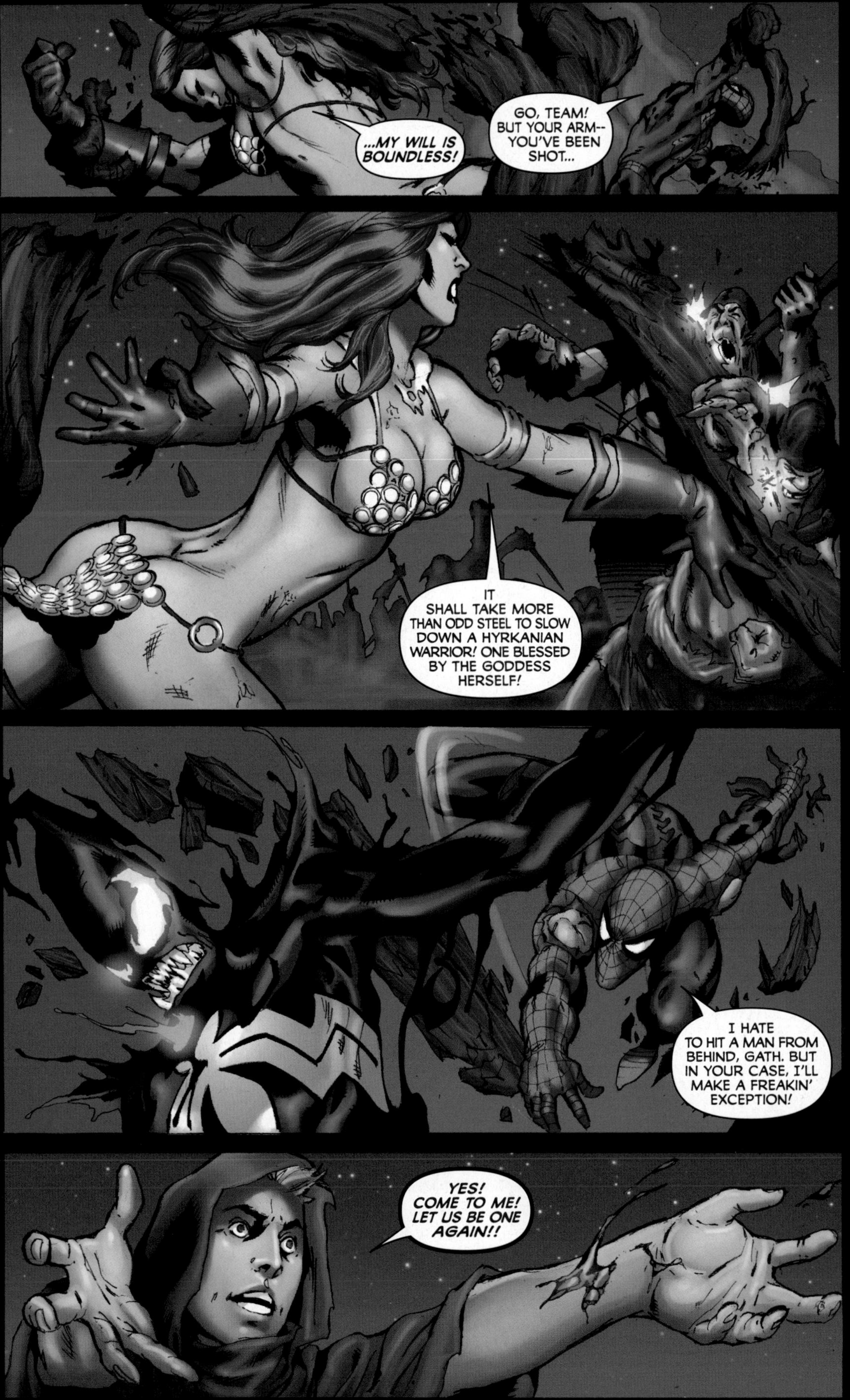
...MY WILL IS BOUNDLESS!
GO, TEAM! BUT YOUR ARM-- YOU'VE BEEN SHOT...
IT SHALL TAKE MORE THAN ODD STEEL TO SLOW DOWN A HYRKANIAN WARRIOR! ONE BLESSED BY THE GODDESS HERSELF!
I HATE TO HIT A MAN FROM BEHIND, GATH. BUT IN YOUR CASE, I'LL MAKE A FREAKIN' EXCEPTION!
YES! COME TO ME! LET US BE ONE AGAIN!!

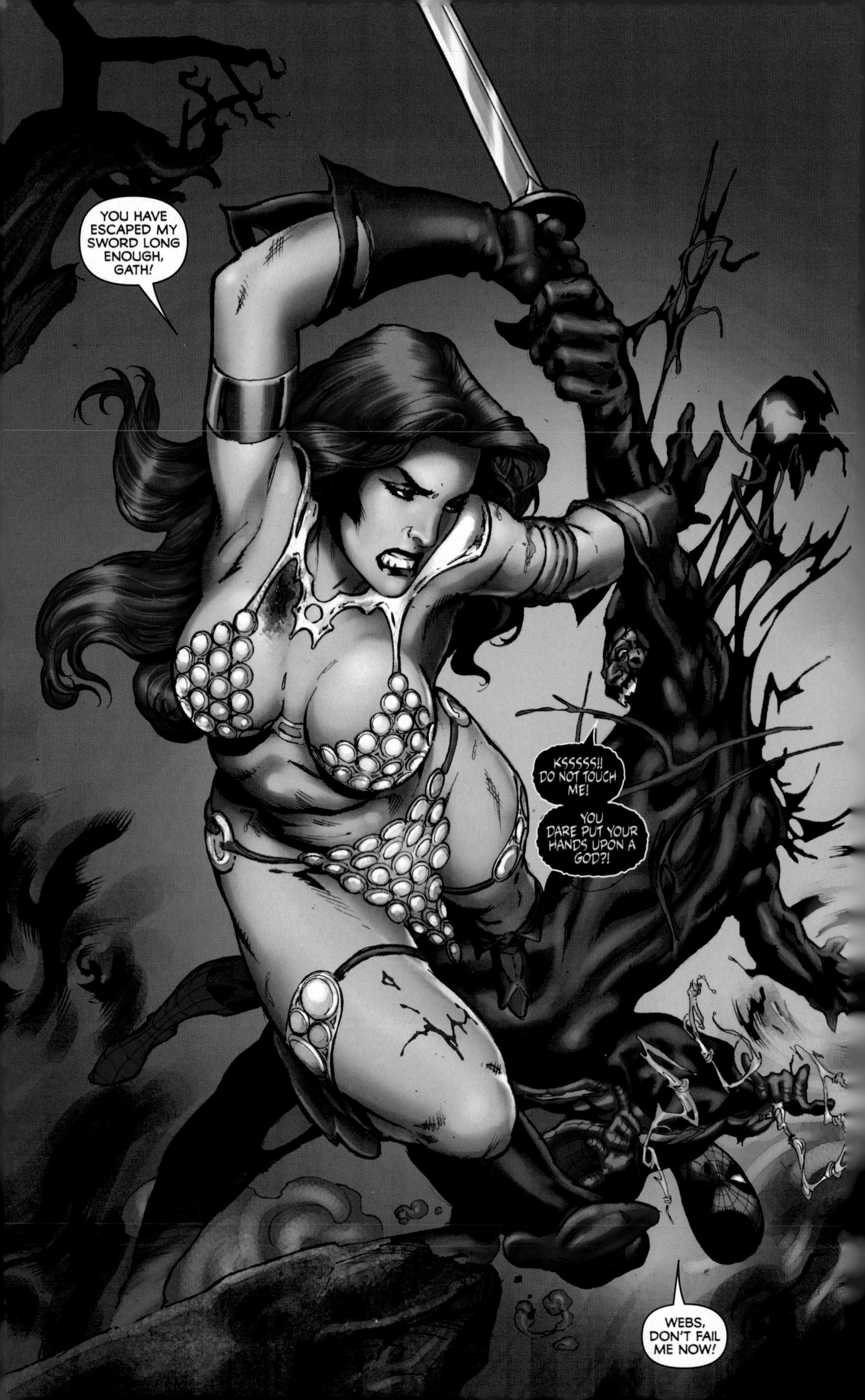
YOU HAVE ESCAPED MY SWORD LONG ENOUGH, GATH!
KSSSSS!! DO NOT TOUCH ME!
YOU DARE PUT YOUR HANDS UPON A GOD?!
WEBS, DON'T FAIL ME NOW!

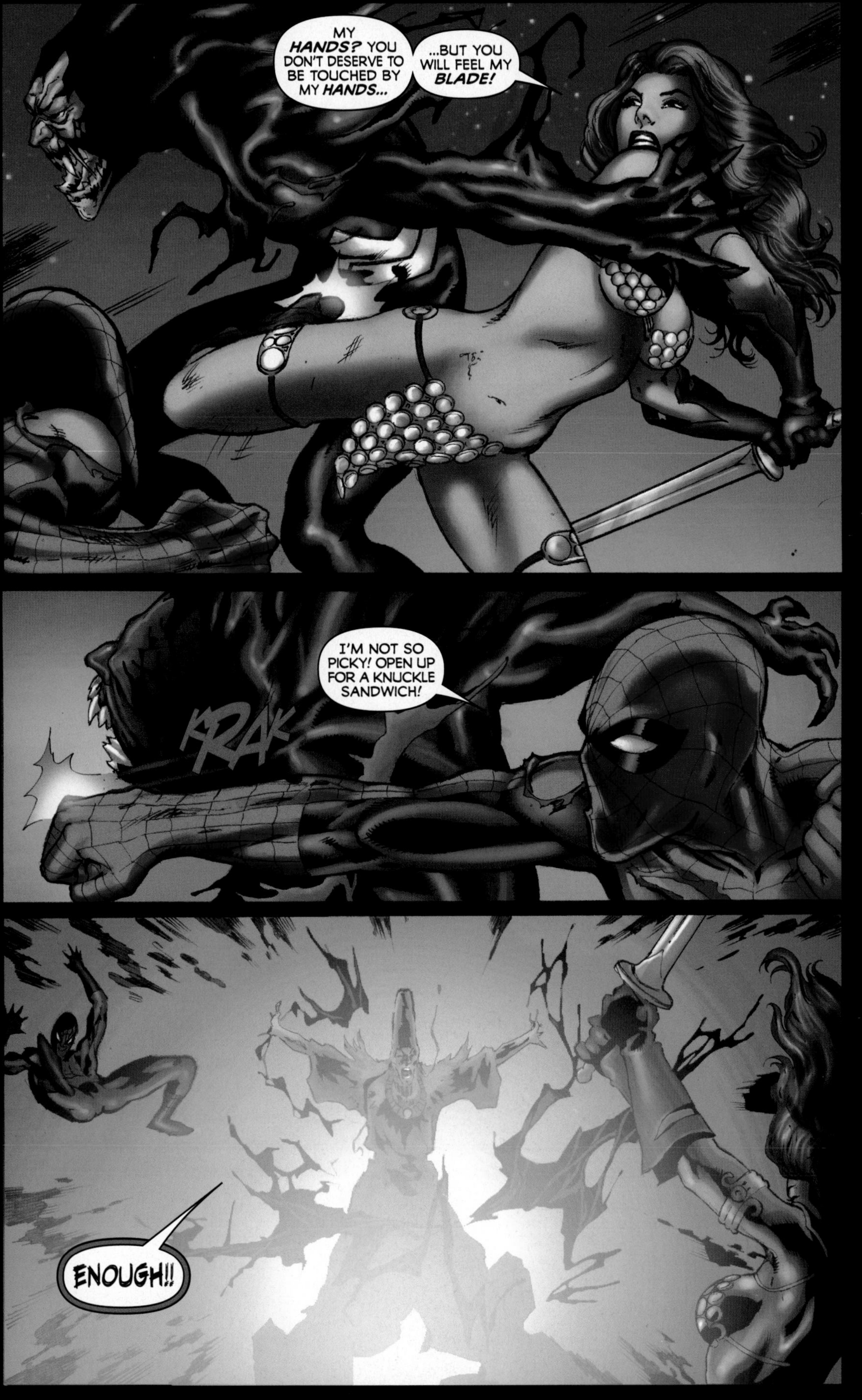
MY HANDS? YOU DON'T DESERVE TO BE TOUCHED BY MY HANDS...
...BUT YOU WILL FEEL MY BLADE!
I'M NOT SO PICKY! OPEN UP FOR A KNUCKLE SANDWICH!
KRAK
ENOUGH!!

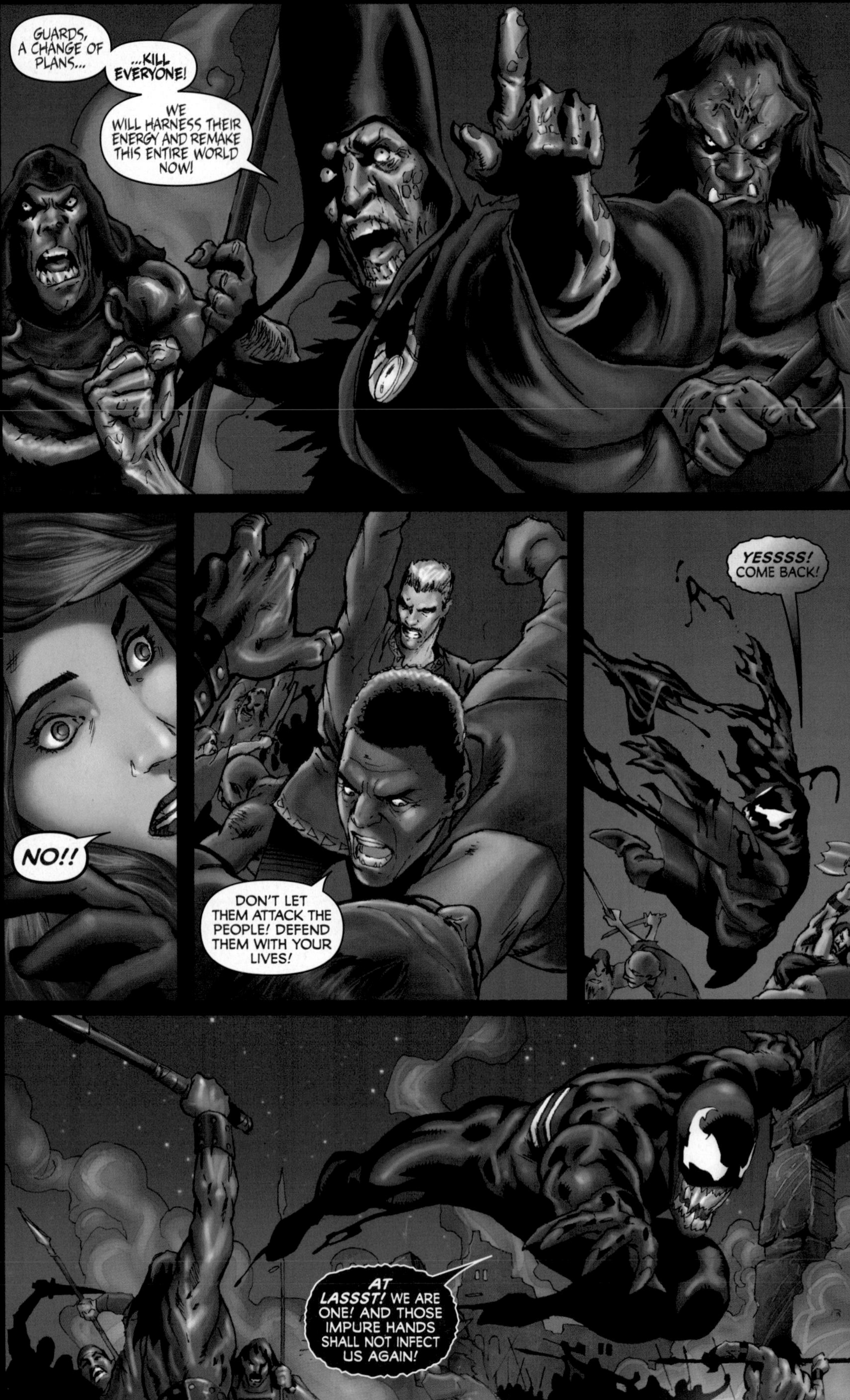
GUARDS, A CHANGE OF PLANS...
...KILL EVERYONE!
WE WILL HARNESS THEIR ENERGY AND REMAKE THIS ENTIRE WORLD NOW!
NO!!
DON'T LET THEM ATTACK THE PEOPLE! DEFEND THEM WITH YOUR LIVES!
YESSSS! COME BACK!
AT LASSST! WE ARE ONE! AND THOSE IMPURE HANDS SHALL NOT INFECT US AGAIN!

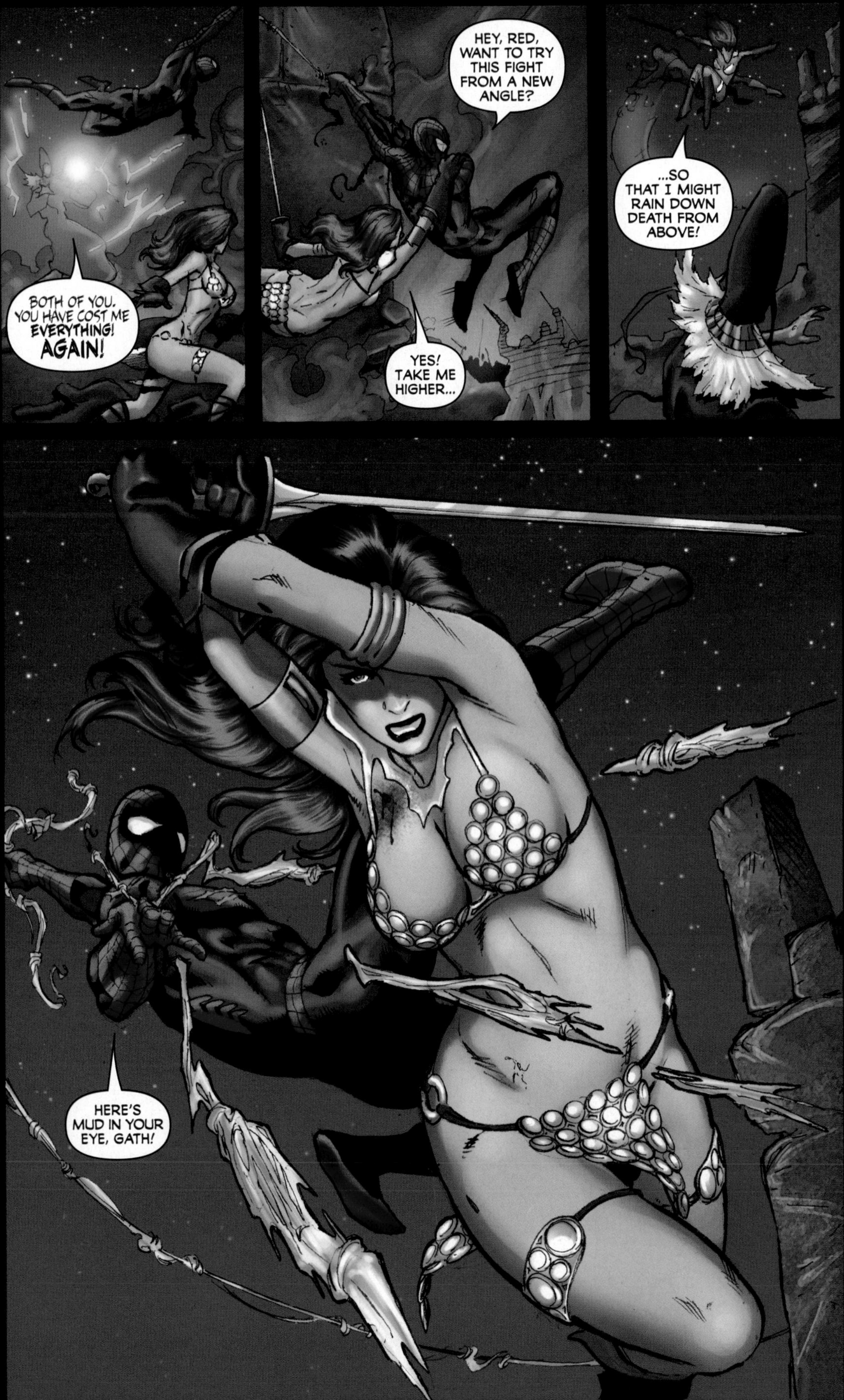
BOTH OF YOU. YOU HAVE COST ME **EVERYTHING! AGAIN!**
HEY, RED, WANT TO TRY THIS FIGHT FROM A NEW ANGLE?
YES! TAKE ME HIGHER...
...SO THAT I MIGHT RAIN DOWN DEATH FROM ABOVE!
HERE'S MUD IN YOUR EYE, GATH!

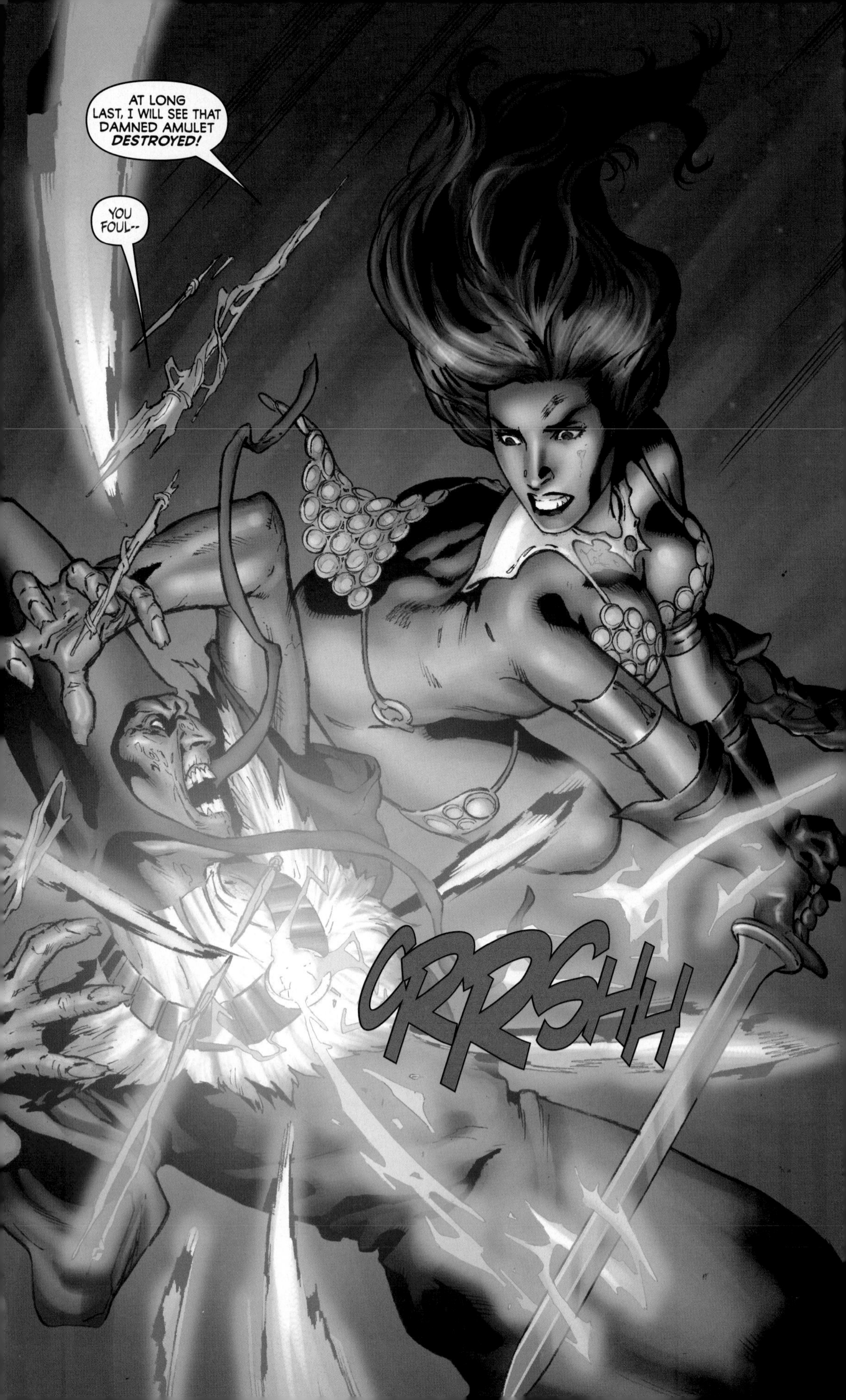
AT LONG LAST, I WILL SEE THAT DAMNED AMULET DESTROYED!
YOU FOUL--
CRRSHH

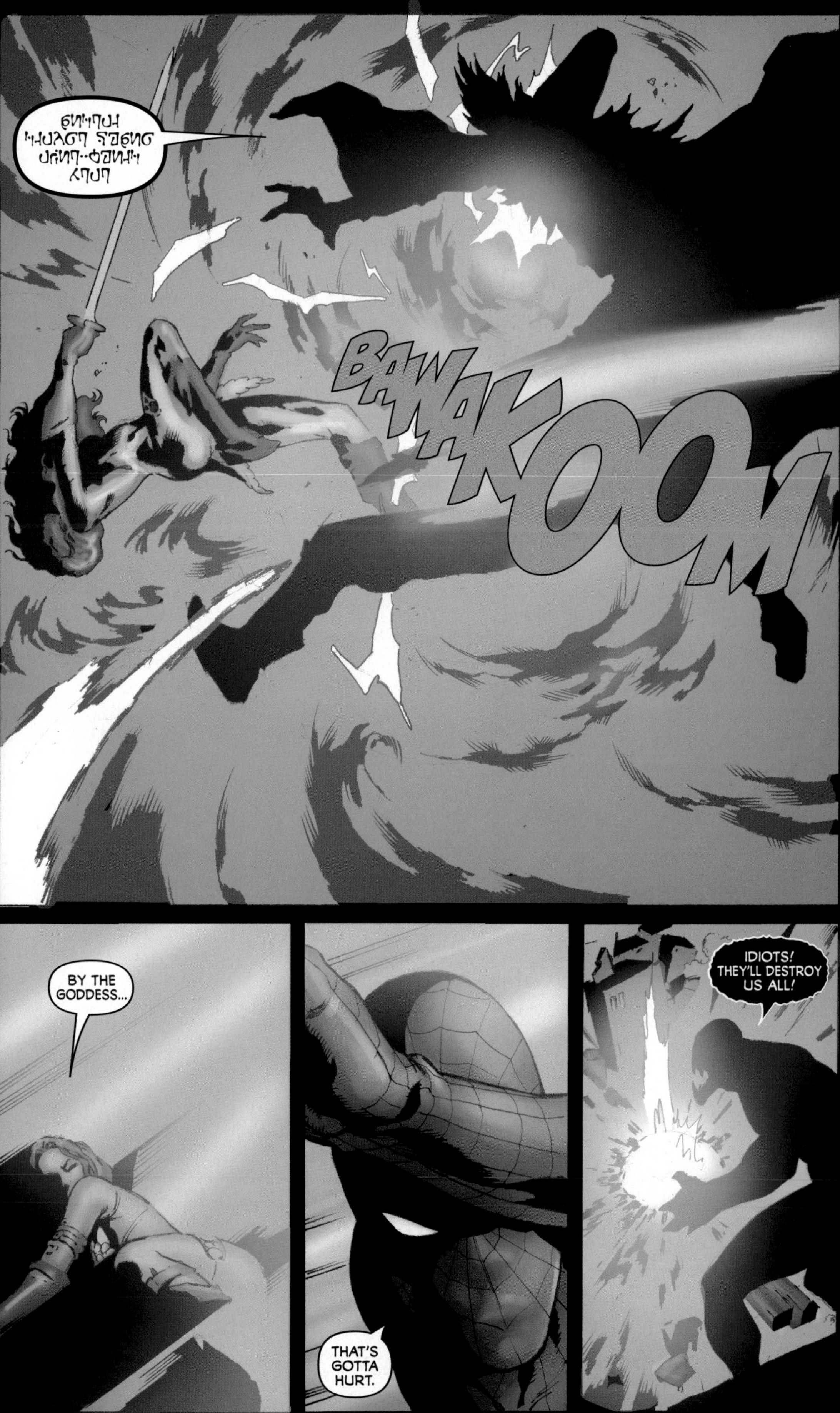
BAWAKOOM
BY THE GODDESS...
THAT'S GOTTA HURT.
IDIOTS! THEY'LL DESTROY US ALL!

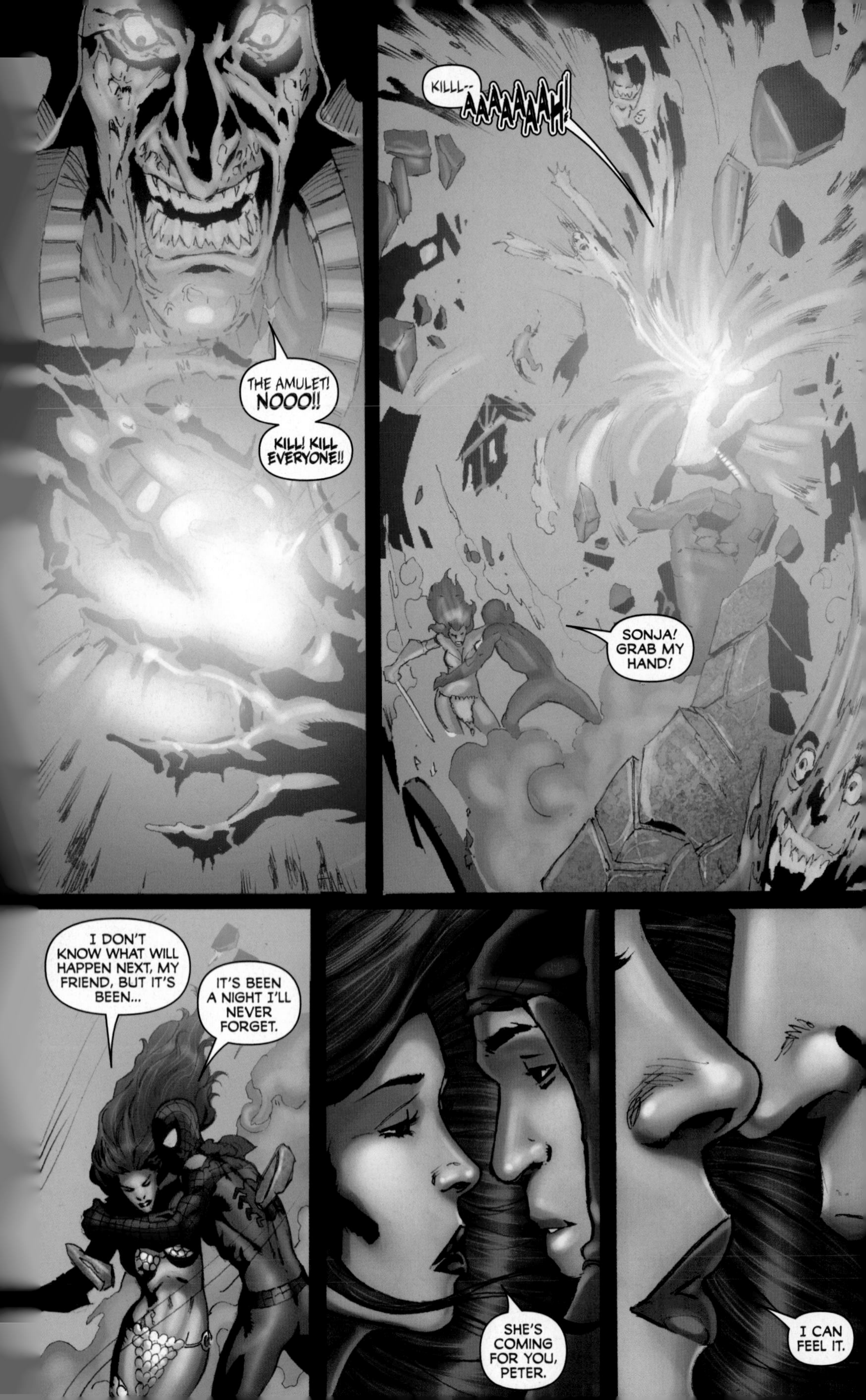
THE AMULET! NOOO!!
KILL! KILL EVERYONE!!
KILLL-- AAAAAAAH!
SONJA! GRAB MY HAND!
I DON'T KNOW WHAT WILL HAPPEN NEXT, MY FRIEND, BUT IT'S BEEN...
IT'S BEEN A NIGHT I'LL NEVER FORGET.
SHE'S COMING FOR YOU, PETER.
I CAN FEEL IT.

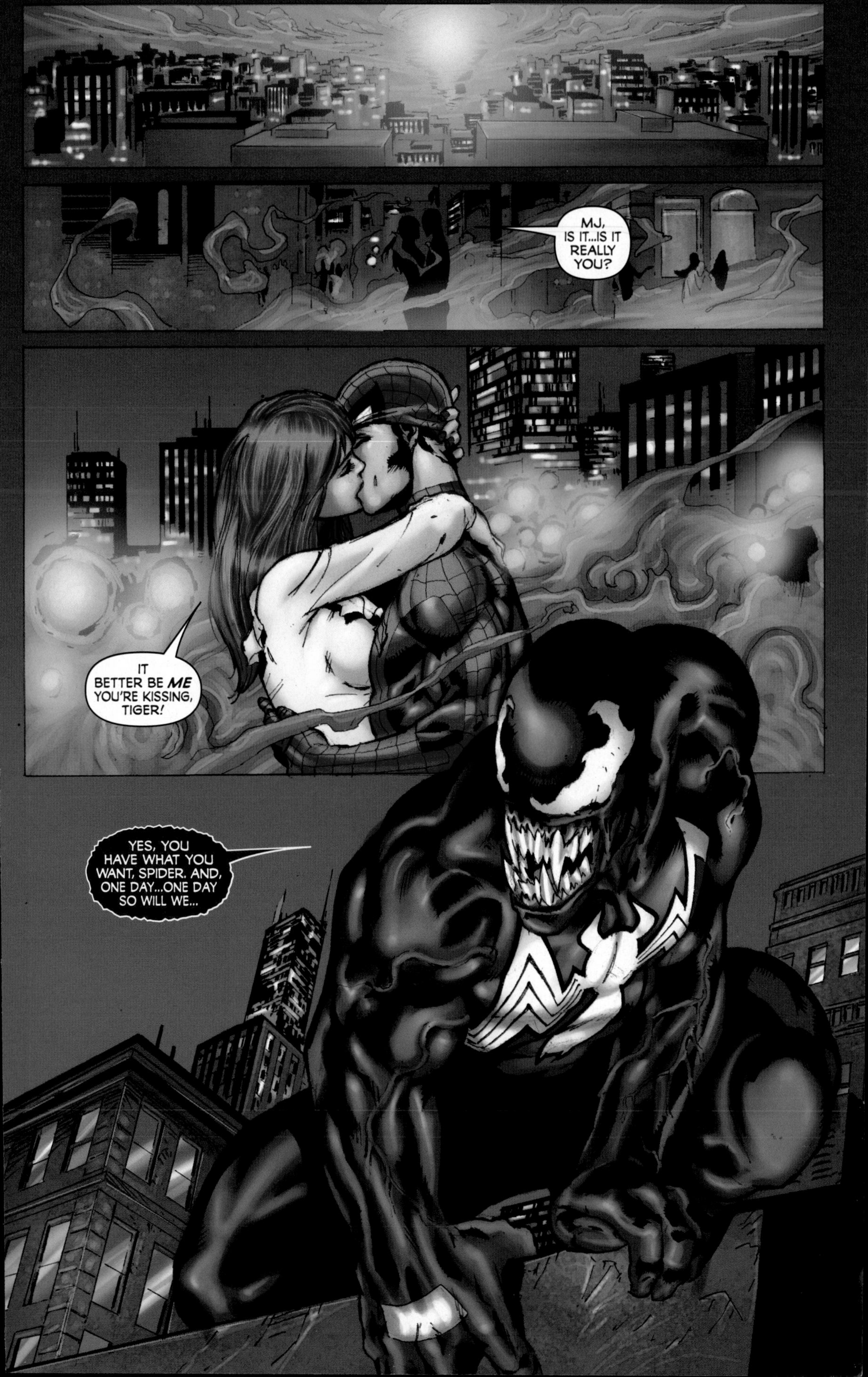
MJ, IS IT...IS IT REALLY YOU?
IT BETTER BE *ME* YOU'RE KISSING, TIGER!
YES, YOU HAVE WHAT YOU WANT, SPIDER. AND, ONE DAY...ONE DAY SO WILL WE...

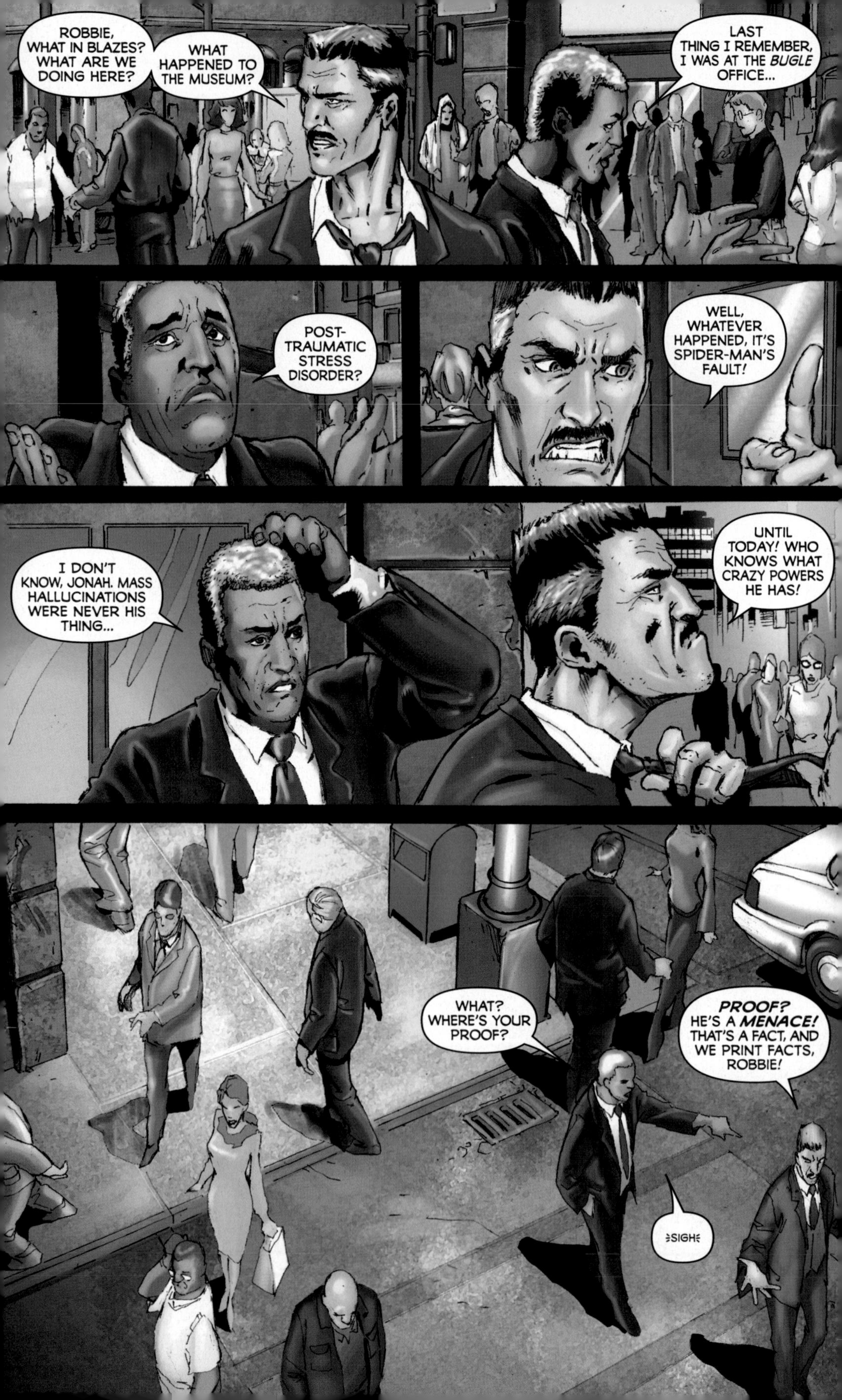
ROBBIE, WHAT IN BLAZES? WHAT ARE WE DOING HERE?
WHAT HAPPENED TO THE MUSEUM?
LAST THING I REMEMBER, I WAS AT THE *BUGLE* OFFICE...
POST-TRAUMATIC STRESS DISORDER?
WELL, WHATEVER HAPPENED, IT'S SPIDER-MAN'S FAULT!
I DON'T KNOW, JONAH. MASS HALLUCINATIONS WERE NEVER HIS THING...
UNTIL TODAY! WHO KNOWS WHAT CRAZY POWERS HE HAS!
WHAT? WHERE'S YOUR PROOF?
*PROOF?* HE'S A *MENACE!* THAT'S A FACT, AND WE PRINT FACTS, ROBBIE!
SIGH

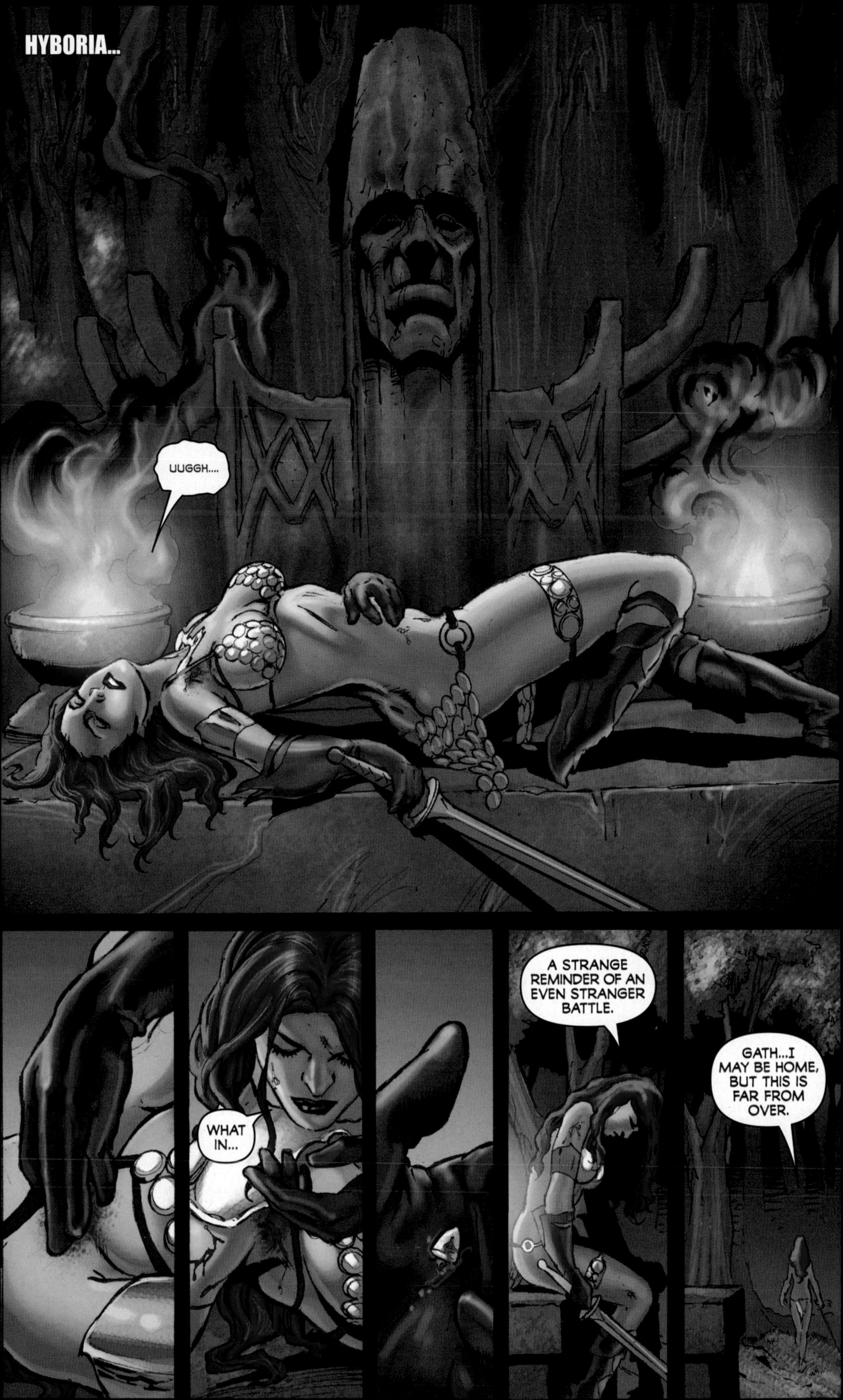
HYBORIA...
UUGGH....
WHAT IN...
A STRANGE REMINDER OF AN EVEN STRANGER BATTLE.
GATH...I MAY BE HOME, BUT THIS IS FAR FROM OVER.

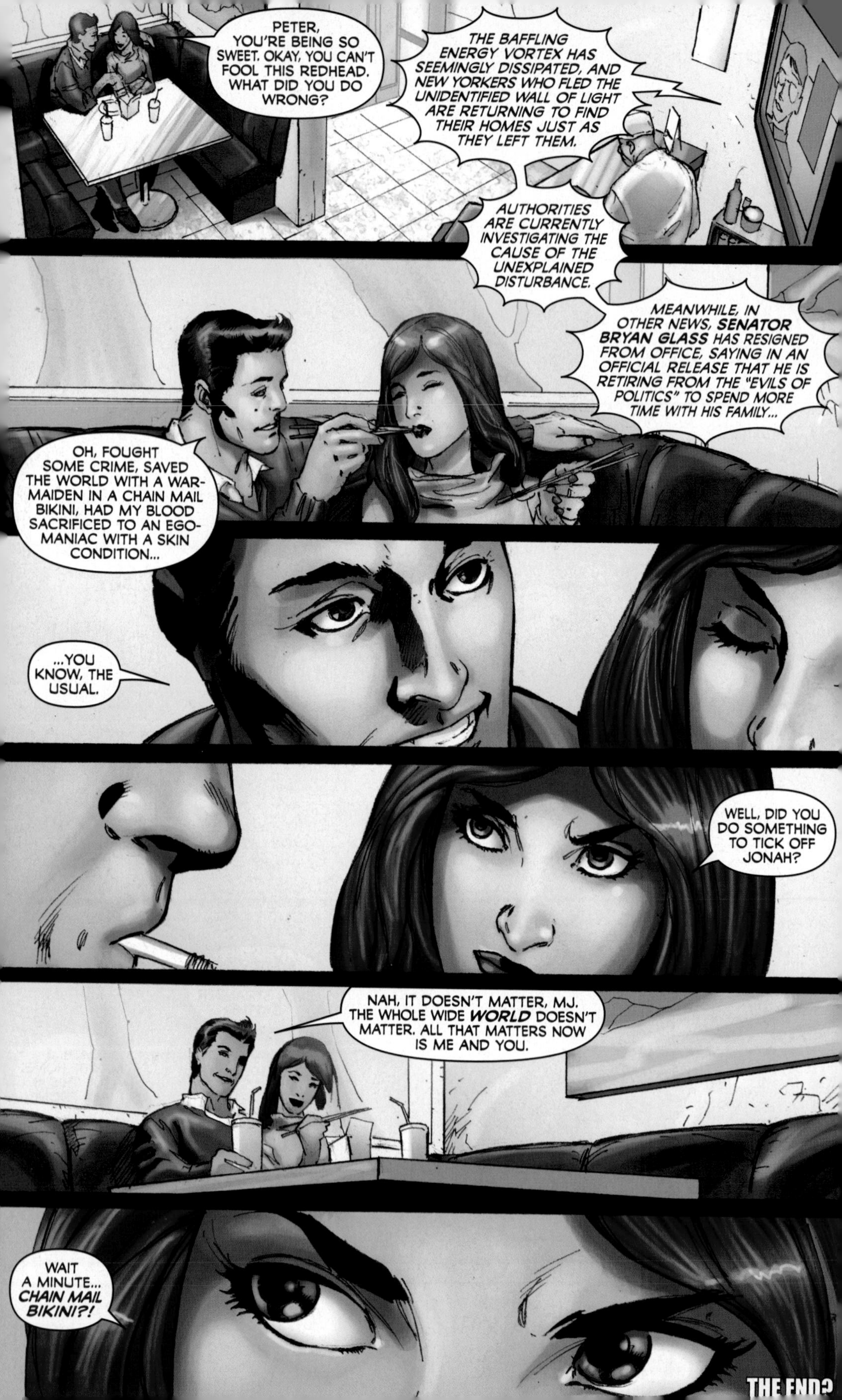
PETER, YOU'RE BEING SO SWEET. OKAY, YOU CAN'T FOOL THIS REDHEAD. WHAT DID YOU DO WRONG?
THE BAFFLING ENERGY VORTEX HAS SEEMINGLY DISSIPATED, AND NEW YORKERS WHO FLED THE UNIDENTIFIED WALL OF LIGHT ARE RETURNING TO FIND THEIR HOMES JUST AS THEY LEFT THEM.
AUTHORITIES ARE CURRENTLY INVESTIGATING THE CAUSE OF THE UNEXPLAINED DISTURBANCE.
MEANWHILE, IN OTHER NEWS, SENATOR BRYAN GLASS HAS RESIGNED FROM OFFICE, SAYING IN AN OFFICIAL RELEASE THAT HE IS RETIRING FROM THE "EVILS OF POLITICS" TO SPEND MORE TIME WITH HIS FAMILY...
OH, FOUGHT SOME CRIME, SAVED THE WORLD WITH A WAR-MAIDEN IN A CHAIN MAIL BIKINI, HAD MY BLOOD SACRIFICED TO AN EGO-MANIAC WITH A SKIN CONDITION...
...YOU KNOW, THE USUAL.
WELL, DID YOU DO SOMETHING TO TICK OFF JONAH?
NAH, IT DOESN'T MATTER, MJ. THE WHOLE WIDE WORLD DOESN'T MATTER. ALL THAT MATTERS NOW IS ME AND YOU.
WAIT A MINUTE... CHAIN MAIL BIKINI?!
THE END?

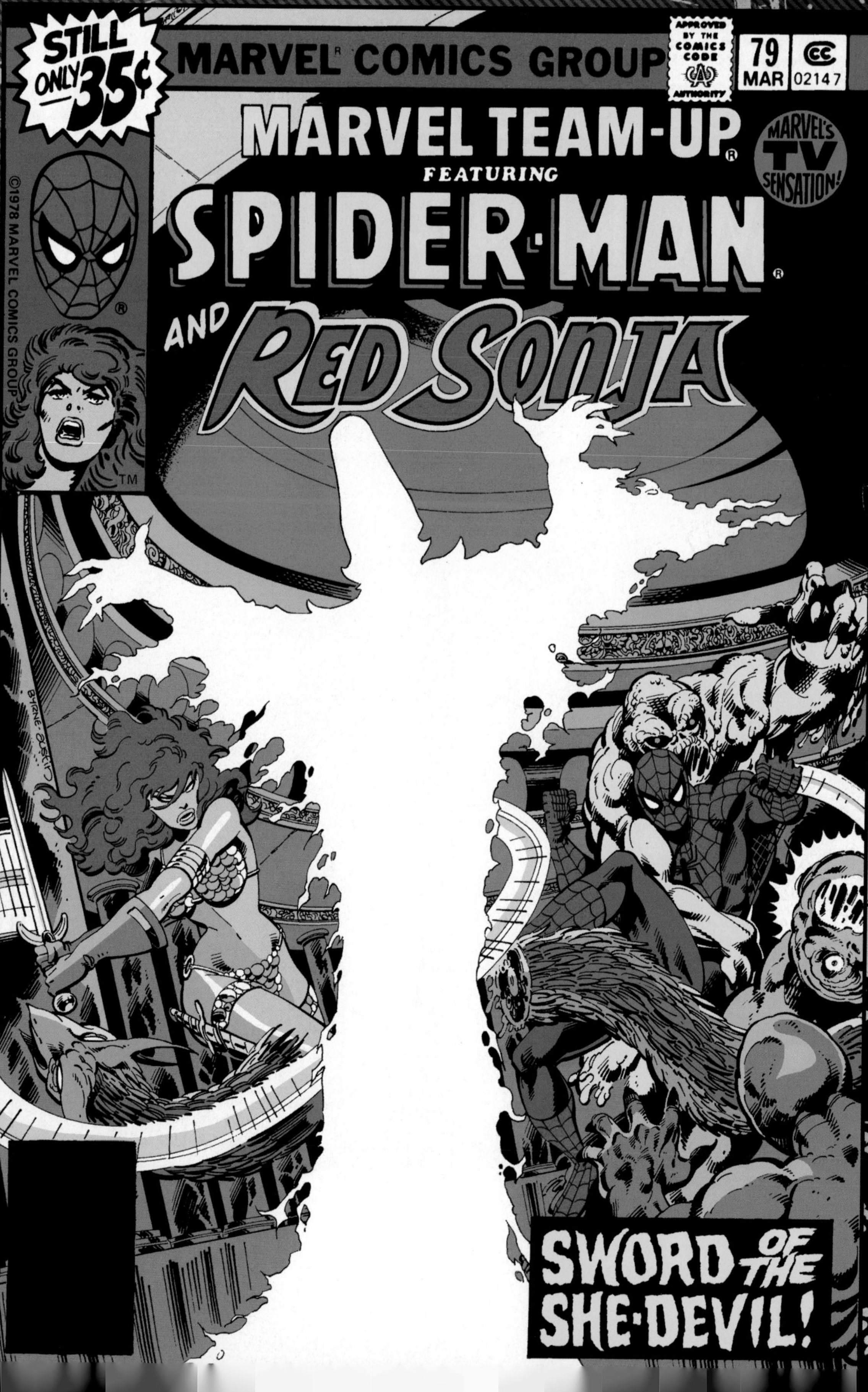
STILL ONLY 35¢
MARVEL COMICS GROUP
APPROVED BY THE COMICS CODE AUTHORITY
79 MAR
CC 02147
MARVEL TEAM-UP
FEATURING
SPIDER-MAN
AND RED SONJA
MARVEL'S TV SENSATION!
©1978 MARVEL COMICS GROUP
SWORD OF THE SHE-DEVIL!

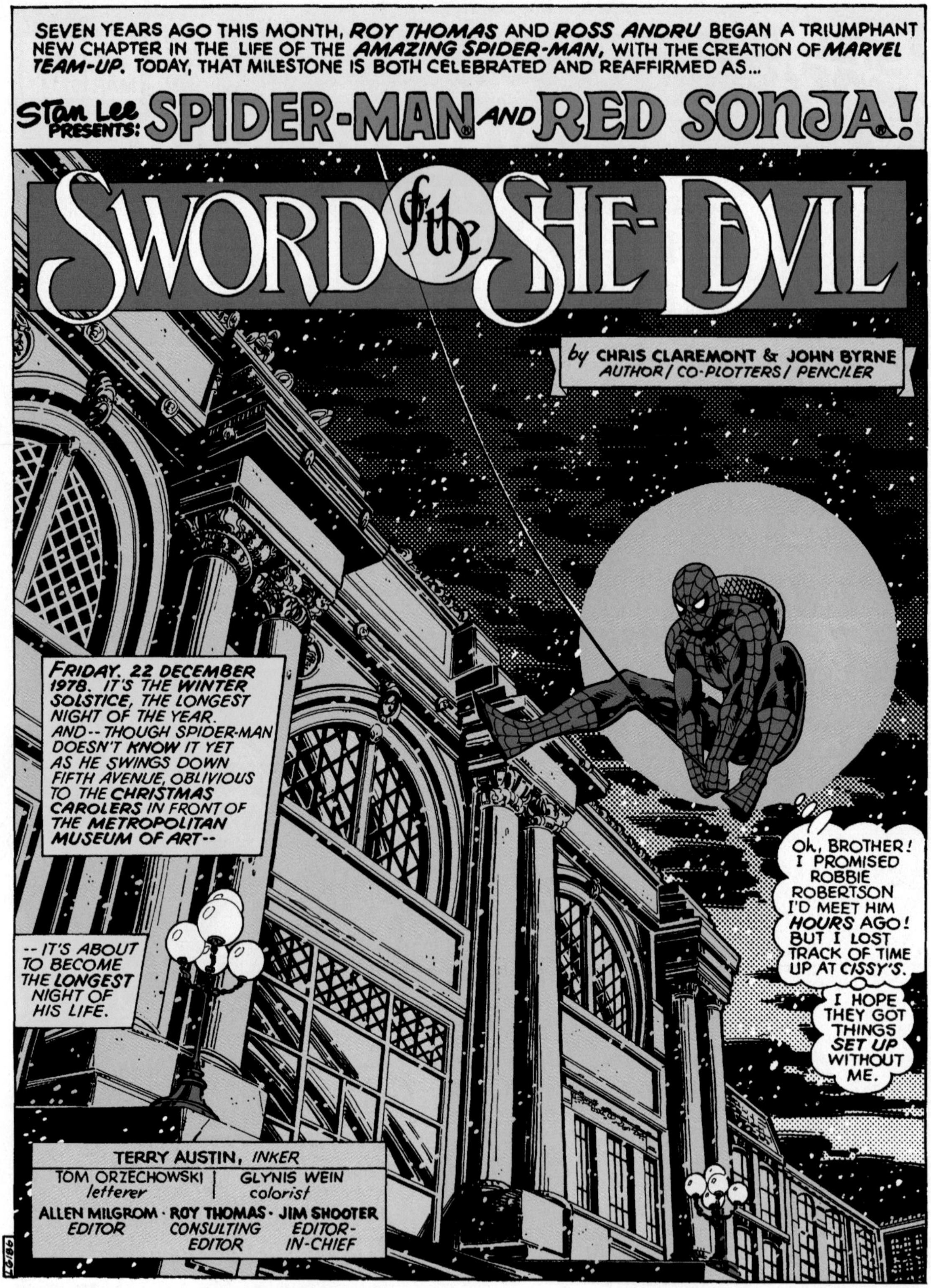
SEVEN YEARS AGO THIS MONTH, ROY THOMAS AND ROSS ANDRU BEGAN A TRIUMPHANT NEW CHAPTER IN THE LIFE OF THE AMAZING SPIDER-MAN, WITH THE CREATION OF MARVEL TEAM-UP. TODAY, THAT MILESTONE IS BOTH CELEBRATED AND REAFFIRMED AS...
STAN LEE PRESENTS: SPIDER-MAN AND RED SONJA!
SWORD of the SHE-DEVIL
by CHRIS CLAREMONT & JOHN BYRNE
AUTHOR / CO-PLOTTERS / PENCILER
FRIDAY, 22 DECEMBER 1978. IT'S THE WINTER SOLSTICE, THE LONGEST NIGHT OF THE YEAR. AND--THOUGH SPIDER-MAN DOESN'T KNOW IT YET AS HE SWINGS DOWN FIFTH AVENUE, OBLIVIOUS TO THE CHRISTMAS CAROLERS IN FRONT OF THE METROPOLITAN MUSEUM OF ART--
--IT'S ABOUT TO BECOME THE LONGEST NIGHT OF HIS LIFE.
OH, BROTHER! I PROMISED ROBBIE ROBERTSON I'D MEET HIM HOURS AGO! BUT I LOST TRACK OF TIME UP AT CISSY'S.
I HOPE THEY GOT THINGS SET UP WITHOUT ME.
TERRY AUSTIN, INKER
TOM ORZECHOWSKI letterer
GLYNIS WEIN colorist
ALLEN MILGROM · ROY THOMAS · JIM SHOOTER
EDITOR
CONSULTING EDITOR
EDITOR-IN-CHIEF
10186

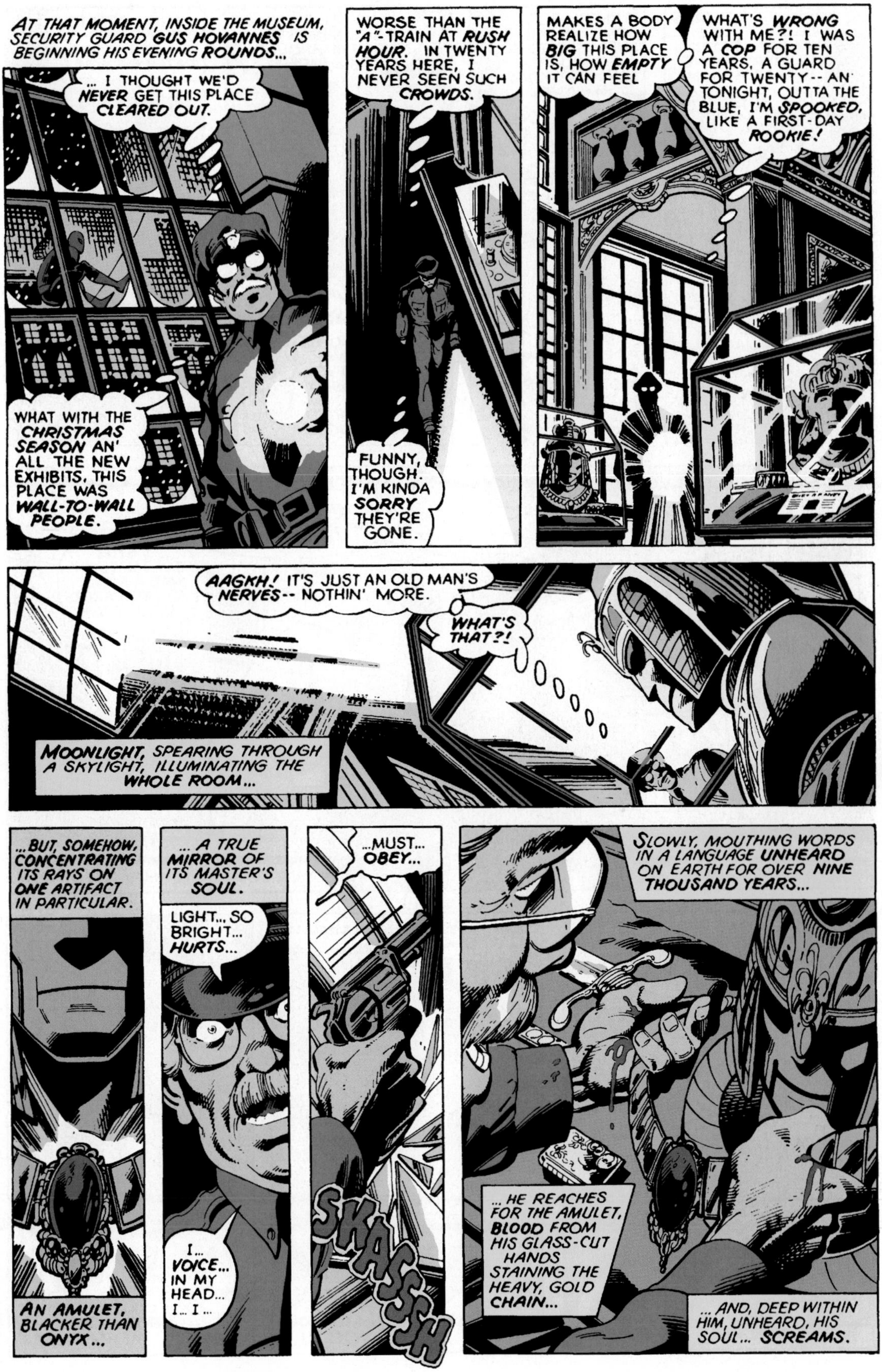
AT THAT MOMENT, INSIDE THE MUSEUM, SECURITY GUARD GUS HOVANNES IS BEGINNING HIS EVENING ROUNDS...
... I THOUGHT WE'D NEVER GET THIS PLACE CLEARED OUT.
WHAT WITH THE CHRISTMAS SEASON AN' ALL THE NEW EXHIBITS, THIS PLACE WAS WALL-TO-WALL PEOPLE.
WORSE THAN THE "A"-TRAIN AT RUSH HOUR. IN TWENTY YEARS HERE, I NEVER SEEN SUCH CROWDS.
FUNNY, THOUGH. I'M KINDA SORRY THEY'RE GONE.
MAKES A BODY REALIZE HOW BIG THIS PLACE IS, HOW EMPTY IT CAN FEEL
WHAT'S WRONG WITH ME?! I WAS A COP FOR TEN YEARS, A GUARD FOR TWENTY-- AN' TONIGHT, OUTTA THE BLUE, I'M SPOOKED, LIKE A FIRST-DAY ROOKIE!
AAGKH! IT'S JUST AN OLD MAN'S NERVES-- NOTHIN' MORE.
WHAT'S THAT?!
MOONLIGHT, SPEARING THROUGH A SKYLIGHT, ILLUMINATING THE WHOLE ROOM...
...BUT, SOMEHOW, CONCENTRATING ITS RAYS ON ONE ARTIFACT IN PARTICULAR.
AN AMULET, BLACKER THAN ONYX...
... A TRUE MIRROR OF ITS MASTER'S SOUL.
LIGHT... SO BRIGHT... HURTS...
I... VOICE... IN MY HEAD... I... I...
...MUST... OBEY...
SKASSSH
SLOWLY, MOUTHING WORDS IN A LANGUAGE UNHEARD ON EARTH FOR OVER NINE THOUSAND YEARS...
...HE REACHES FOR THE AMULET, BLOOD FROM HIS GLASS-CUT HANDS STAINING THE HEAVY, GOLD CHAIN...
... AND, DEEP WITHIN HIM, UNHEARD, HIS SOUL... SCREAMS.

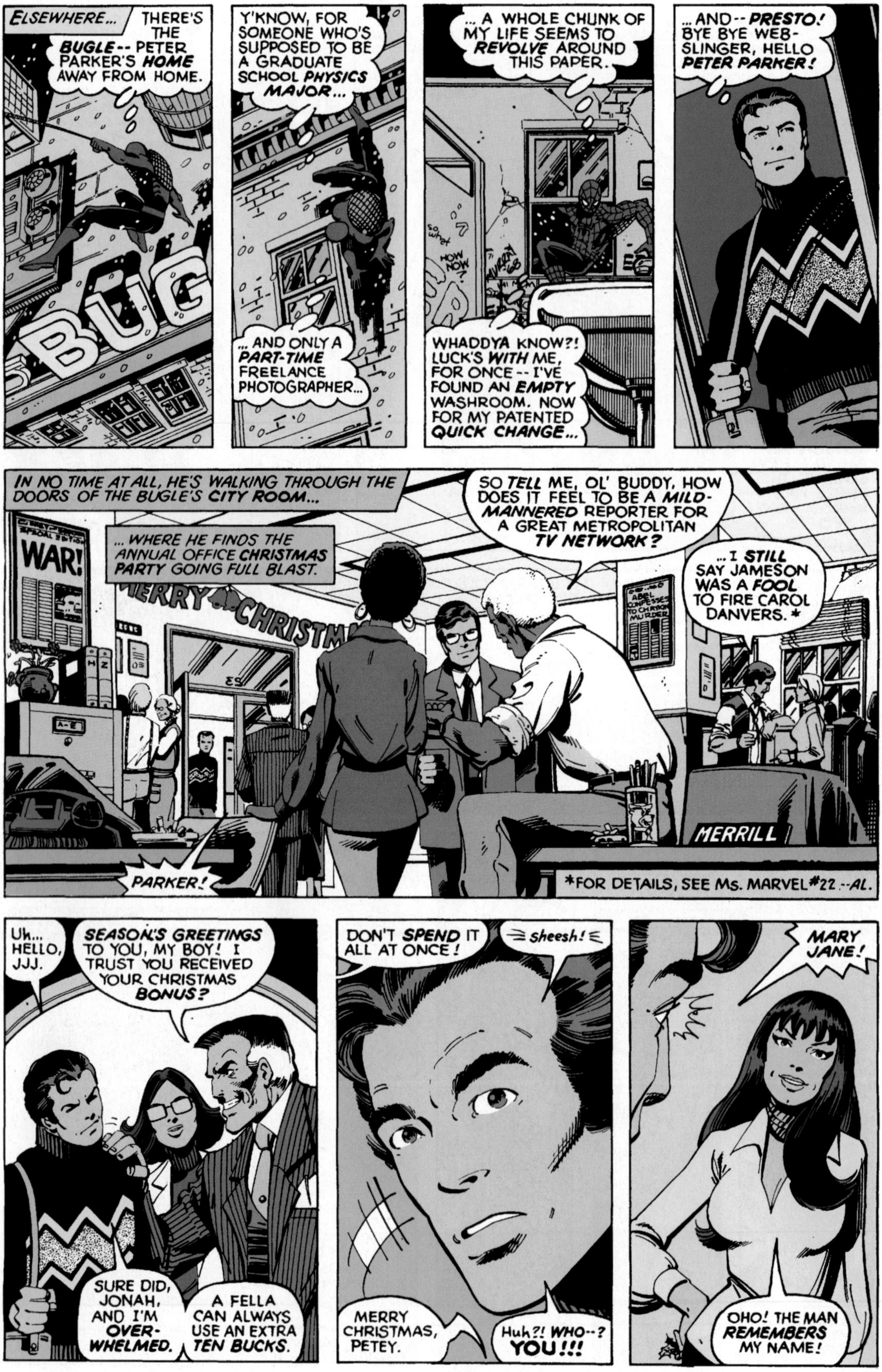
ELSEWHERE...
THERE'S THE BUGLE-- PETER PARKER'S HOME AWAY FROM HOME.
Y'KNOW, FOR SOMEONE WHO'S SUPPOSED TO BE A GRADUATE SCHOOL PHYSICS MAJOR...
...AND ONLY A PART-TIME FREELANCE PHOTOGRAPHER...
...A WHOLE CHUNK OF MY LIFE SEEMS TO REVOLVE AROUND THIS PAPER.
WHADDYA KNOW?! LUCK'S WITH ME, FOR ONCE -- I'VE FOUND AN EMPTY WASHROOM. NOW FOR MY PATENTED QUICK CHANGE...
...AND -- PRESTO! BYE BYE WEB-SLINGER, HELLO PETER PARKER!
IN NO TIME AT ALL, HE'S WALKING THROUGH THE DOORS OF THE BUGLE'S CITY ROOM...
...WHERE HE FINDS THE ANNUAL OFFICE CHRISTMAS PARTY GOING FULL BLAST.
WAR!
MERRY CHRISTMAS
SO TELL ME, OL' BUDDY, HOW DOES IT FEEL TO BE A MILD-MANNERED REPORTER FOR A GREAT METROPOLITAN TV NETWORK?
...I STILL SAY JAMESON WAS A FOOL TO FIRE CAROL DANVERS.*
MERRILL
PARKER!
*FOR DETAILS, SEE Ms. MARVEL #22.--AL.
Uh... HELLO, JJJ.
SEASON'S GREETINGS TO YOU, MY BOY! I TRUST YOU RECEIVED YOUR CHRISTMAS BONUS?
SURE DID, JONAH, AND I'M OVER-WHELMED.
A FELLA CAN ALWAYS USE AN EXTRA TEN BUCKS.
DON'T SPEND IT ALL AT ONCE!
sheesh!
MERRY CHRISTMAS, PETEY.
Huh?! WHO--? YOU!!!
MARY JANE!
OHO! THE MAN REMEMBERS MY NAME!

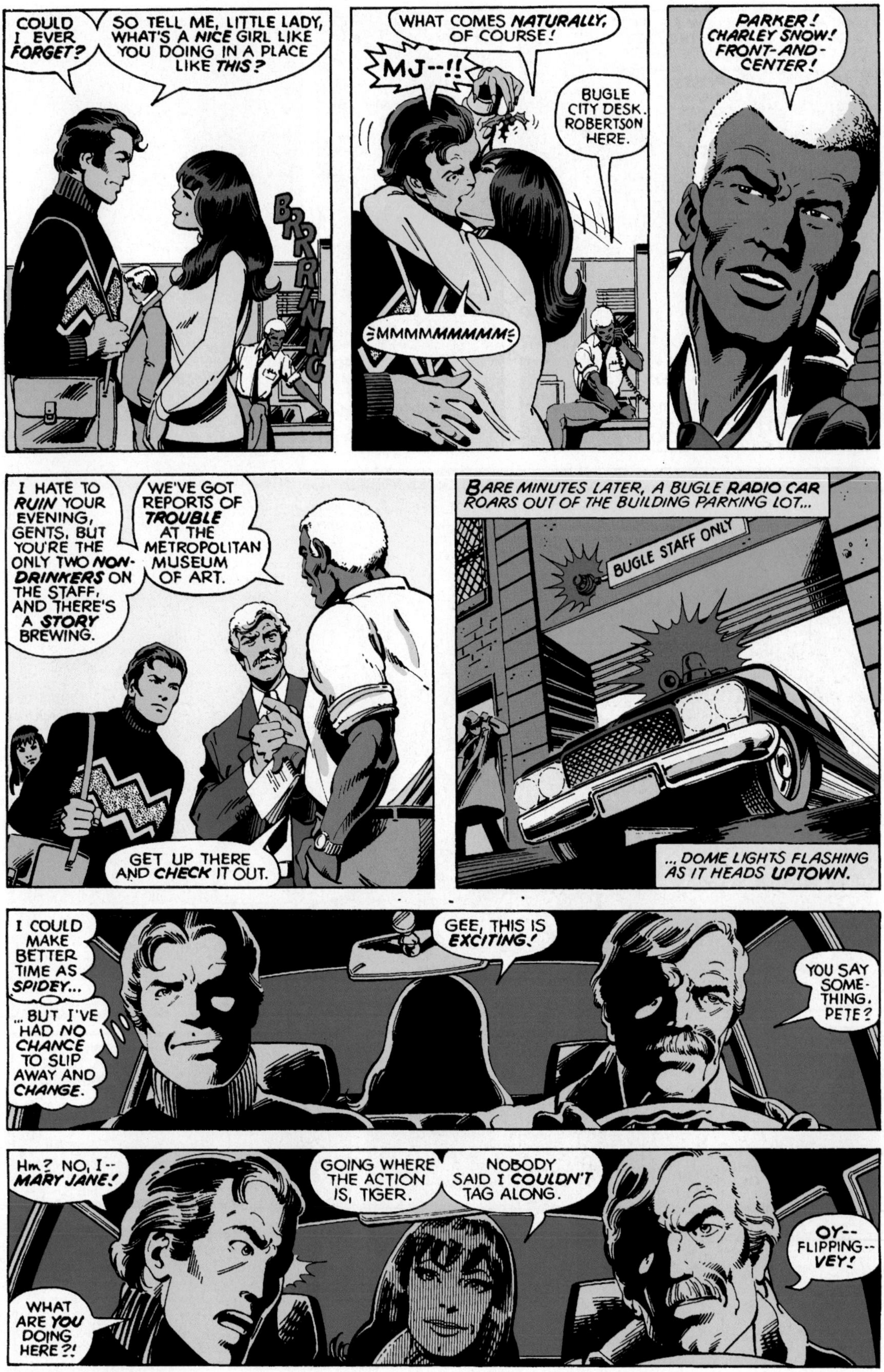

COULD I EVER FORGET?
SO TELL ME, LITTLE LADY, WHAT'S A NICE GIRL LIKE YOU DOING IN A PLACE LIKE THIS?
BRRRRINNNG
WHAT COMES NATURALLY, OF COURSE!
MJ--!!
MMMMMMMMM
BUGLE CITY DESK. ROBERTSON HERE.
PARKER! CHARLEY SNOW! FRONT-AND-CENTER!
I HATE TO RUIN YOUR EVENING, GENTS, BUT YOU'RE THE ONLY TWO NON-DRINKERS ON THE STAFF, AND THERE'S A STORY BREWING.
WE'VE GOT REPORTS OF TROUBLE AT THE METROPOLITAN MUSEUM OF ART.
GET UP THERE AND CHECK IT OUT.
BARE MINUTES LATER, A BUGLE RADIO CAR ROARS OUT OF THE BUILDING PARKING LOT...
BUGLE STAFF ONLY
...DOME LIGHTS FLASHING AS IT HEADS UPTOWN.
I COULD MAKE BETTER TIME AS SPIDEY...
...BUT I'VE HAD NO CHANCE TO SLIP AWAY AND CHANGE.
GEE, THIS IS EXCITING!
YOU SAY SOME-THING, PETE?
Hm? NO, I-- MARY JANE!
WHAT ARE YOU DOING HERE?!
GOING WHERE THE ACTION IS, TIGER.
NOBODY SAID I COULDN'T TAG ALONG.
OY-- FLIPPING-- VEY!

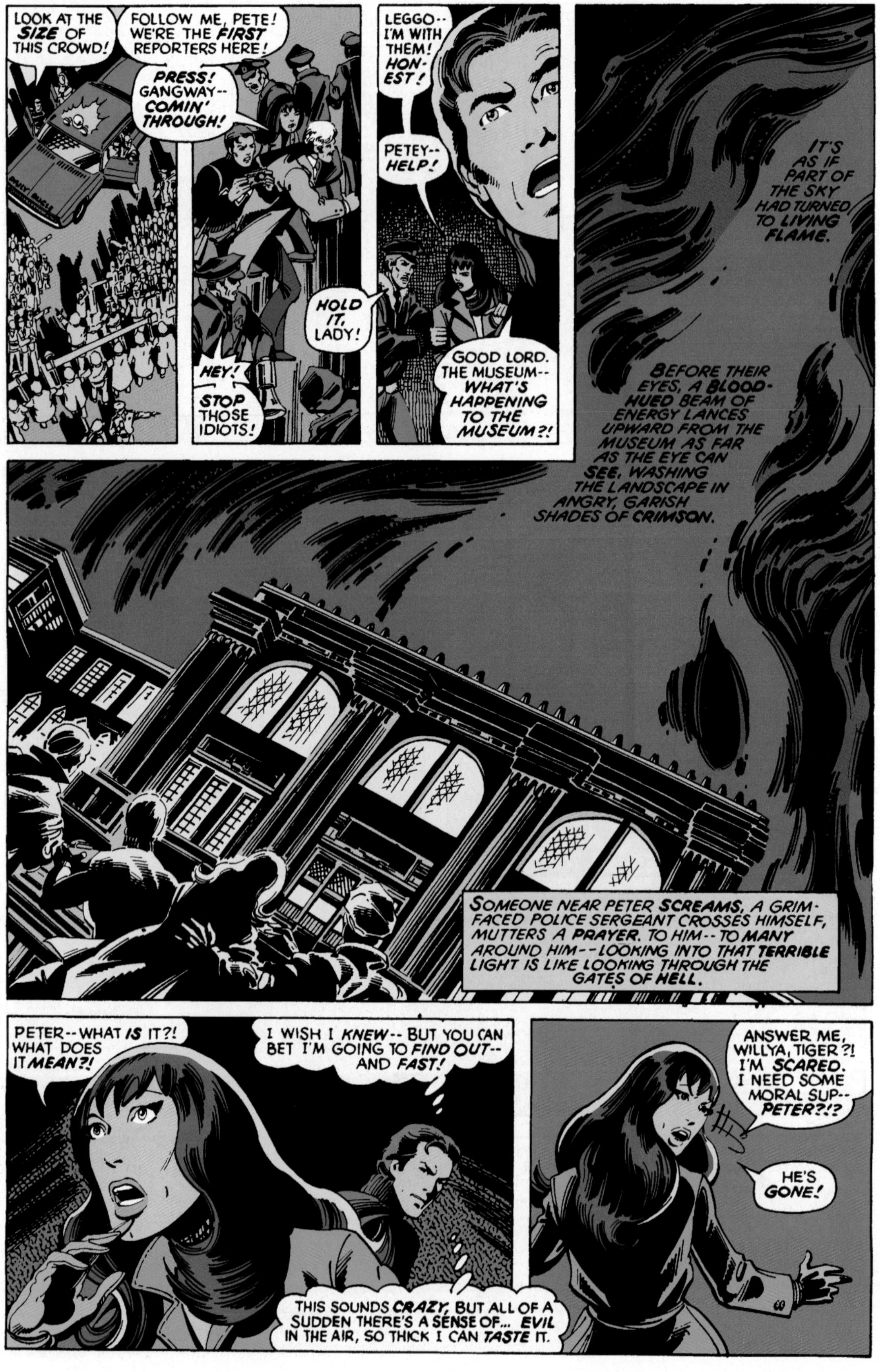
LOOK AT THE SIZE OF THIS CROWD!
FOLLOW ME, PETE! WE'RE THE FIRST REPORTERS HERE!
PRESS! GANGWAY-- COMIN' THROUGH!
HEY! STOP THOSE IDIOTS!
LEGGO-- I'M WITH THEM! HON-EST!
PETEY-- HELP!
HOLD IT, LADY!
GOOD LORD. THE MUSEUM-- WHAT'S HAPPENING TO THE MUSEUM?!
IT'S AS IF PART OF THE SKY HAD TURNED TO LIVING FLAME.
BEFORE THEIR EYES, A BLOOD-HUED BEAM OF ENERGY LANCES UPWARD FROM THE MUSEUM AS FAR AS THE EYE CAN SEE, WASHING THE LANDSCAPE IN ANGRY, GARISH SHADES OF CRIMSON.
SOMEONE NEAR PETER SCREAMS, A GRIM-FACED POLICE SERGEANT CROSSES HIMSELF, MUTTERS A PRAYER. TO HIM--TO MANY AROUND HIM--LOOKING INTO THAT TERRIBLE LIGHT IS LIKE LOOKING THROUGH THE GATES OF HELL.
PETER--WHAT IS IT?! WHAT DOES IT MEAN?!
I WISH I KNEW-- BUT YOU CAN BET I'M GOING TO FIND OUT-- AND FAST!
THIS SOUNDS CRAZY, BUT ALL OF A SUDDEN THERE'S A SENSE OF... EVIL IN THE AIR, SO THICK I CAN TASTE IT.
ANSWER ME, WILLYA, TIGER?! I'M SCARED. I NEED SOME MORAL SUP-- PETER?!?
HE'S GONE!

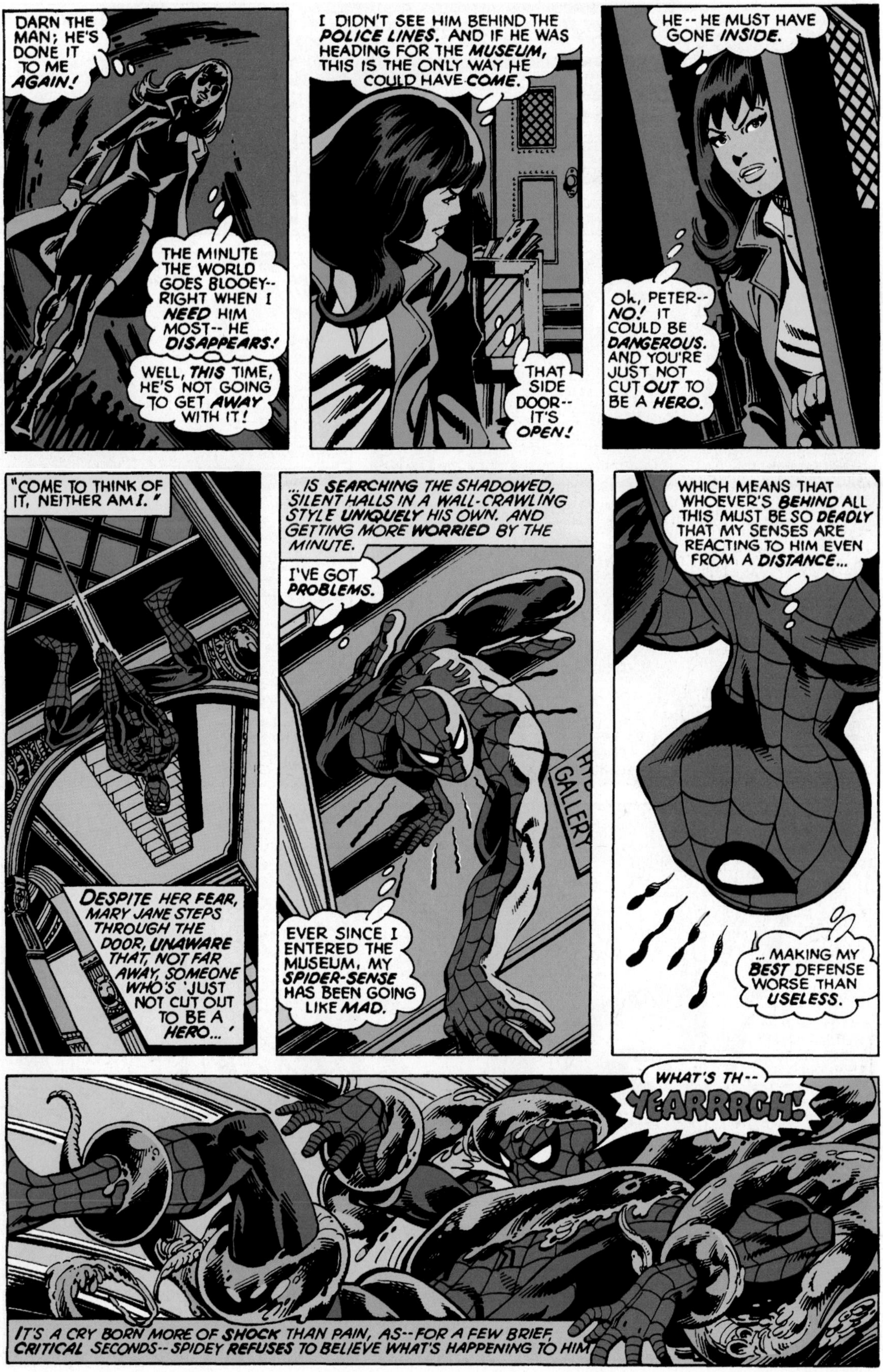
DARN THE MAN; HE'S DONE IT TO ME AGAIN!
THE MINUTE THE WORLD GOES BLOOEY-- RIGHT WHEN I NEED HIM MOST-- HE DISAPPEARS!
WELL, THIS TIME, HE'S NOT GOING TO GET AWAY WITH IT!
I DIDN'T SEE HIM BEHIND THE POLICE LINES. AND IF HE WAS HEADING FOR THE MUSEUM, THIS IS THE ONLY WAY HE COULD HAVE COME.
THAT SIDE DOOR-- IT'S OPEN!
HE-- HE MUST HAVE GONE INSIDE.
Oh, PETER-- NO! IT COULD BE DANGEROUS. AND YOU'RE JUST NOT CUT OUT TO BE A HERO.
"COME TO THINK OF IT, NEITHER AM I."
DESPITE HER FEAR, MARY JANE STEPS THROUGH THE DOOR, UNAWARE THAT, NOT FAR AWAY, SOMEONE WHO'S 'JUST NOT CUT OUT TO BE A HERO...'
...IS SEARCHING THE SHADOWED, SILENT HALLS IN A WALL-CRAWLING STYLE UNIQUELY HIS OWN. AND GETTING MORE WORRIED BY THE MINUTE.
I'VE GOT PROBLEMS.
GALLERY
EVER SINCE I ENTERED THE MUSEUM, MY SPIDER-SENSE HAS BEEN GOING LIKE MAD.
WHICH MEANS THAT WHOEVER'S BEHIND ALL THIS MUST BE SO DEADLY THAT MY SENSES ARE REACTING TO HIM EVEN FROM A DISTANCE...
...MAKING MY BEST DEFENSE WORSE THAN USELESS.
WHAT'S TH--
YEARRRGH!
IT'S A CRY BORN MORE OF SHOCK THAN PAIN, AS--FOR A FEW BRIEF, CRITICAL SECONDS-- SPIDEY REFUSES TO BELIEVE WHAT'S HAPPENING TO HIM

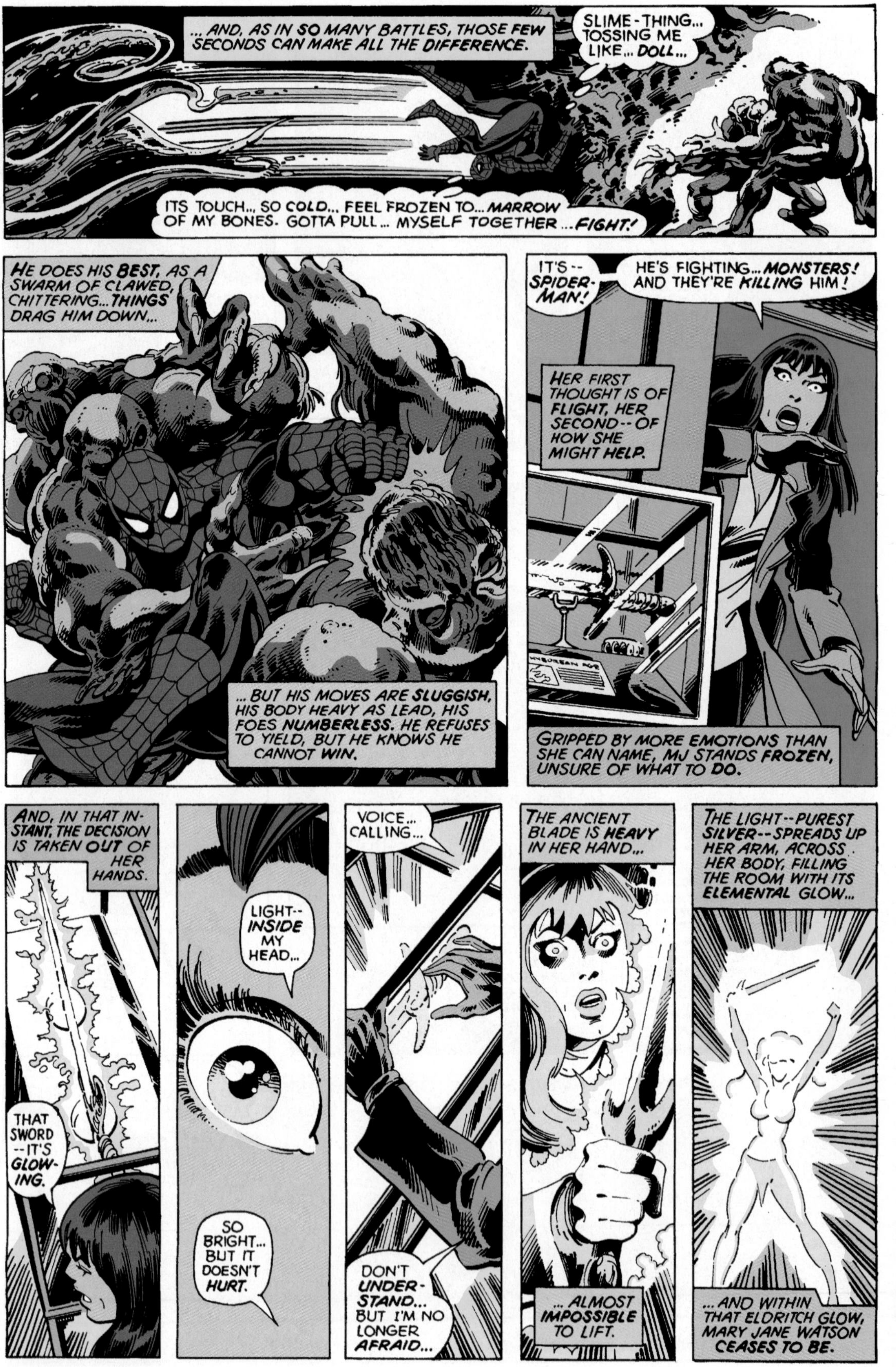

... AND, AS IN SO MANY BATTLES, THOSE FEW SECONDS CAN MAKE ALL THE DIFFERENCE.
SLIME-THING... TOSSING ME LIKE... DOLL...
ITS TOUCH... SO COLD... FEEL FROZEN TO... MARROW OF MY BONES. GOTTA PULL... MYSELF TOGETHER ... FIGHT!
HE DOES HIS BEST, AS A SWARM OF CLAWED, CHITTERING... THINGS DRAG HIM DOWN...
... BUT HIS MOVES ARE SLUGGISH, HIS BODY HEAVY AS LEAD, HIS FOES NUMBERLESS. HE REFUSES TO YIELD, BUT HE KNOWS HE CANNOT WIN.
IT'S -- SPIDER-MAN!
HE'S FIGHTING... MONSTERS! AND THEY'RE KILLING HIM!
HER FIRST THOUGHT IS OF FLIGHT, HER SECOND -- OF HOW SHE MIGHT HELP.
GRIPPED BY MORE EMOTIONS THAN SHE CAN NAME, MJ STANDS FROZEN, UNSURE OF WHAT TO DO.
AND, IN THAT INSTANT, THE DECISION IS TAKEN OUT OF HER HANDS.
THAT SWORD -- IT'S GLOWING.
LIGHT-- INSIDE MY HEAD...
SO BRIGHT... BUT IT DOESN'T HURT.
VOICE... CALLING...
DON'T UNDERSTAND... BUT I'M NO LONGER AFRAID...
THE ANCIENT BLADE IS HEAVY IN HER HAND...
... ALMOST IMPOSSIBLE TO LIFT.
THE LIGHT -- PUREST SILVER -- SPREADS UP HER ARM, ACROSS HER BODY, FILLING THE ROOM WITH ITS ELEMENTAL GLOW...
... AND WITHIN THAT ELDRITCH GLOW, MARY JANE WATSON CEASES TO BE.

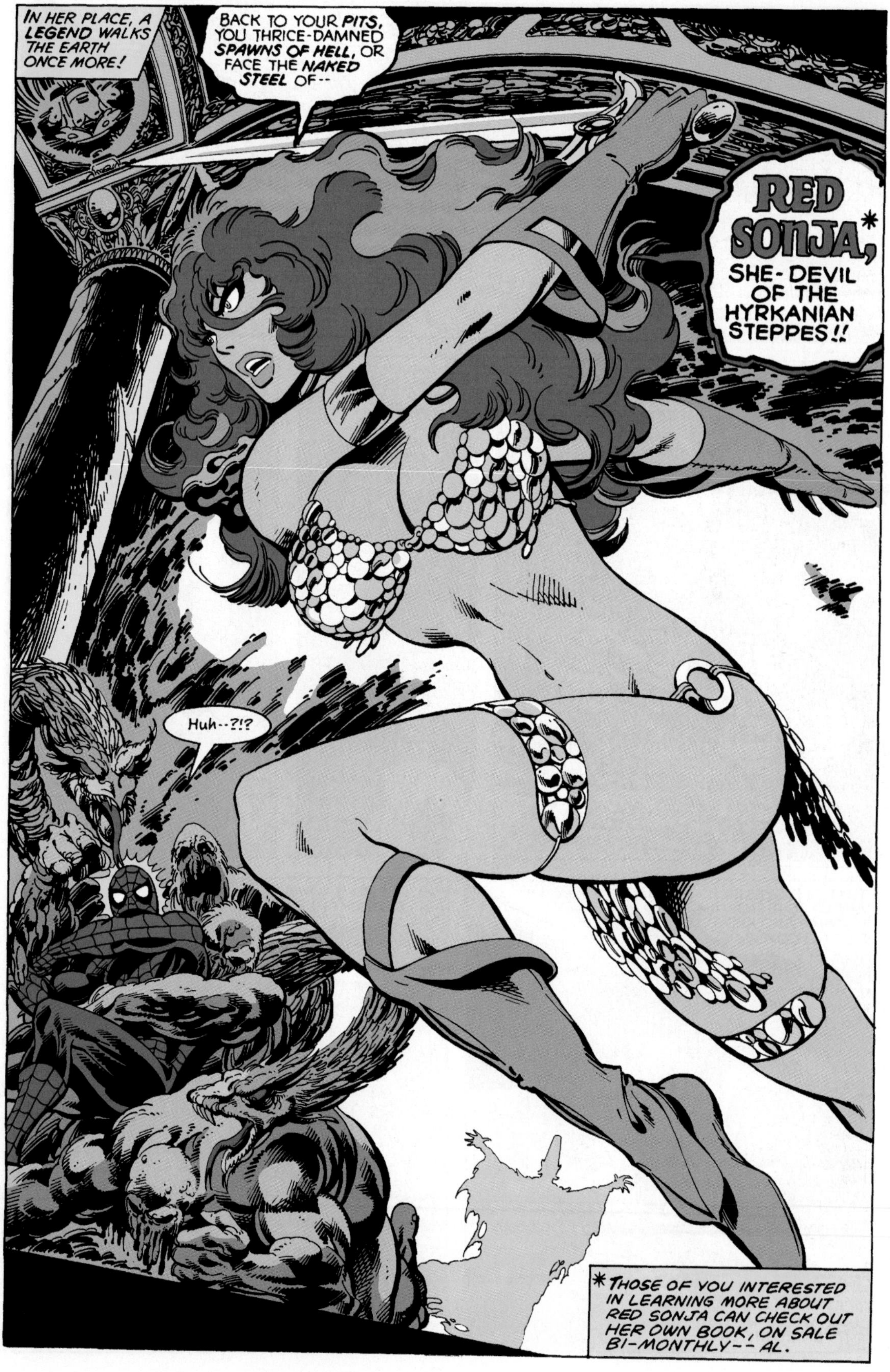

IN HER PLACE, A LEGEND WALKS THE EARTH ONCE MORE!
BACK TO YOUR PITS, YOU THRICE-DAMNED SPAWNS OF HELL, OR FACE THE NAKED STEEL OF--
RED SONJA,* SHE-DEVIL OF THE HYRKANIAN STEPPES!!
Huh--?!?
*THOSE OF YOU INTERESTED IN LEARNING MORE ABOUT RED SONJA CAN CHECK OUT HER OWN BOOK, ON SALE BI-MONTHLY-- AL.

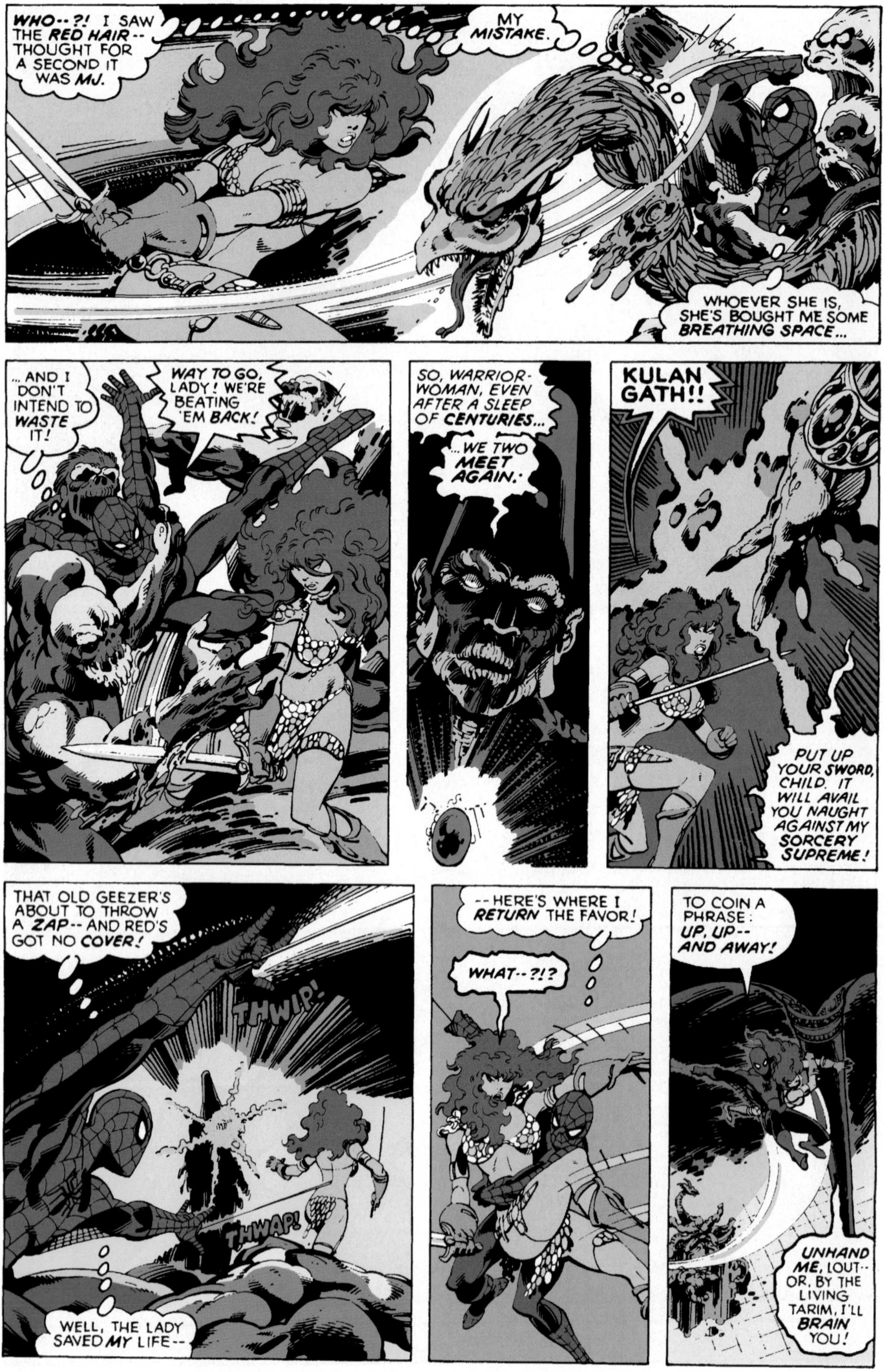
WHO--?! I SAW THE RED HAIR-- THOUGHT FOR A SECOND IT WAS MJ.
MY MISTAKE.
WHOEVER SHE IS, SHE'S BOUGHT ME SOME BREATHING SPACE...
...AND I DON'T INTEND TO WASTE IT!
WAY TO GO, LADY! WE'RE BEATING 'EM BACK!
SO, WARRIOR-WOMAN, EVEN AFTER A SLEEP OF CENTURIES...
...WE TWO MEET AGAIN.
KULAN GATH!!
PUT UP YOUR SWORD, CHILD. IT WILL AVAIL YOU NAUGHT AGAINST MY SORCERY SUPREME!
THAT OLD GEEZER'S ABOUT TO THROW A ZAP-- AND RED'S GOT NO COVER!
THWIP!
THWAP!
WELL, THE LADY SAVED MY LIFE--
--HERE'S WHERE I RETURN THE FAVOR!
WHAT--?!?
TO COIN A PHRASE: UP, UP-- AND AWAY!
UNHAND ME, LOUT-- OR, BY THE LIVING TARIM, I'LL BRAIN YOU!

ISHTAR'S GIRDLE! I THOUGHT THIS MERELY A *WARRIOR* CLAD IN SOME *OUTLANDISH* HARNESS.

BUT HE *RUNS* UP THE WALL-- ACROSS THE CEILING--LIKE SOME HUMAN *SPIDER!*

QUIT *STRUGGLING*, LADY--OH, WHAT'S THE *USE*?! SHE DOESN'T SPEAK *ENGLISH*, AND HER LANGUAGE SOUNDS LIKE *GIBBERISH* TO ME.

BETTER TRY SOMETHING ELSE-- *HABLES ESPANOL? PARLEZ-VOUS FRANCAIS?* UH... *SPRECHEN SIE DEUTSCH?* NO DICE.

MITRA TAKE ME FOR A *FOOL!* THIS CAN'T BE A *MAN!*

HEY! WHAT'RE YOU DO-- *UNNNGNH!*

YOU MAY *HAVE* ME, MONSTER. BUT YOU'LL NOT *KEEP* ME WITHOUT A *FIGHT!*

YOU... *CRAZY--!* DON'T HIT-- YOU'LL MAKE US...

*SAAAAA!*

*THWIP!*

IT'S ANOTHER OF KULAN GATH'S *DEMONS*, WEARING A MAN'S *SHAPE!* AND I PLAYED RIGHT INTO ITS *HANDS!*

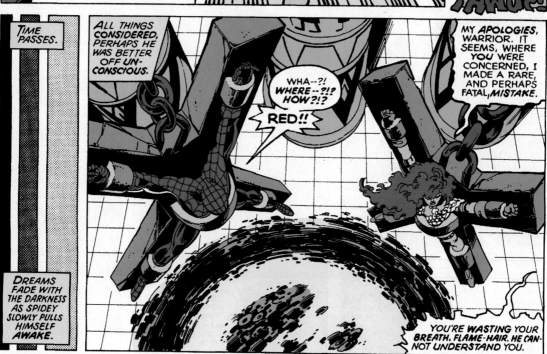

TIME PASSES.

DREAMS FADE WITH THE DARKNESS AS SPIDEY SLOWLY PULLS HIMSELF AWAKE.

ALL THINGS CONSIDERED, PERHAPS HE WAS BETTER OFF UNCONSCIOUS.

WHA--?! WHERE-- ?!? HOW?!?

*RED!!*

MY *APOLOGIES*, WARRIOR. IT SEEMS, WHERE *YOU* WERE CONCERNED, I MADE A RARE, AND PERHAPS FATAL, *MISTAKE.*

YOU'RE *WASTING* YOUR BREATH, FLAME-HAIR. HE CANNOT UNDERSTAND YOU.

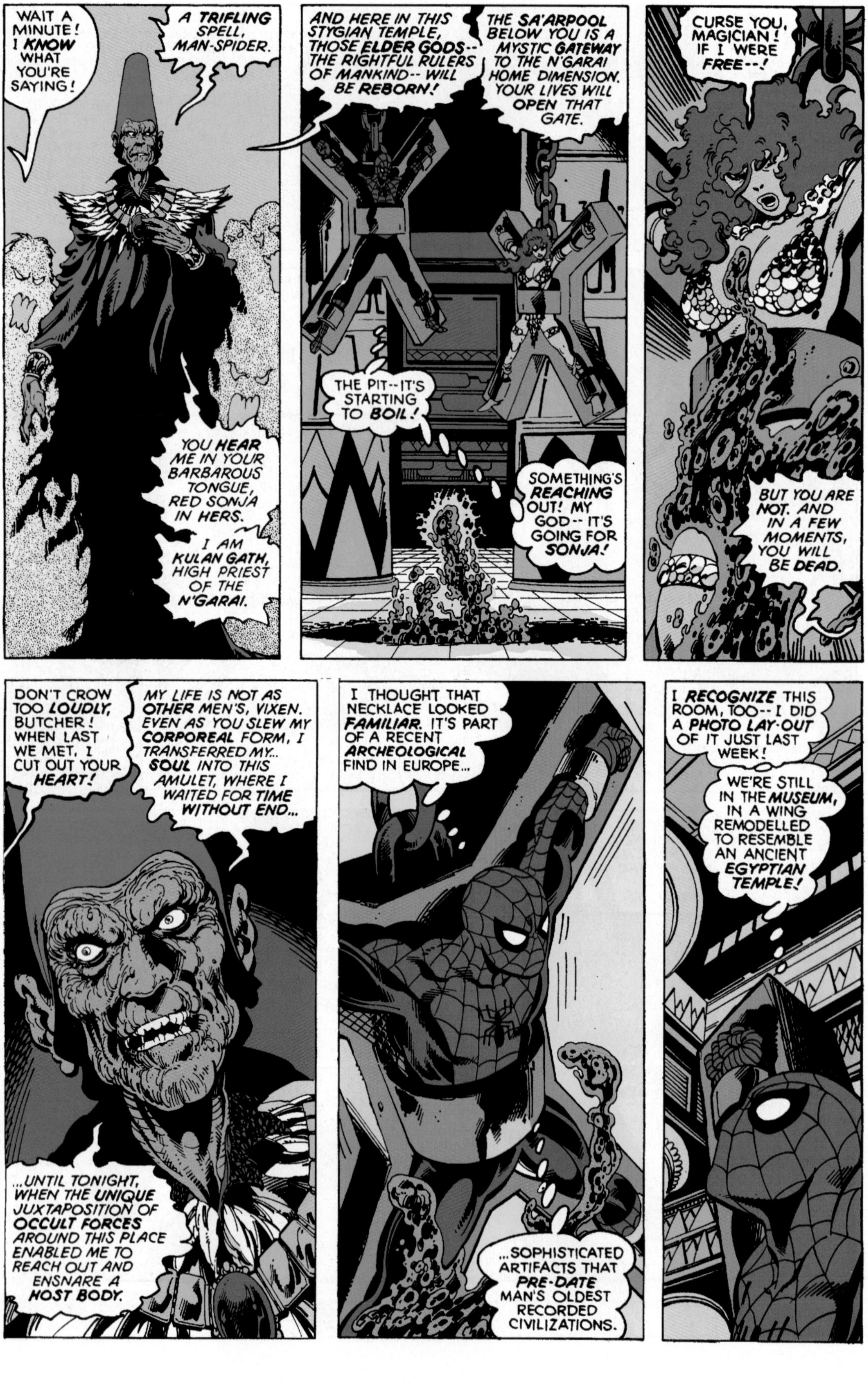

WAIT A MINUTE! I KNOW WHAT YOU'RE SAYING!
A TRIFLING SPELL, MAN-SPIDER.
YOU HEAR ME IN YOUR BARBAROUS TONGUE, RED SONJA IN HERS.
I AM KULAN GATH, HIGH PRIEST OF THE N'GARAI.
AND HERE IN THIS STYGIAN TEMPLE, THOSE ELDER GODS-- THE RIGHTFUL RULERS OF MANKIND-- WILL BE REBORN!
THE SA'ARPOOL BELOW YOU IS A MYSTIC GATEWAY TO THE N'GARAI HOME DIMENSION. YOUR LIVES WILL OPEN THAT GATE.
THE PIT--IT'S STARTING TO BOIL!
SOMETHING'S REACHING OUT! MY GOD-- IT'S GOING FOR SONJA!
CURSE YOU, MAGICIAN! IF I WERE FREE--!
BUT YOU ARE NOT. AND IN A FEW MOMENTS, YOU WILL BE DEAD.
DON'T CROW TOO LOUDLY, BUTCHER! WHEN LAST WE MET, I CUT OUT YOUR HEART!
MY LIFE IS NOT AS OTHER MEN'S, VIXEN. EVEN AS YOU SLEW MY CORPOREAL FORM, I TRANSFERRED MY... SOUL INTO THIS AMULET, WHERE I WAITED FOR TIME WITHOUT END...
...UNTIL TONIGHT, WHEN THE UNIQUE JUXTAPOSITION OF OCCULT FORCES AROUND THIS PLACE ENABLED ME TO REACH OUT AND ENSNARE A HOST BODY.
I THOUGHT THAT NECKLACE LOOKED FAMILIAR. IT'S PART OF A RECENT ARCHEOLOGICAL FIND IN EUROPE...
...SOPHISTICATED ARTIFACTS THAT PRE-DATE MAN'S OLDEST RECORDED CIVILIZATIONS.
I RECOGNIZE THIS ROOM, TOO-- I DID A PHOTO LAY-OUT OF IT JUST LAST WEEK!
WE'RE STILL IN THE MUSEUM, IN A WING REMODELLED TO RESEMBLE AN ANCIENT EGYPTIAN TEMPLE!

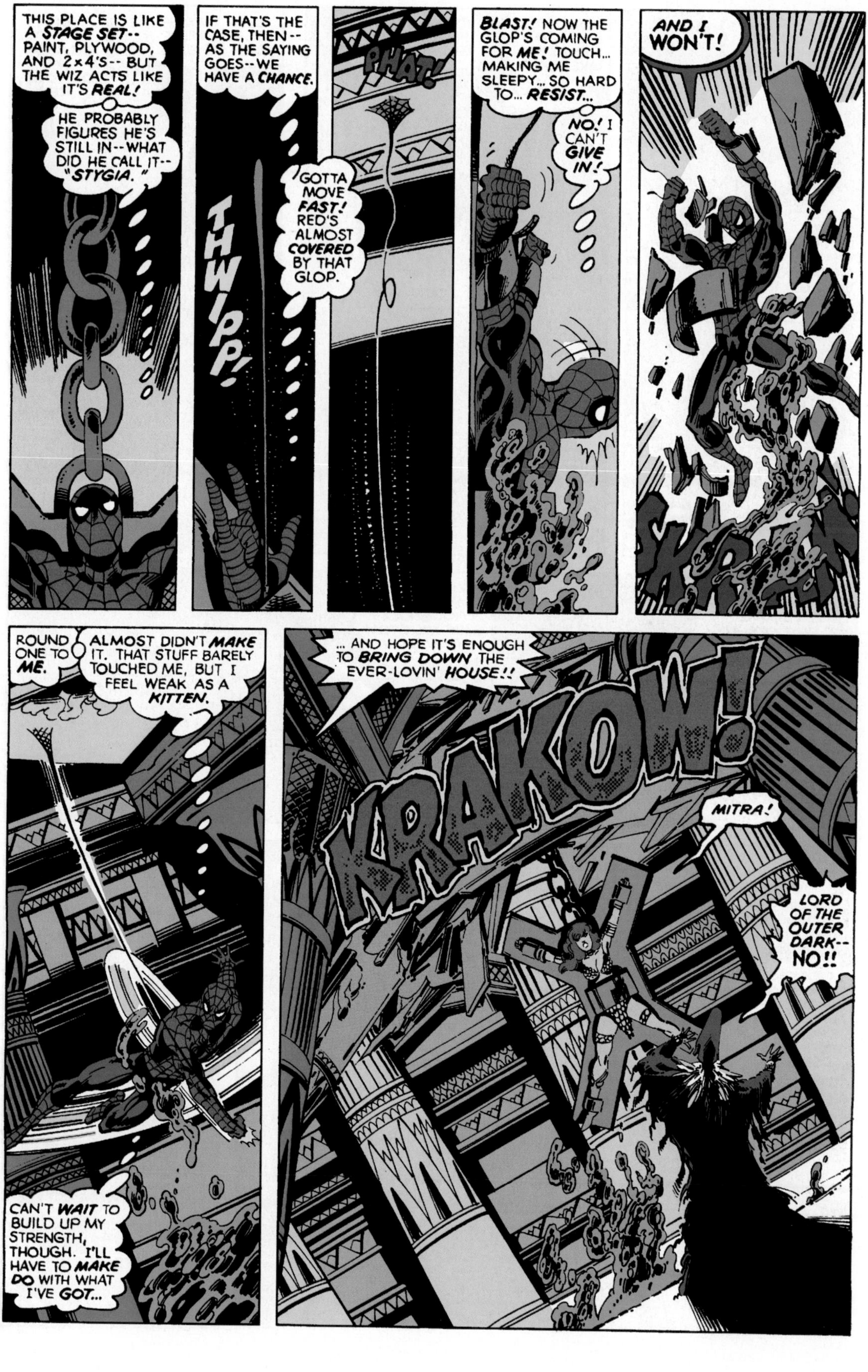
THIS PLACE IS LIKE A STAGE SET-- PAINT, PLYWOOD, AND 2x4'S-- BUT THE WIZ ACTS LIKE IT'S REAL!
HE PROBABLY FIGURES HE'S STILL IN--WHAT DID HE CALL IT-- "STYGIA."
IF THAT'S THE CASE, THEN-- AS THE SAYING GOES--WE HAVE A CHANCE.
THWIPP!
PHAT!
GOTTA MOVE FAST! RED'S ALMOST COVERED BY THAT GLOP.
BLAST! NOW THE GLOP'S COMING FOR ME! TOUCH... MAKING ME SLEEPY... SO HARD TO... RESIST...
NO! I CAN'T GIVE IN!
AND I WON'T!
SKREEEM
ROUND ONE TO ME.
ALMOST DIDN'T MAKE IT. THAT STUFF BARELY TOUCHED ME, BUT I FEEL WEAK AS A KITTEN.
CAN'T WAIT TO BUILD UP MY STRENGTH, THOUGH. I'LL HAVE TO MAKE DO WITH WHAT I'VE GOT...
... AND HOPE IT'S ENOUGH TO BRING DOWN THE EVER-LOVIN' HOUSE!!
KRAKOW!
MITRA!
LORD OF THE OUTER DARK-- NO!!

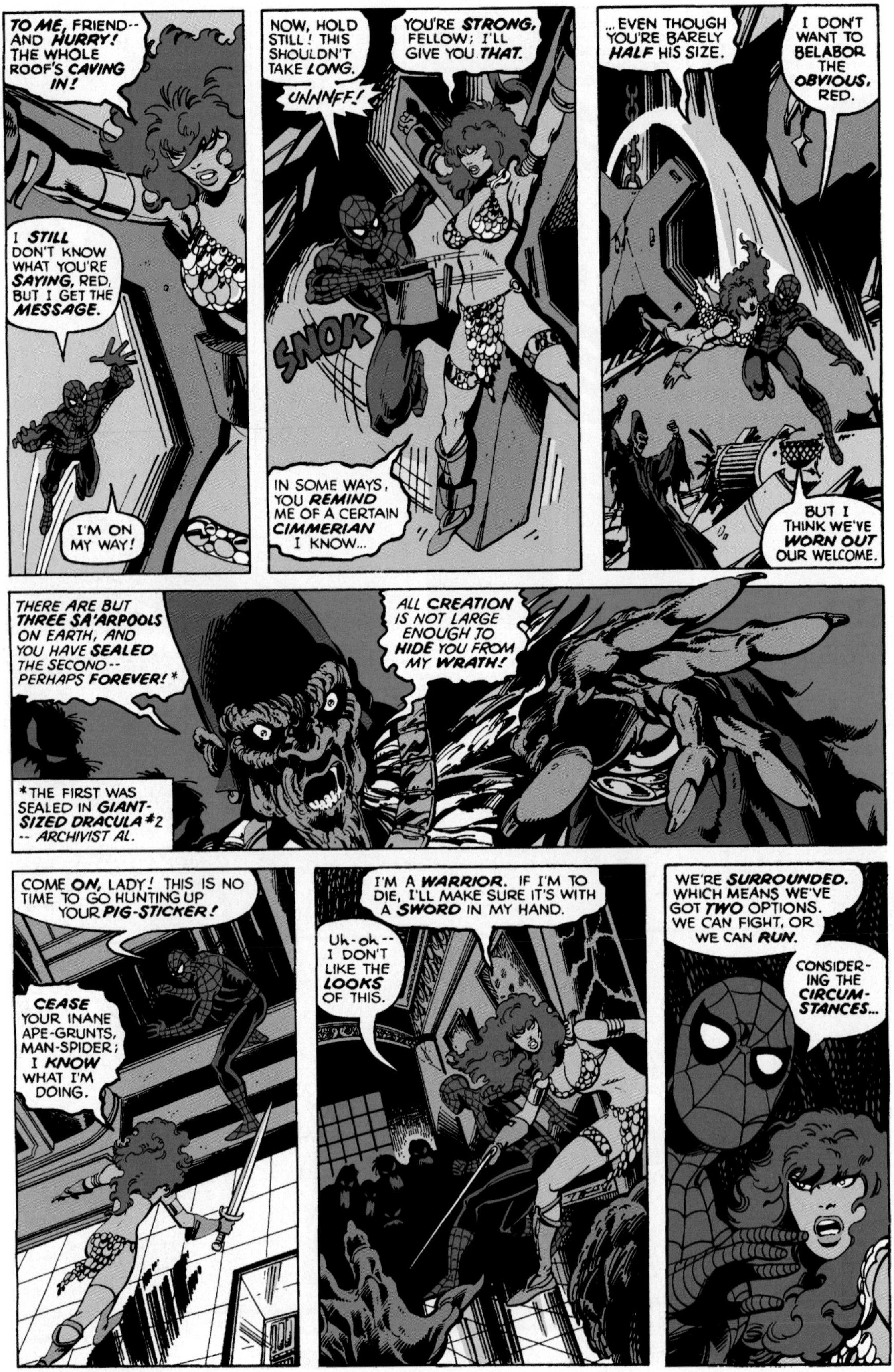
TO ME, FRIEND-- AND HURRY! THE WHOLE ROOF'S CAVING IN!
I STILL DON'T KNOW WHAT YOU'RE SAYING, RED, BUT I GET THE MESSAGE.
I'M ON MY WAY!
NOW, HOLD STILL! THIS SHOULDN'T TAKE LONG.
YOU'RE STRONG, FELLOW; I'LL GIVE YOU THAT.
UNNNFF!
SNOK
IN SOME WAYS, YOU REMIND ME OF A CERTAIN CIMMERIAN I KNOW...
...EVEN THOUGH YOU'RE BARELY HALF HIS SIZE.
I DON'T WANT TO BELABOR THE OBVIOUS, RED.
BUT I THINK WE'VE WORN OUT OUR WELCOME.
THERE ARE BUT THREE SA'ARPOOLS ON EARTH, AND YOU HAVE SEALED THE SECOND -- PERHAPS FOREVER! *
ALL CREATION IS NOT LARGE ENOUGH TO HIDE YOU FROM MY WRATH!
*THE FIRST WAS SEALED IN GIANT-SIZED DRACULA #2 -- ARCHIVIST AL.
COME ON, LADY! THIS IS NO TIME TO GO HUNTING UP YOUR PIG-STICKER!
CEASE YOUR INANE APE-GRUNTS, MAN-SPIDER; I KNOW WHAT I'M DOING.
I'M A WARRIOR. IF I'M TO DIE, I'LL MAKE SURE IT'S WITH A SWORD IN MY HAND.
Uh-oh -- I DON'T LIKE THE LOOKS OF THIS.
WE'RE SURROUNDED. WHICH MEANS WE'VE GOT TWO OPTIONS. WE CAN FIGHT, OR WE CAN RUN.
CONSIDERING THE CIRCUMSTANCES...

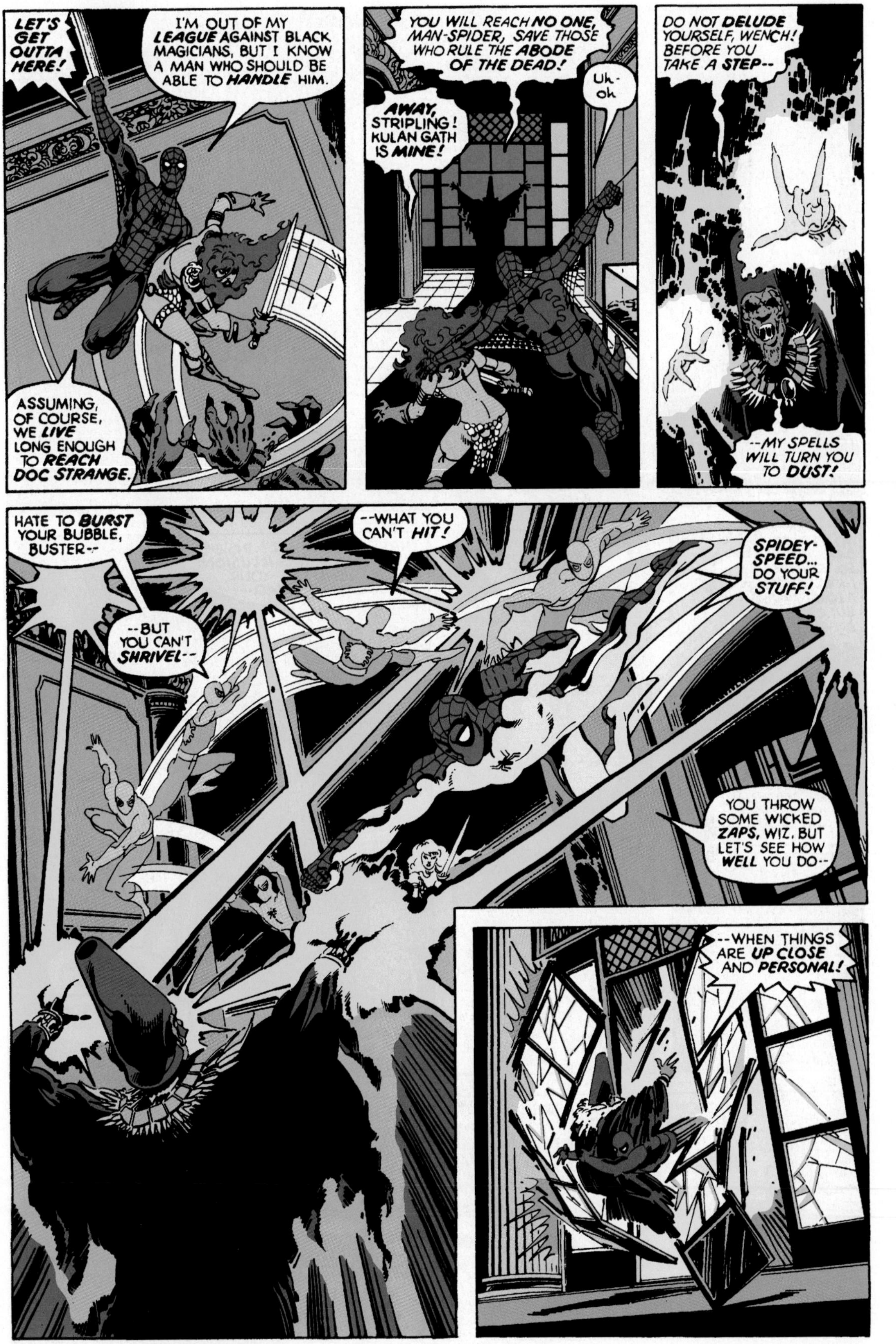
LET'S GET OUTTA HERE!
I'M OUT OF MY LEAGUE AGAINST BLACK MAGICIANS, BUT I KNOW A MAN WHO SHOULD BE ABLE TO HANDLE HIM.
ASSUMING, OF COURSE, WE LIVE LONG ENOUGH TO REACH DOC STRANGE.
YOU WILL REACH NO ONE, MAN-SPIDER, SAVE THOSE WHO RULE THE ABODE OF THE DEAD!
Uh-oh
AWAY, STRIPLING! KULAN GATH IS MINE!
DO NOT DELUDE YOURSELF, WENCH! BEFORE YOU TAKE A STEP--
--MY SPELLS WILL TURN YOU TO DUST!
HATE TO BURST YOUR BUBBLE, BUSTER--
--BUT YOU CAN'T SHRIVEL--
--WHAT YOU CAN'T HIT!
SPIDEY-SPEED... DO YOUR STUFF!
YOU THROW SOME WICKED ZAPS, WIZ. BUT LET'S SEE HOW WELL YOU DO--
--WHEN THINGS ARE UP CLOSE AND PERSONAL!

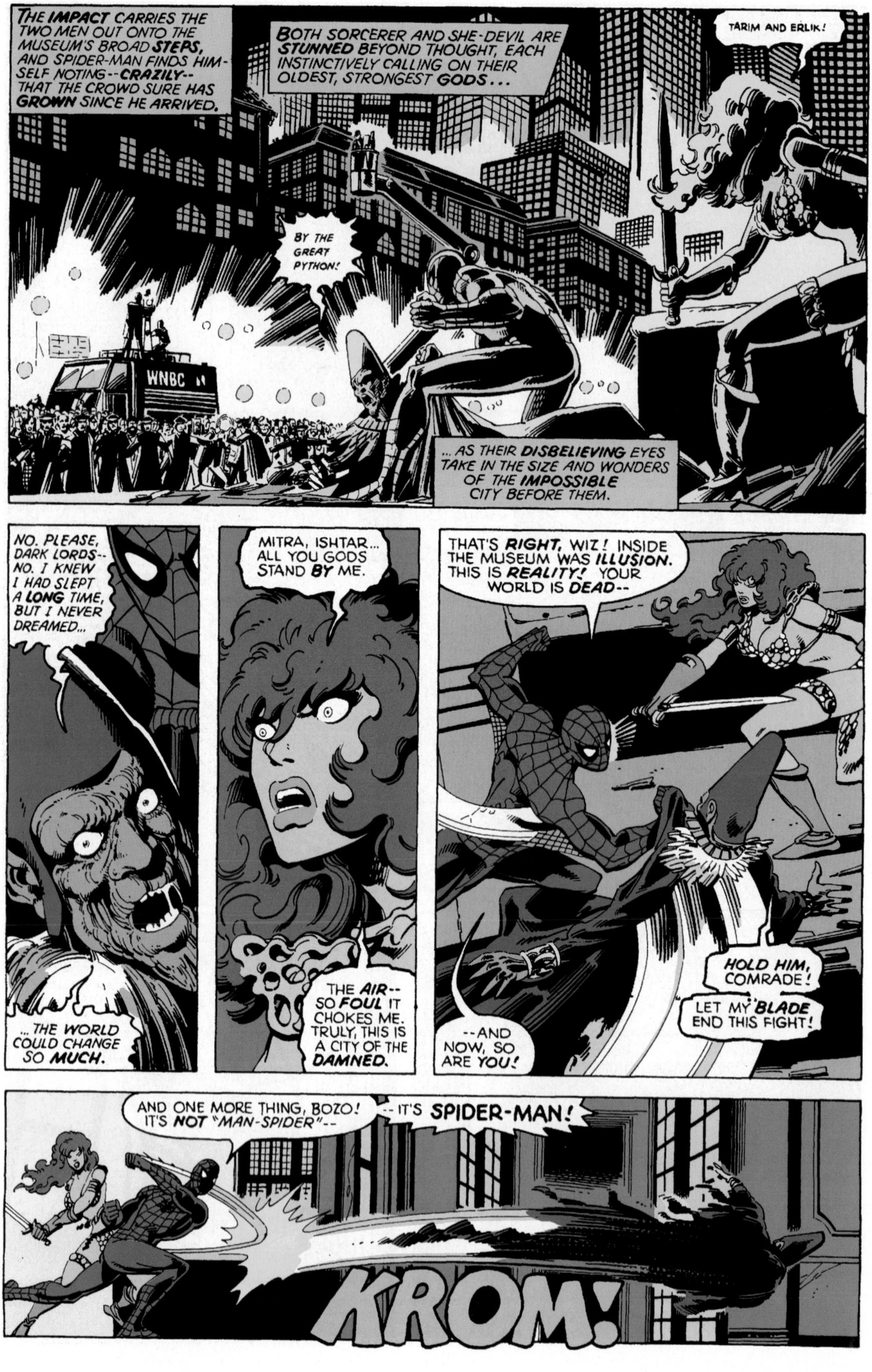
THE IMPACT CARRIES THE TWO MEN OUT ONTO THE MUSEUM'S BROAD STEPS, AND SPIDER-MAN FINDS HIMSELF NOTING--CRAZILY--THAT THE CROWD SURE HAS GROWN SINCE HE ARRIVED.
BOTH SORCERER AND SHE-DEVIL ARE STUNNED BEYOND THOUGHT, EACH INSTINCTIVELY CALLING ON THEIR OLDEST, STRONGEST GODS...
TARIM AND ERLIK!
BY THE GREAT PYTHON!
WNBC
...AS THEIR DISBELIEVING EYES TAKE IN THE SIZE AND WONDERS OF THE IMPOSSIBLE CITY BEFORE THEM.
NO. PLEASE, DARK LORDS--NO. I KNEW I HAD SLEPT A LONG TIME, BUT I NEVER DREAMED...
...THE WORLD COULD CHANGE SO MUCH.
MITRA, ISHTAR... ALL YOU GODS STAND BY ME.
THE AIR--SO FOUL IT CHOKES ME. TRULY, THIS IS A CITY OF THE DAMNED.
THAT'S RIGHT, WIZ! INSIDE THE MUSEUM WAS ILLUSION. THIS IS REALITY! YOUR WORLD IS DEAD--
--AND NOW, SO ARE YOU!
HOLD HIM, COMRADE!
LET MY BLADE END THIS FIGHT!
AND ONE MORE THING, BOZO! IT'S NOT "MAN-SPIDER"--
--IT'S SPIDER-MAN!
KROM!

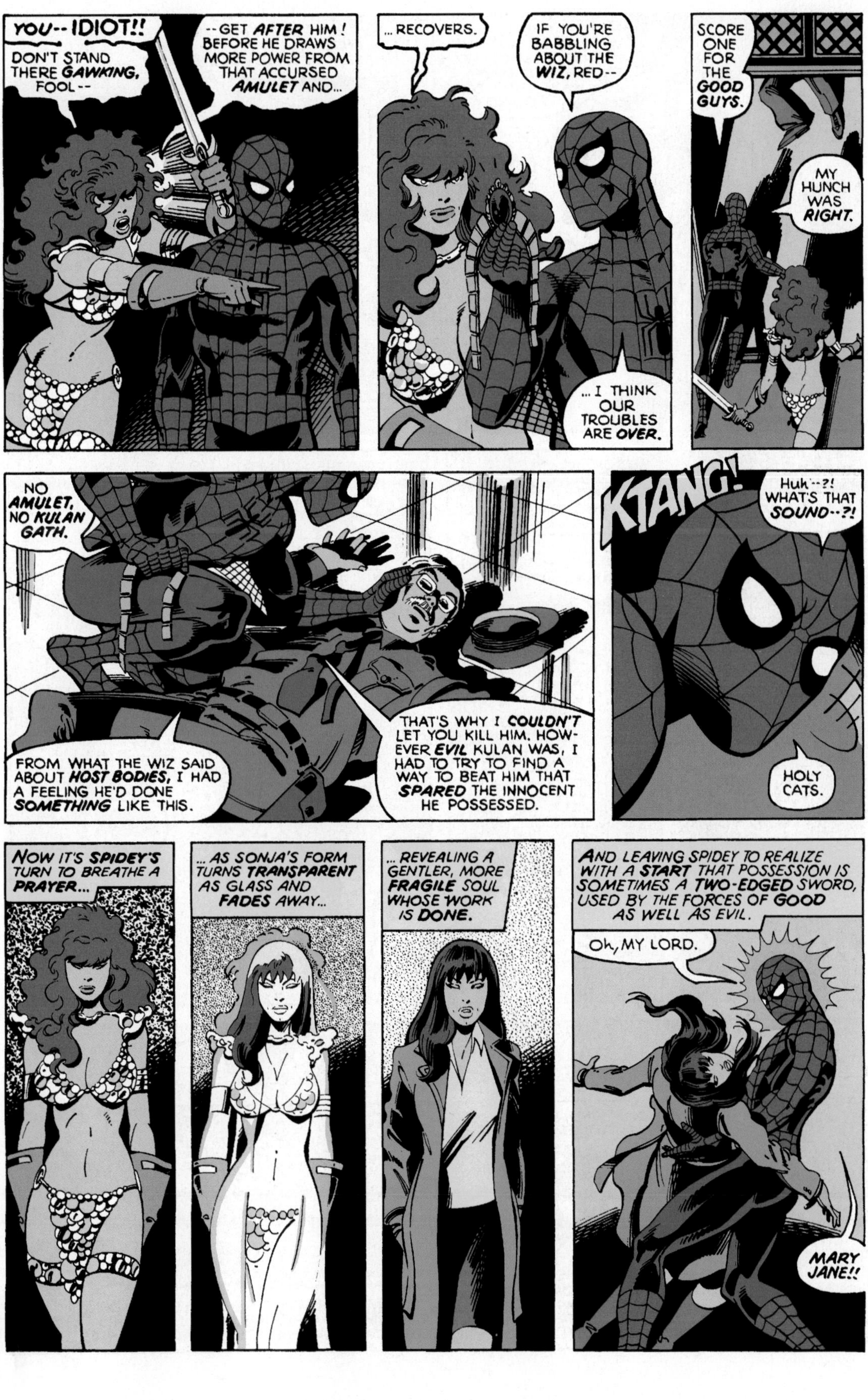
YOU--IDIOT!!
DON'T STAND THERE GAWKING, FOOL--
--GET AFTER HIM! BEFORE HE DRAWS MORE POWER FROM THAT ACCURSED AMULET AND...
...RECOVERS.
IF YOU'RE BABBLING ABOUT THE WIZ, RED--
...I THINK OUR TROUBLES ARE OVER.
SCORE ONE FOR THE GOOD GUYS.
MY HUNCH WAS RIGHT.
NO AMULET, NO KULAN GATH.
FROM WHAT THE WIZ SAID ABOUT HOST BODIES, I HAD A FEELING HE'D DONE SOMETHING LIKE THIS.
THAT'S WHY I COULDN'T LET YOU KILL HIM. HOWEVER EVIL KULAN WAS, I HAD TO TRY TO FIND A WAY TO BEAT HIM THAT SPARED THE INNOCENT HE POSSESSED.
KTANG!
Huh--?! WHAT'S THAT SOUND--?!
HOLY CATS.
NOW IT'S SPIDEY'S TURN TO BREATHE A PRAYER...
...AS SONJA'S FORM TURNS TRANSPARENT AS GLASS AND FADES AWAY...
...REVEALING A GENTLER, MORE FRAGILE SOUL WHOSE WORK IS DONE.
AND LEAVING SPIDEY TO REALIZE WITH A START THAT POSSESSION IS SOMETIMES A TWO-EDGED SWORD, USED BY THE FORCES OF GOOD AS WELL AS EVIL.
Oh, MY LORD.
MARY JANE!!

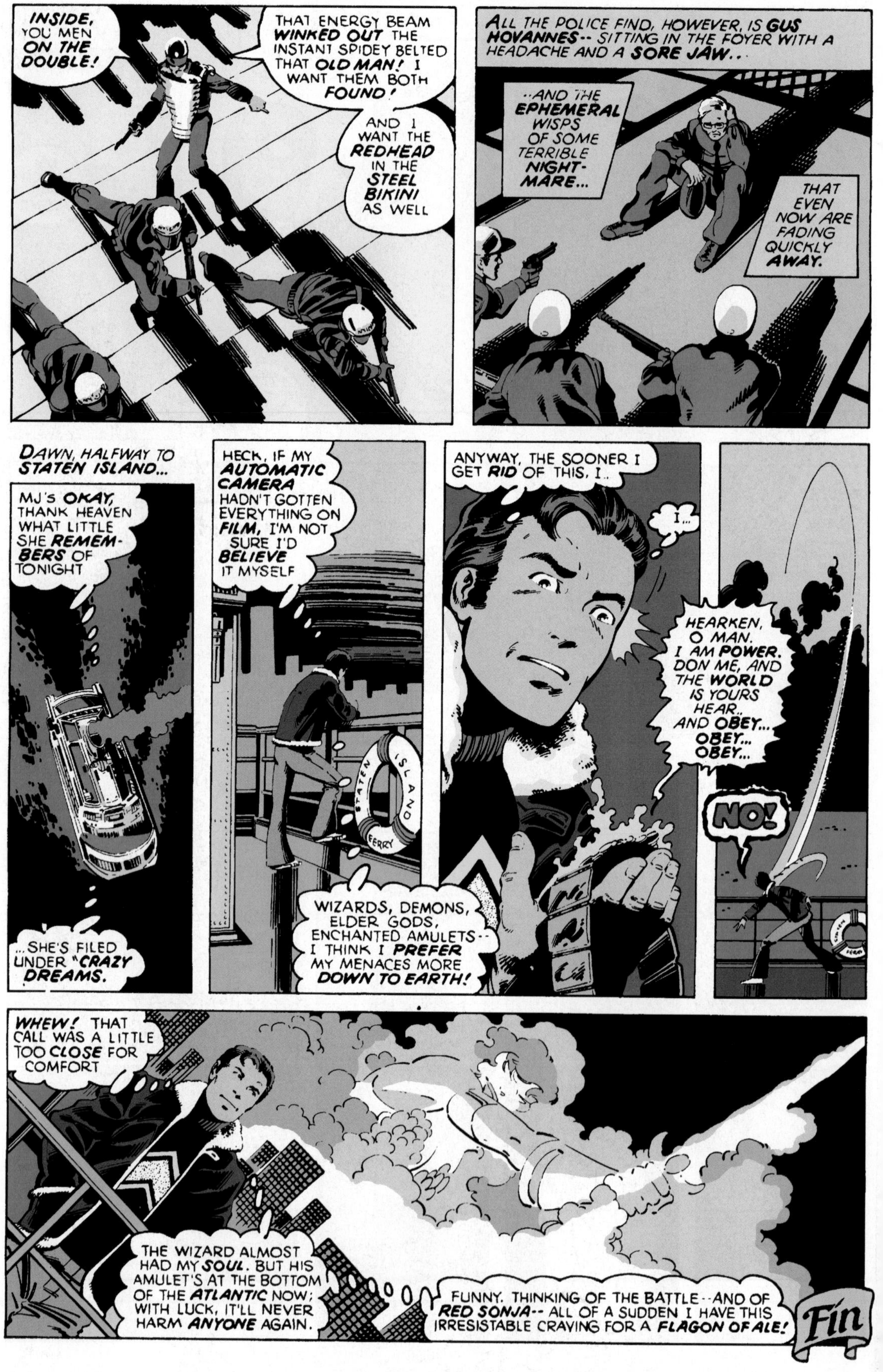
INSIDE, YOU MEN ON THE DOUBLE!
THAT ENERGY BEAM WINKED OUT THE INSTANT SPIDEY BELTED THAT OLD MAN! I WANT THEM BOTH FOUND!
AND I WANT THE REDHEAD IN THE STEEL BIKINI AS WELL
ALL THE POLICE FIND, HOWEVER, IS GUS HOVANNES-- SITTING IN THE FOYER WITH A HEADACHE AND A SORE JAW..
..AND THE EPHEMERAL WISPS OF SOME TERRIBLE NIGHT-MARE...
THAT EVEN NOW ARE FADING QUICKLY AWAY.
DAWN, HALFWAY TO STATEN ISLAND...
MJ'S OKAY, THANK HEAVEN WHAT LITTLE SHE REMEM-BERS OF TONIGHT
...SHE'S FILED UNDER "CRAZY DREAMS.
HECK, IF MY AUTOMATIC CAMERA HADN'T GOTTEN EVERYTHING ON FILM, I'M NOT SURE I'D BELIEVE IT MYSELF
STATEN ISLAND FERRY
WIZARDS, DEMONS, ELDER GODS, ENCHANTED AMULETS-- I THINK I PREFER MY MENACES MORE DOWN TO EARTH!
ANYWAY, THE SOONER I GET RID OF THIS, I..
I...
HEARKEN, O MAN. I AM POWER. DON ME, AND THE WORLD IS YOURS HEAR.. AND OBEY... OBEY... OBEY...
NO!
WHEW! THAT CALL WAS A LITTLE TOO CLOSE FOR COMFORT
THE WIZARD ALMOST HAD MY SOUL. BUT HIS AMULET'S AT THE BOTTOM OF THE ATLANTIC NOW; WITH LUCK, IT'LL NEVER HARM ANYONE AGAIN.
FUNNY. THINKING OF THE BATTLE--AND OF RED SONJA-- ALL OF A SUDDEN I HAVE THIS IRRESISTABLE CRAVING FOR A FLAGON OF ALE!
Fin

# CHARACTER SKETCHES
*by mel rubi*

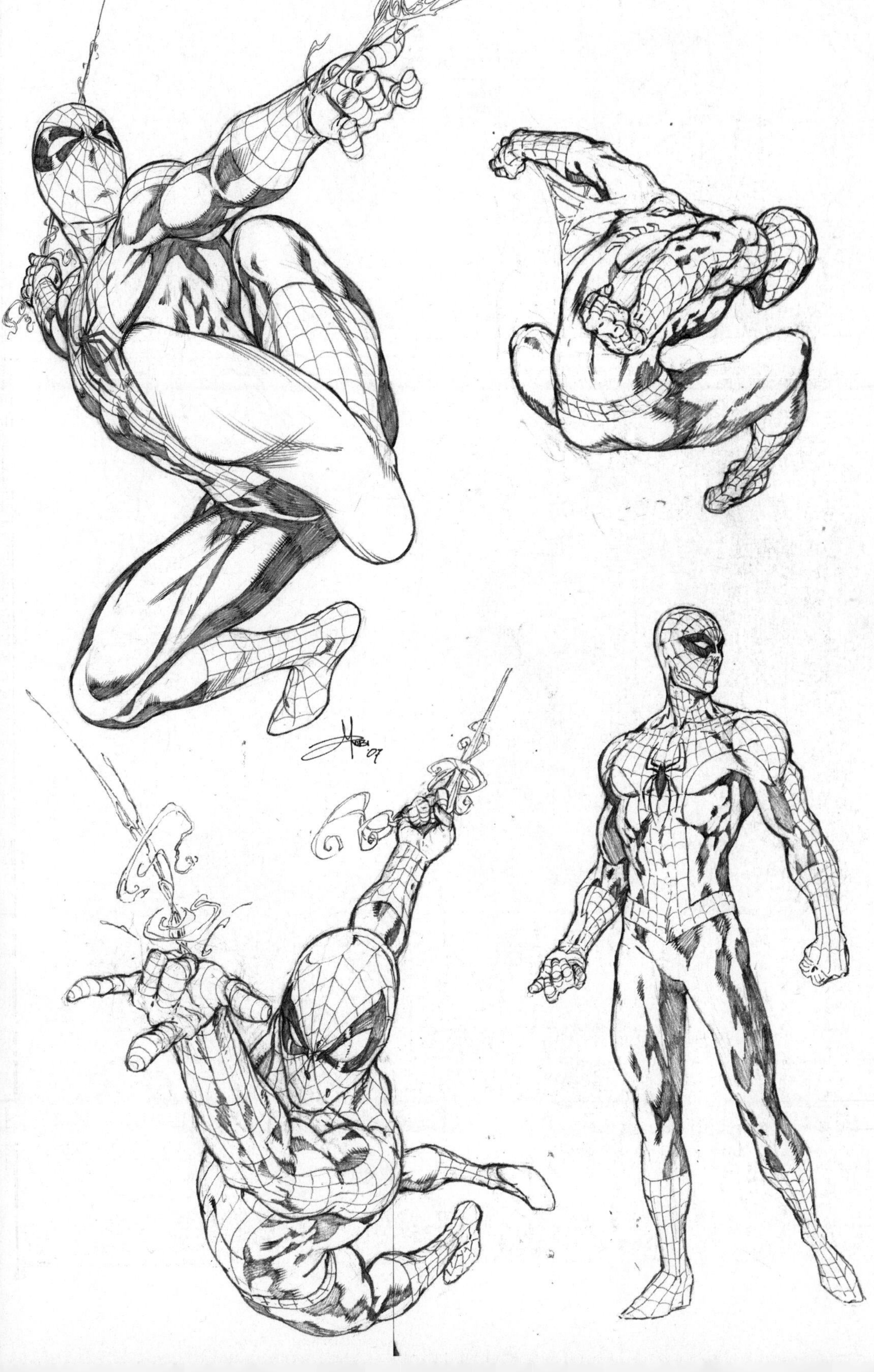

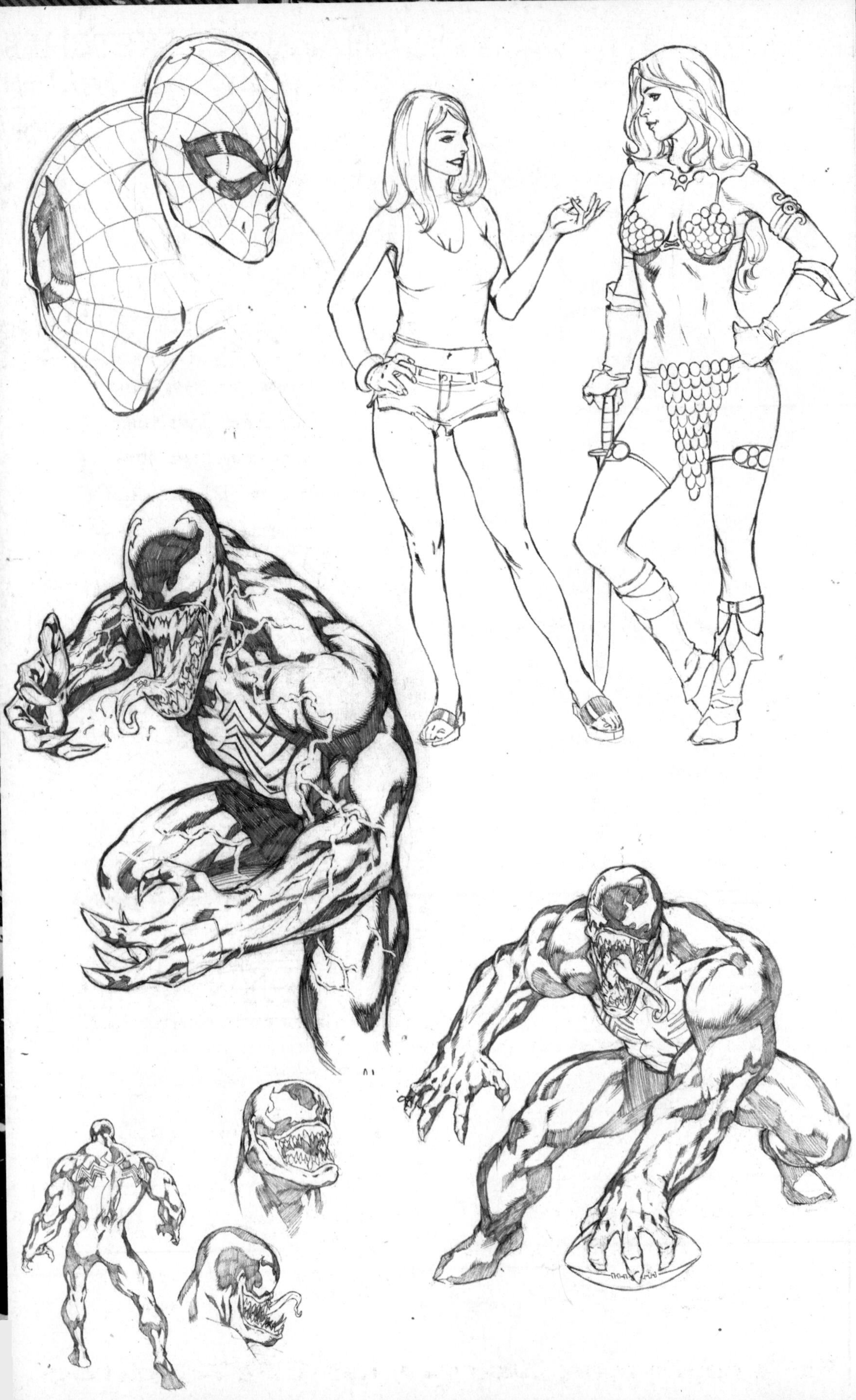